BAD MACHINERY™

THE CASE OF THE LONELY ONE

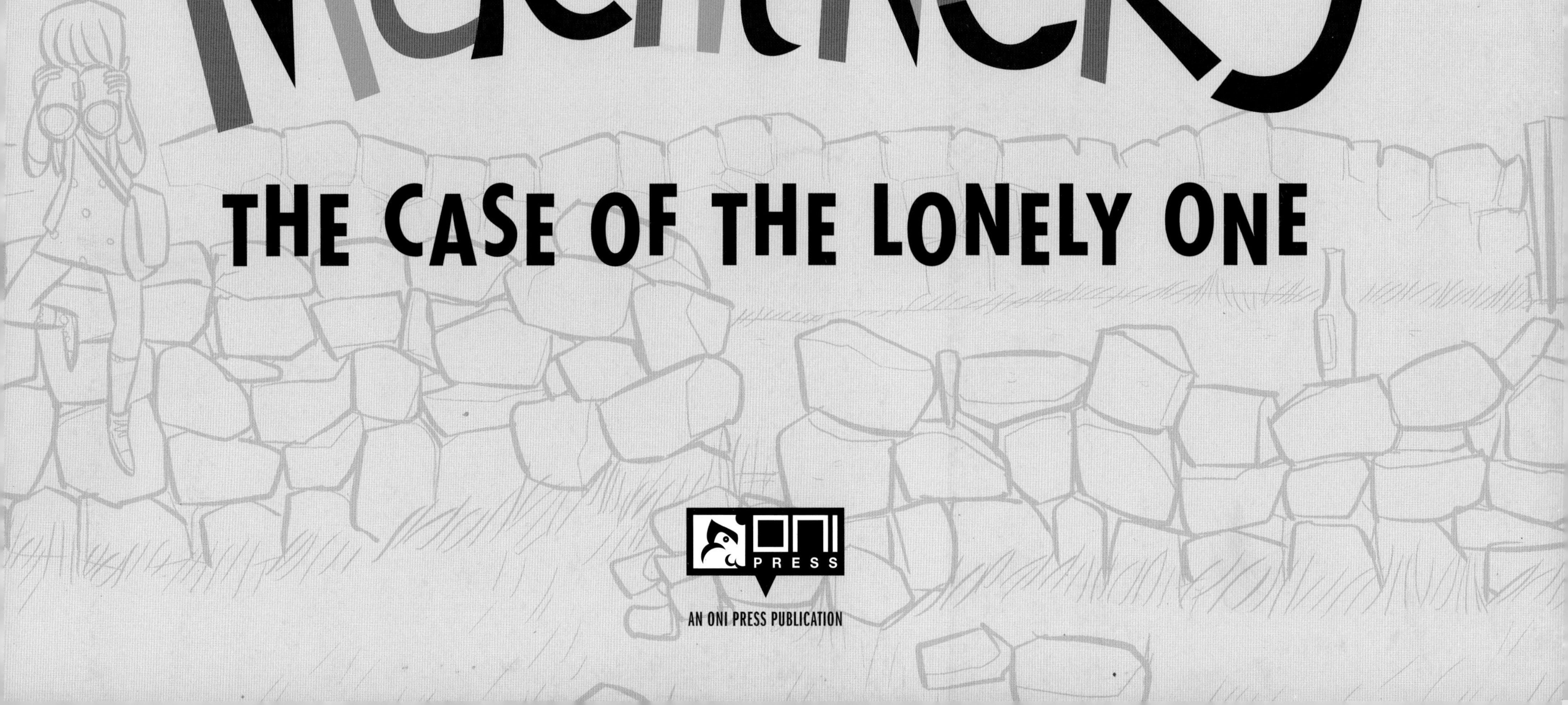

ONI PRESS
AN ONI PRESS PUBLICATION

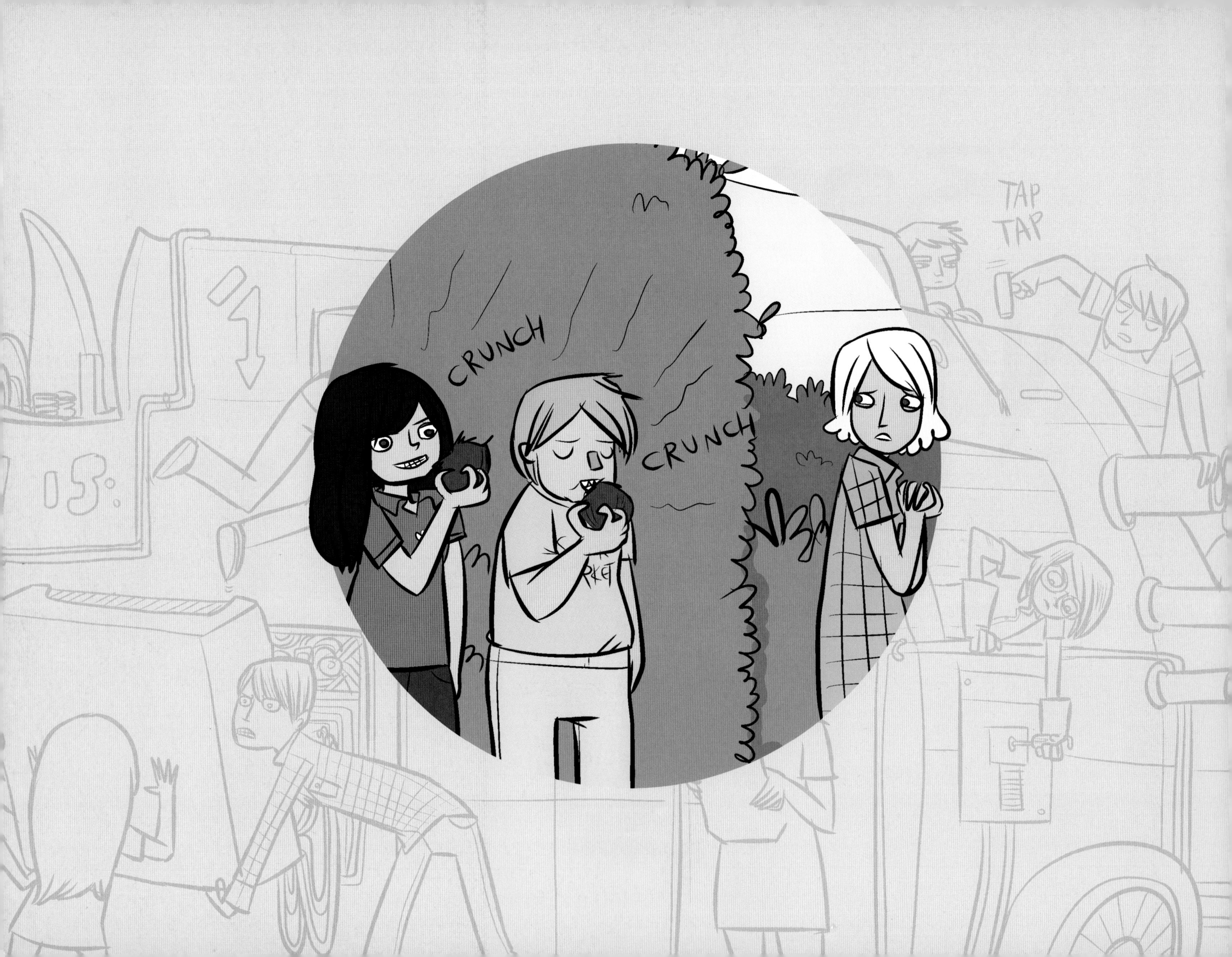

TAP
TAP
CRUNCH
CRUNCH

Bad Machinery™

THE CASE OF THE LONELY ONE

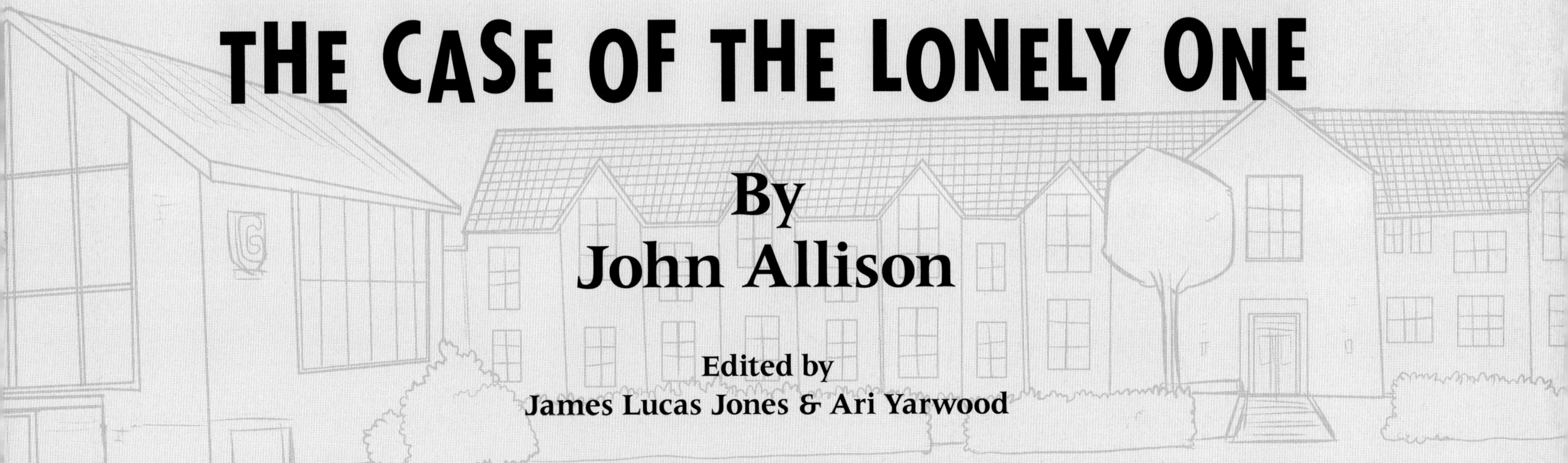

By
John Allison

Edited by
James Lucas Jones & Ari Yarwood

Designed by
Hilary Thompson

Colour Assists by
Adam Cadwell

Oni Press, Inc.
publisher, Joe Nozemack
editor in chief, James Lucas Jones
director of sales, Cheyenne Allott
director of publicity, Fred Reckling
production manager, Troy Look
graphic designer, Hilary Thompson
production assistant, Jared Jones
senior editor, Charlie Chu
editor, Robin Herrera
associate editor, Ari Yarwood
inventory coordinator, Brad Rooks
office assistant, Jung Lee

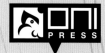

onipress.com
facebook.com/onipress
twitter.com/onipress
onipress.tumblr.com
instagram.com/onipress
badmachinery.com

First Edition: October 2015

ISBN 978-1-62010-212-1
eISBN 978-1-62010-213-8

Bad Machinery Volume Four: The Case of the Lonely One, October 2015. Published by Oni Press, Inc. 1305 SE Martin Luther King Jr. Blvd., Suite A, Portland, OR 97214.

Printed in China.

Library of Congress Control Number: 2012953355

1 2 3 4 5 6 7 8 9 10

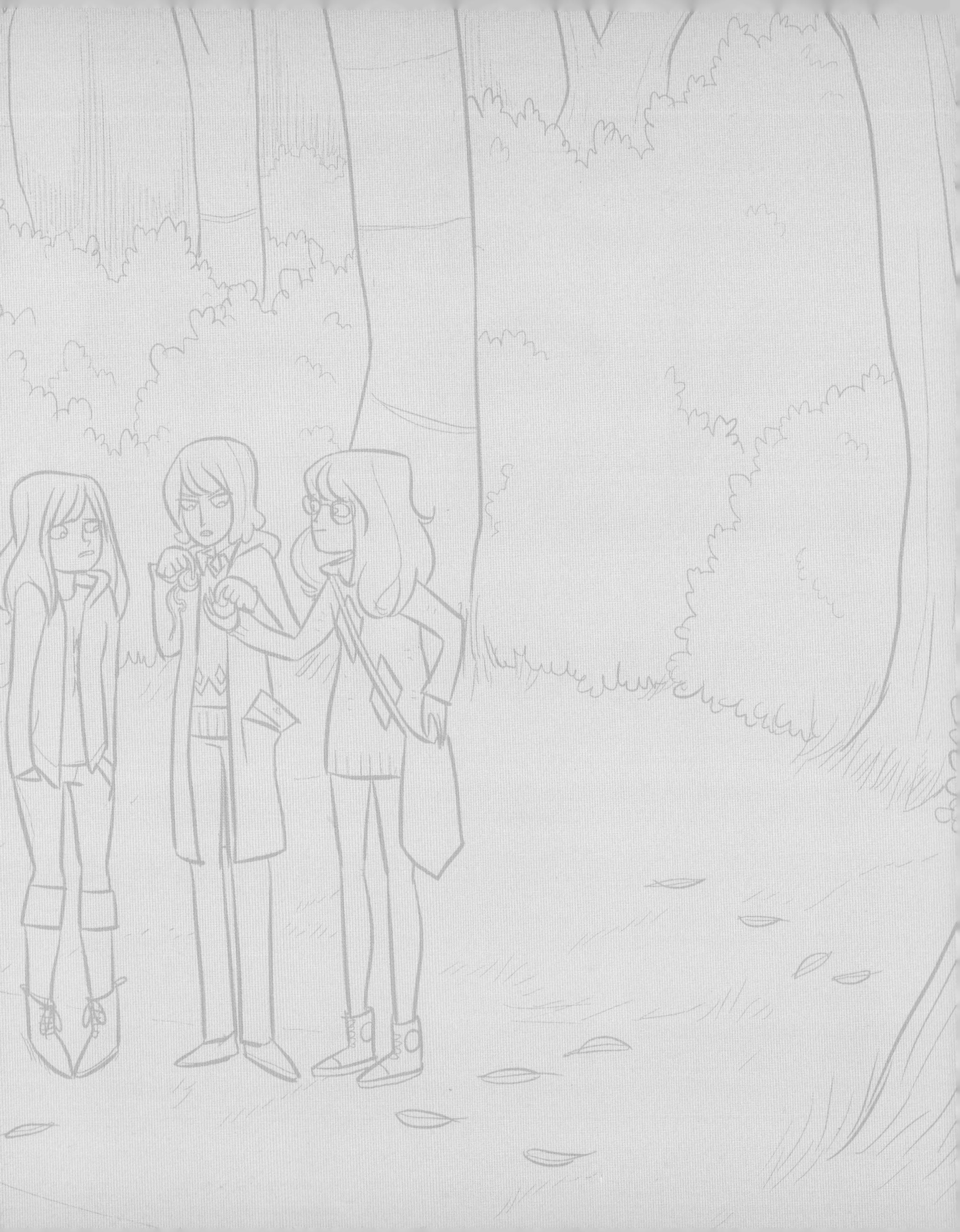

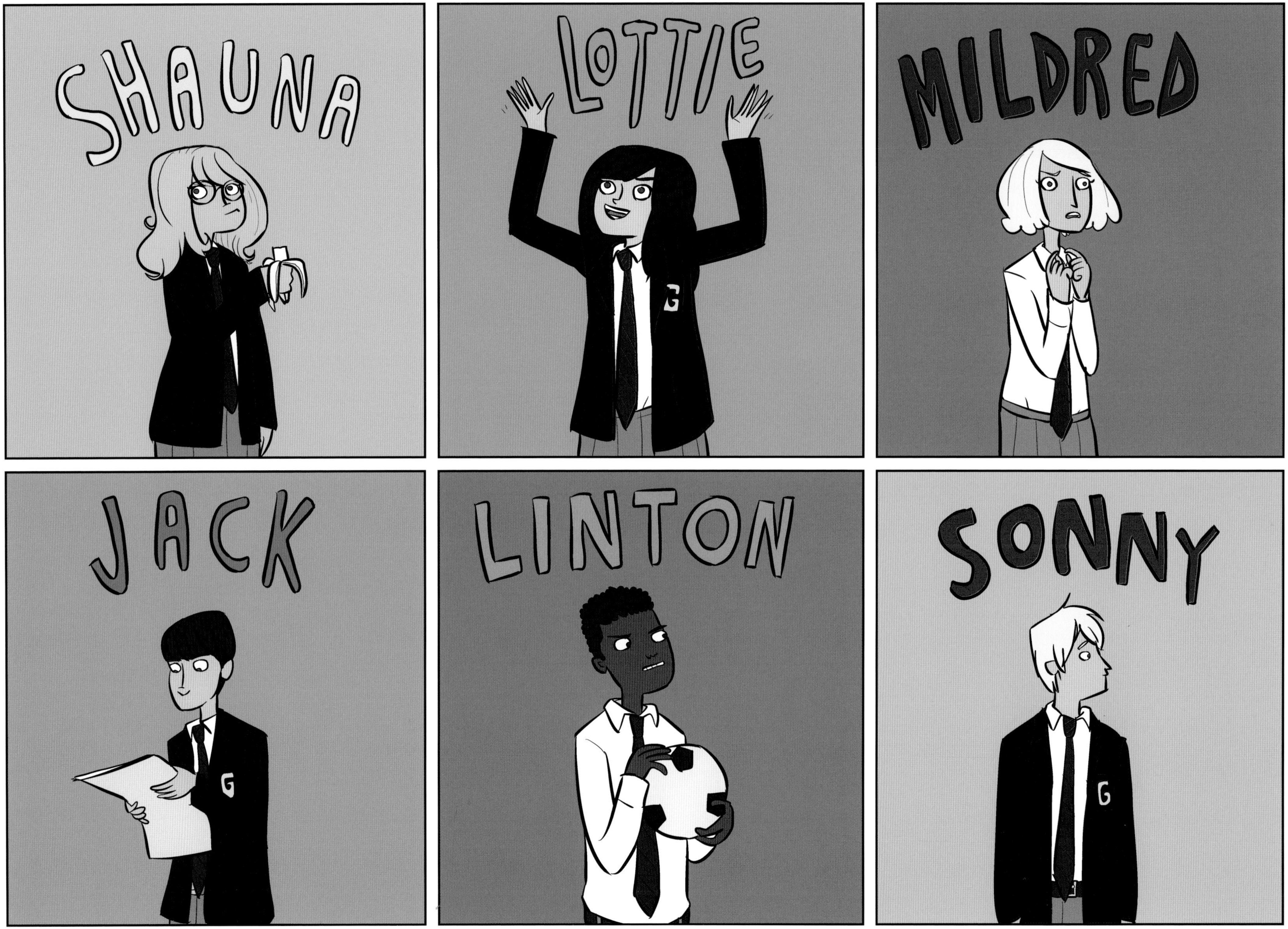
SHAUNA
LOTTIE
MILDRED
JACK
LINTON
SONNY

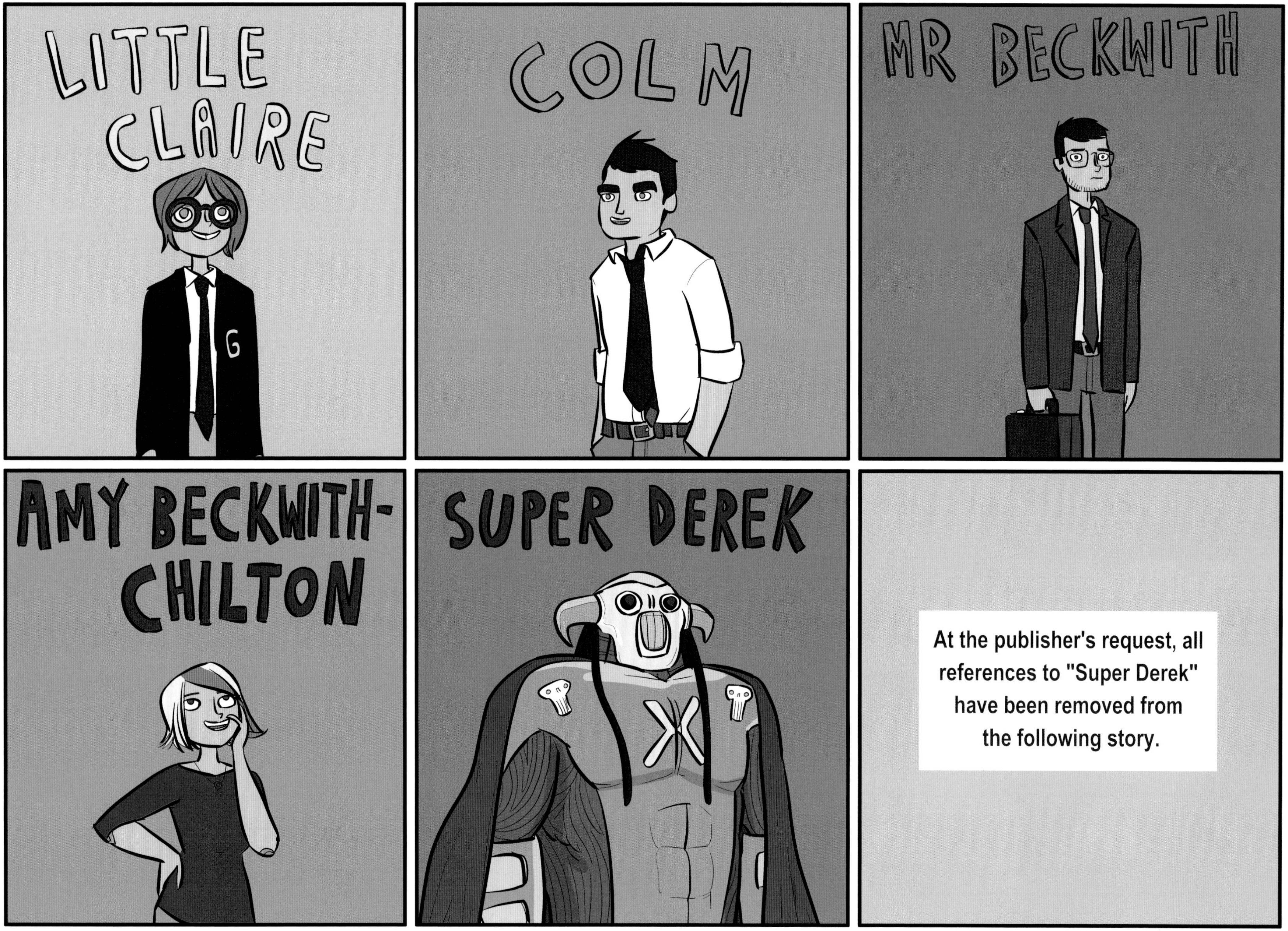
LITTLE CLAIRE
G
COLM
MR BECKWITH
AMY BECKWITH-CHILTON
SUPER DEREK
X
At the publisher's request, all references to "Super Derek" have been removed from the following story.

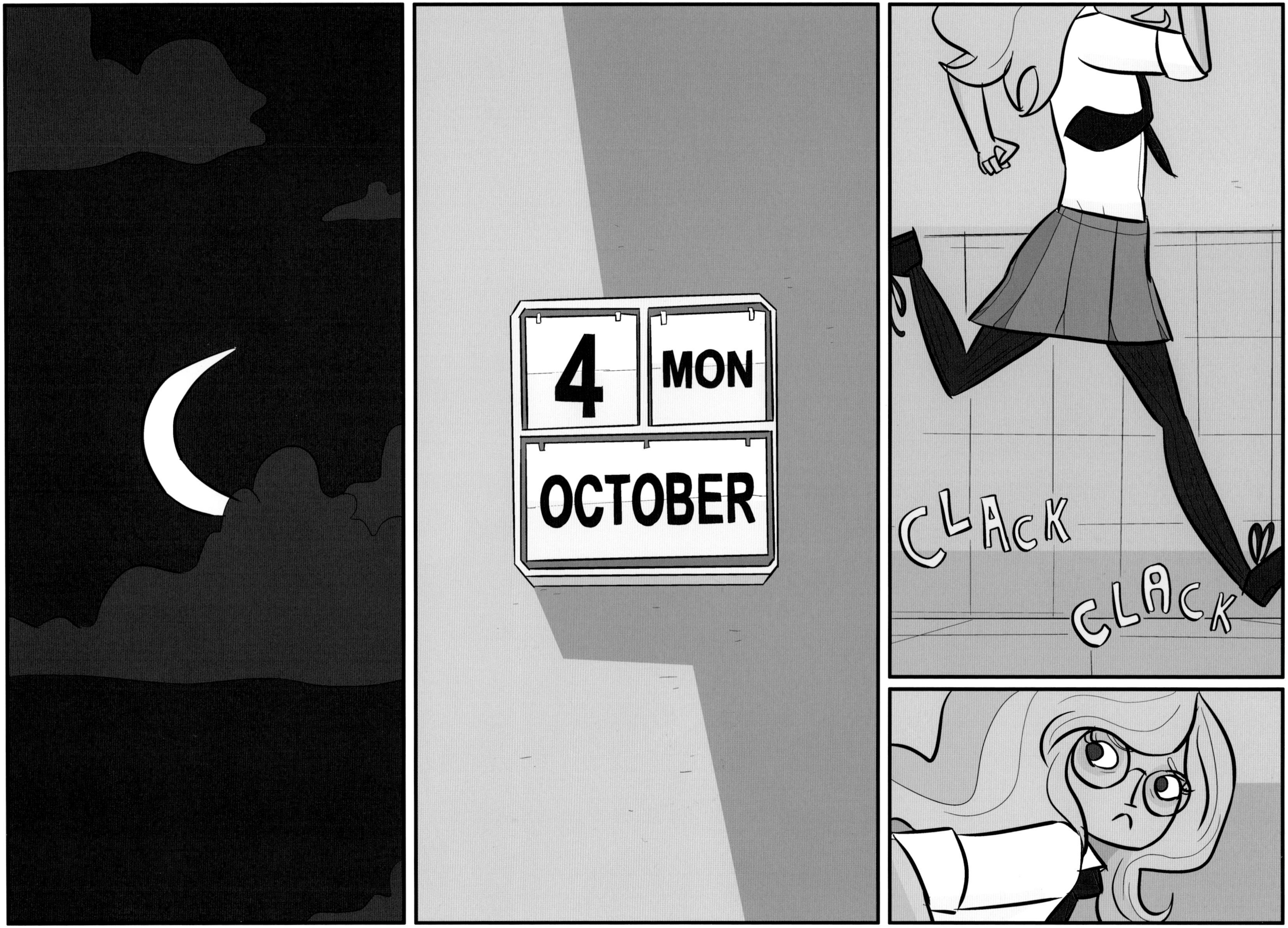
4 MON
OCTOBER
CLACK
CLACK

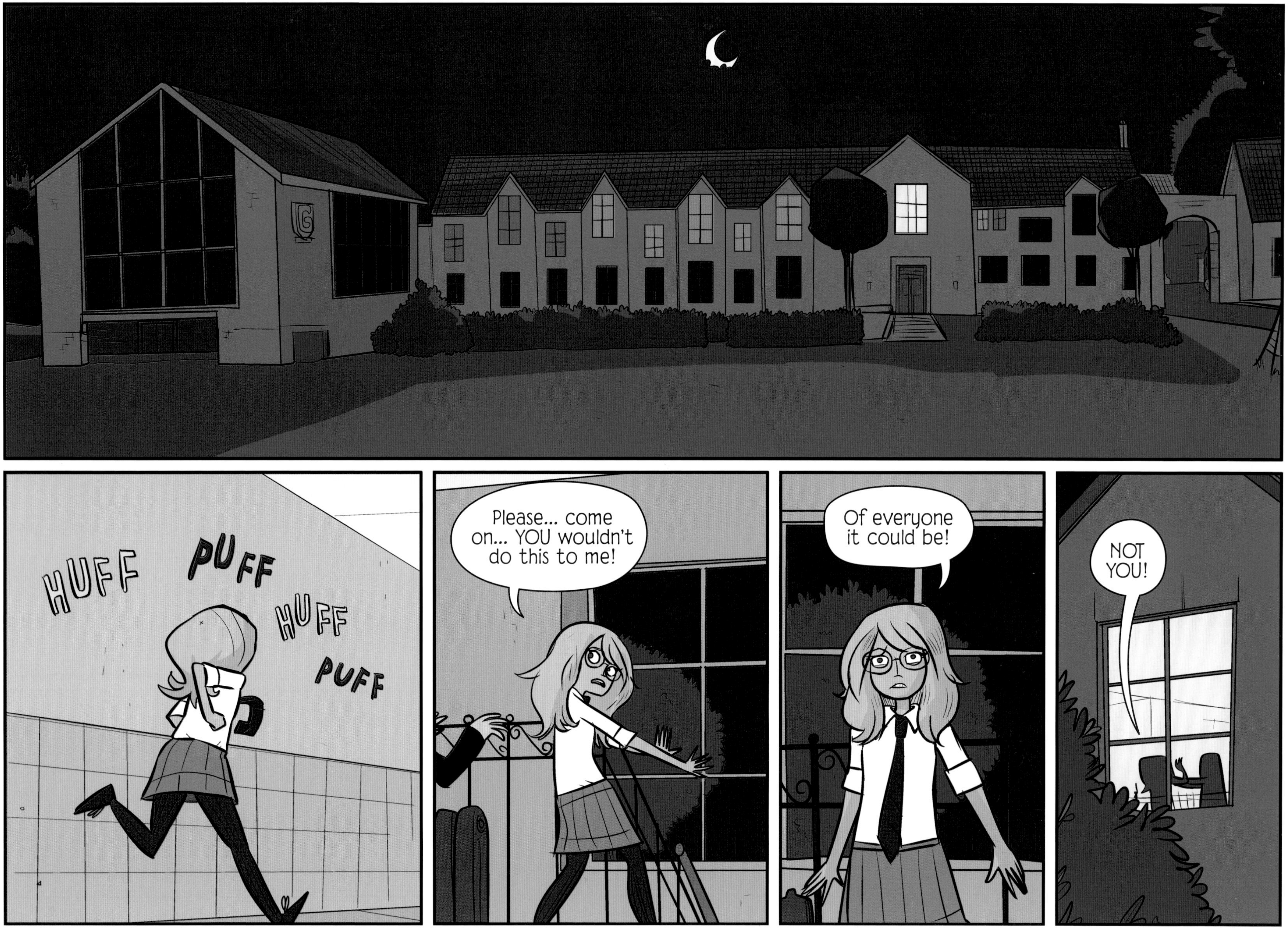
HUFF
PUFF
HUFF
PUFF
Please... come on... YOU wouldn't do this to me!
Of everyone it could be!
NOT YOU!

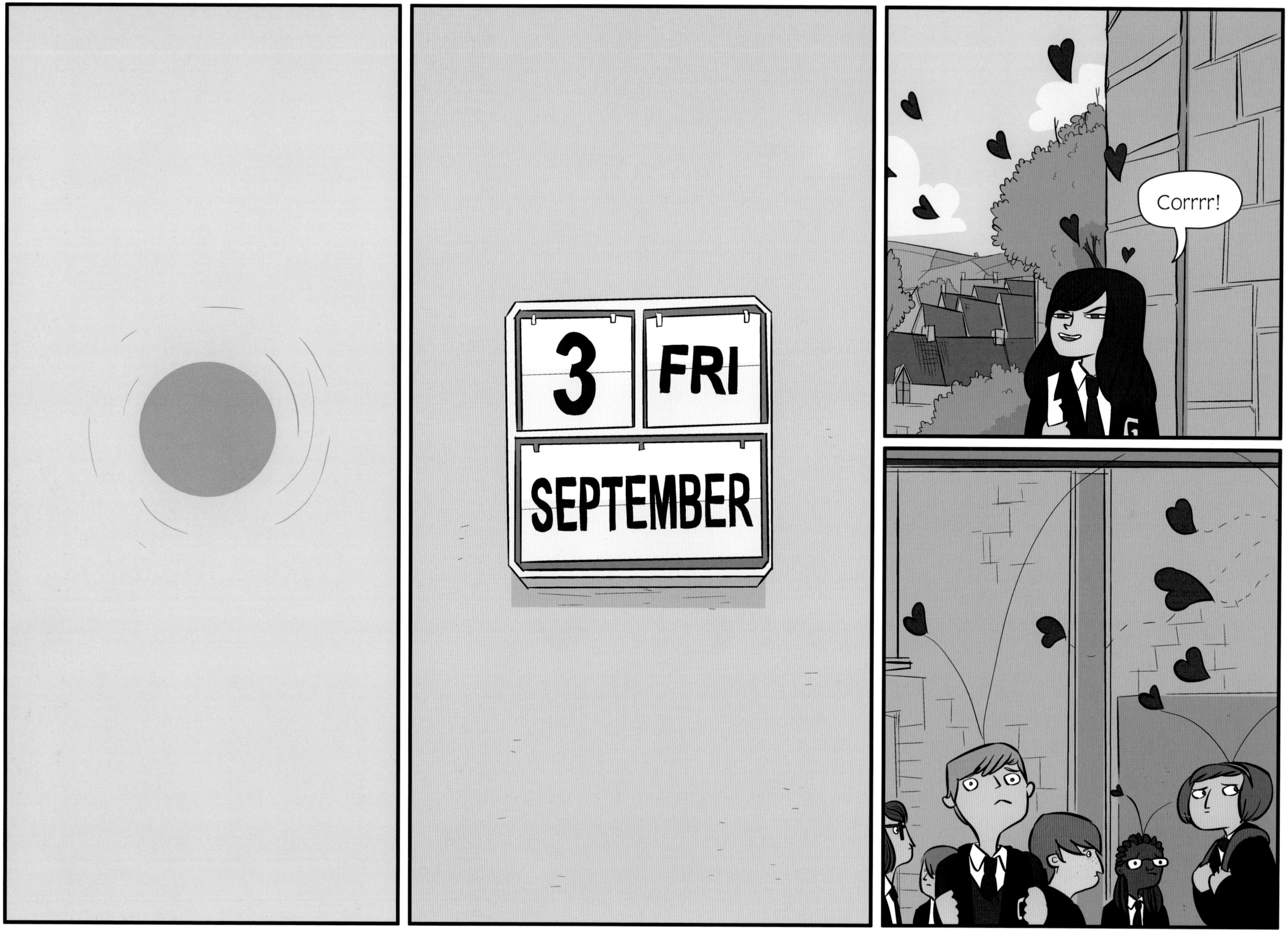
3 FRI
SEPTEMBER
Corrrr!

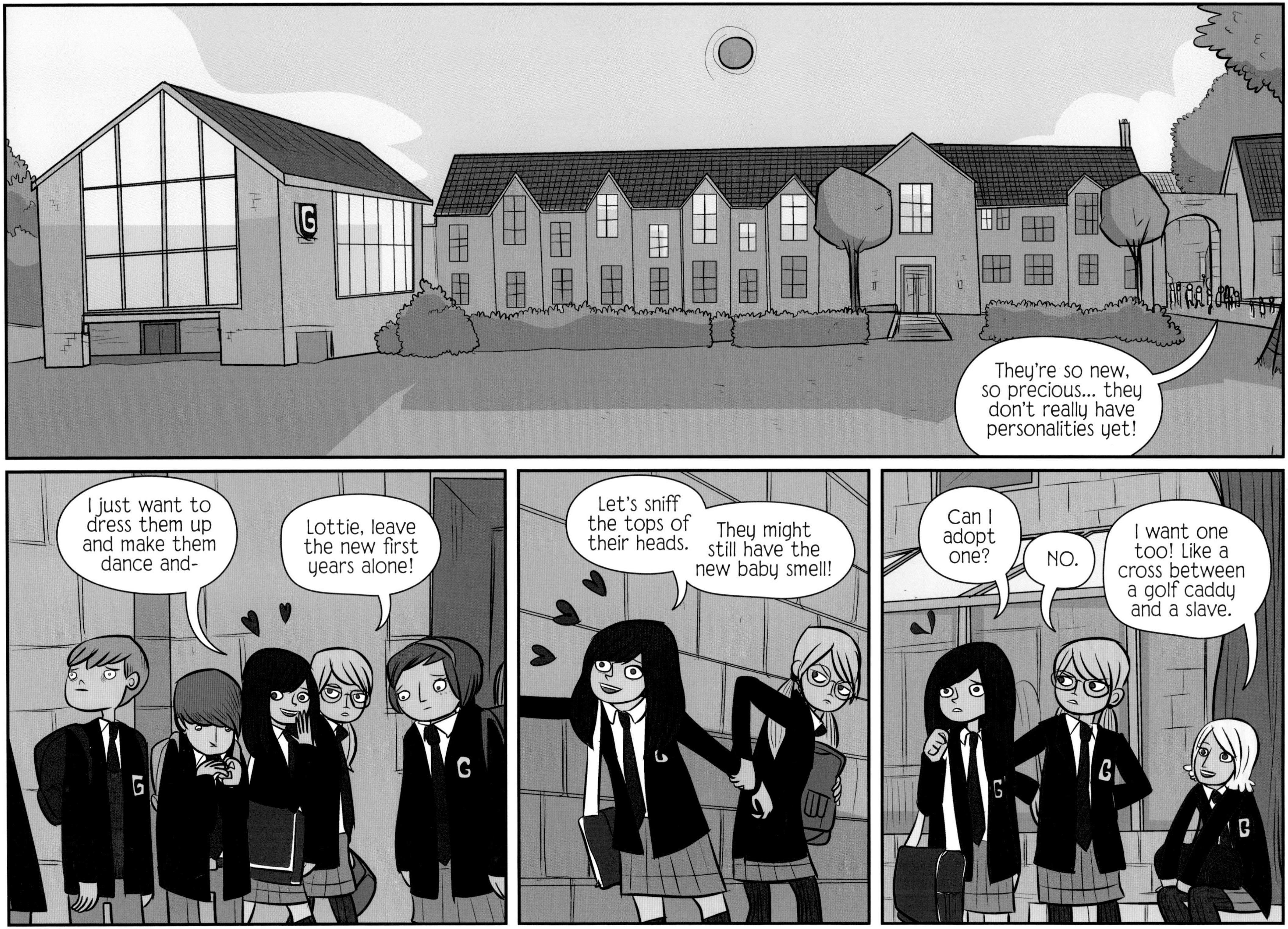
They're so new, so precious... they don't really have personalities yet!
I just want to dress them up and make them dance and-
Lottie, leave the new first years alone!
Let's sniff the tops of their heads.
They might still have the new baby smell!
Can I adopt one?
NO.
I want one too! Like a cross between a golf caddy and a slave.

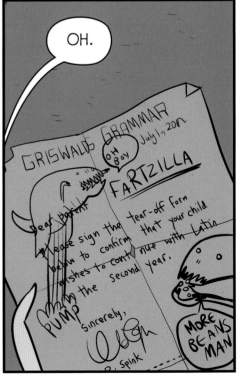

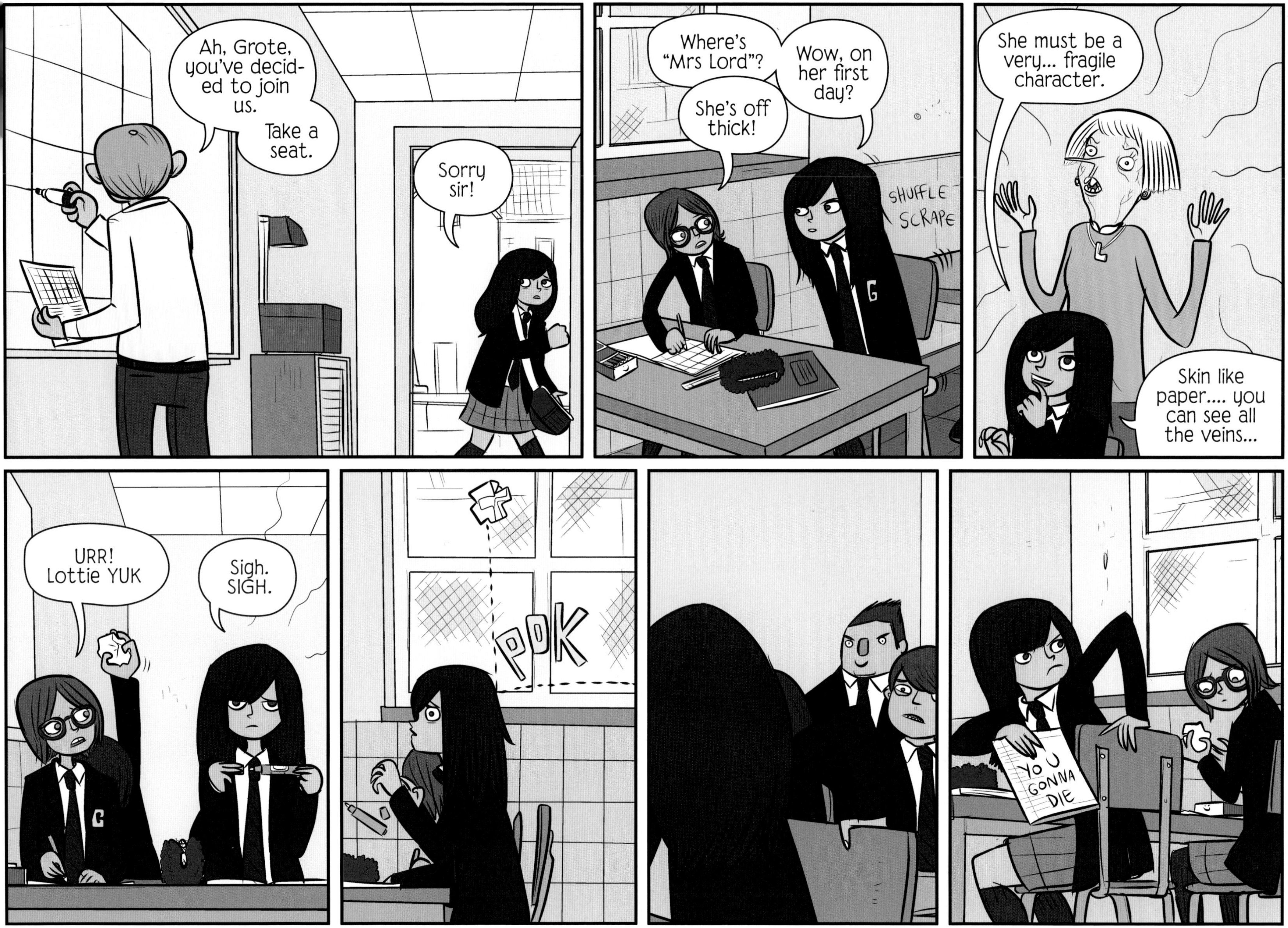
Ah, Grote, you've decid-ed to join us.
Take a seat.
Sorry sir!
Where's "Mrs Lord"?
She's off thick!
Wow, on her first day?
SHUFFLE
SCRAPE
She must be a very... fragile character.
Skin like paper.... you can see all the veins...
URR! Lottie YUK
Sigh. SIGH.
POK
YO U GONNA DIE

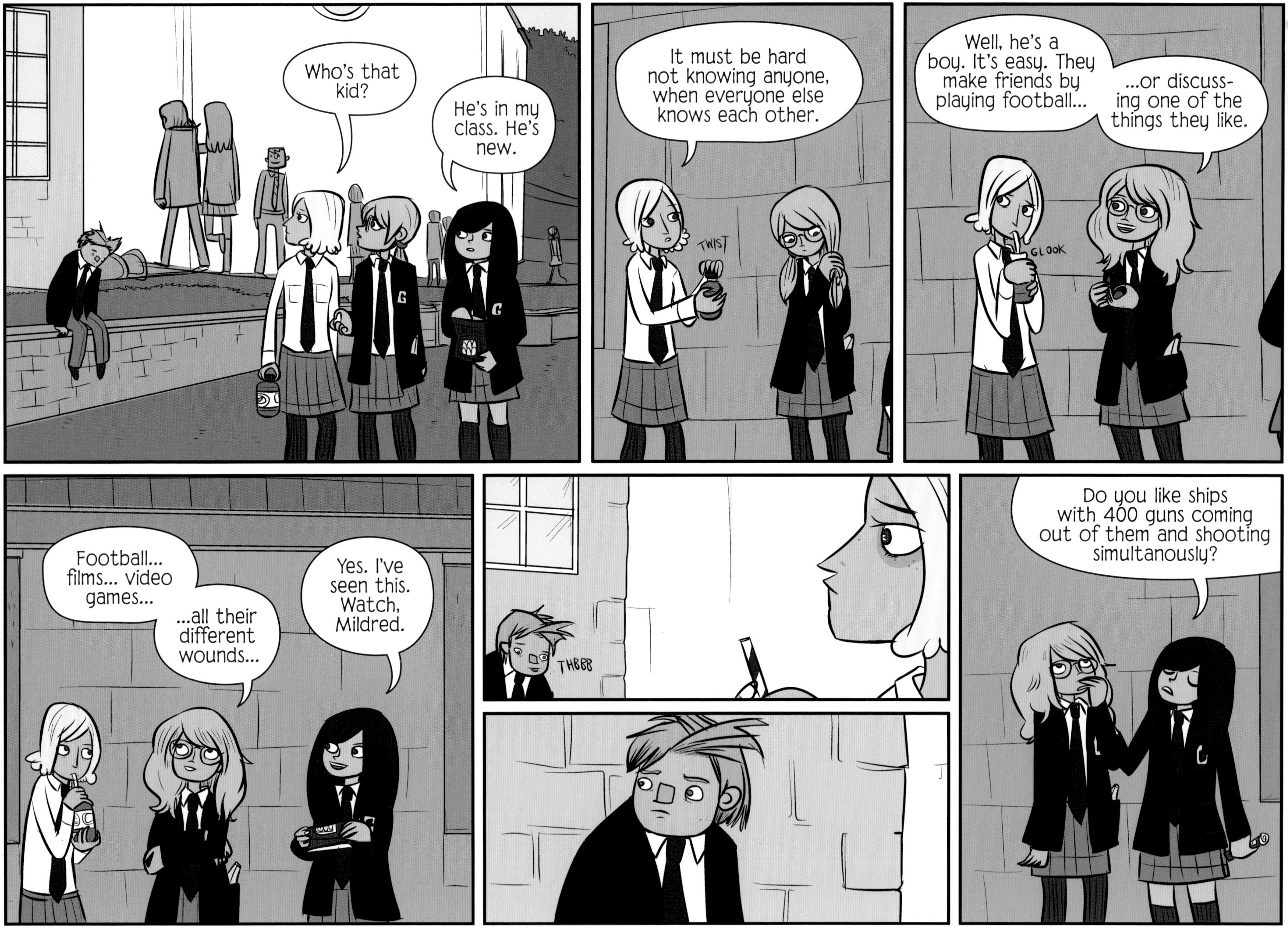
Who's that kid?
He's in my class. He's new.
It must be hard not knowing anyone, when everyone else knows each other.
TWIST
Well, he's a boy. It's easy. They make friends by playing football...
...or discuss-ing one of the things they like.
GLOOK
Football... films... video games...
...all their different wounds...
Yes. I've seen this. Watch, Mildred.
THBBB
Do you like ships with 400 guns coming out of them and shooting simultanously?

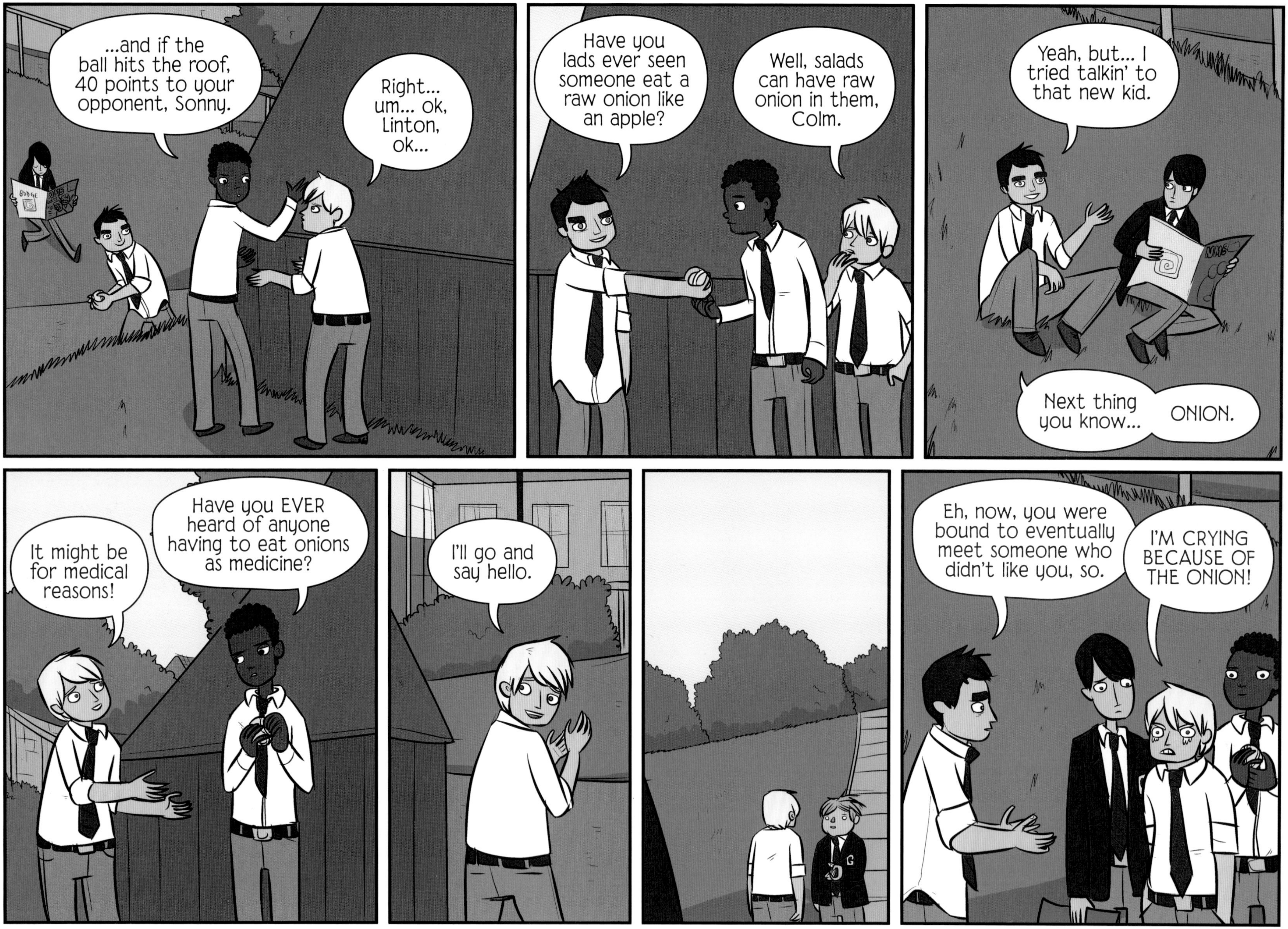
...and if the ball hits the roof, 40 points to your opponent, Sonny.
Right... um... ok, Linton, ok...
Have you lads ever seen someone eat a raw onion like an apple?
Well, salads can have raw onion in them, Colm.
Yeah, but... I tried talkin' to that new kid.
Next thing you know...
ONION.
It might be for medical reasons!
Have you EVER heard of anyone having to eat onions as medicine?
I'll go and say hello.
Eh, now, you were bound to eventually meet someone who didn't like you, so.
I'M CRYING BECAUSE OF THE ONION!

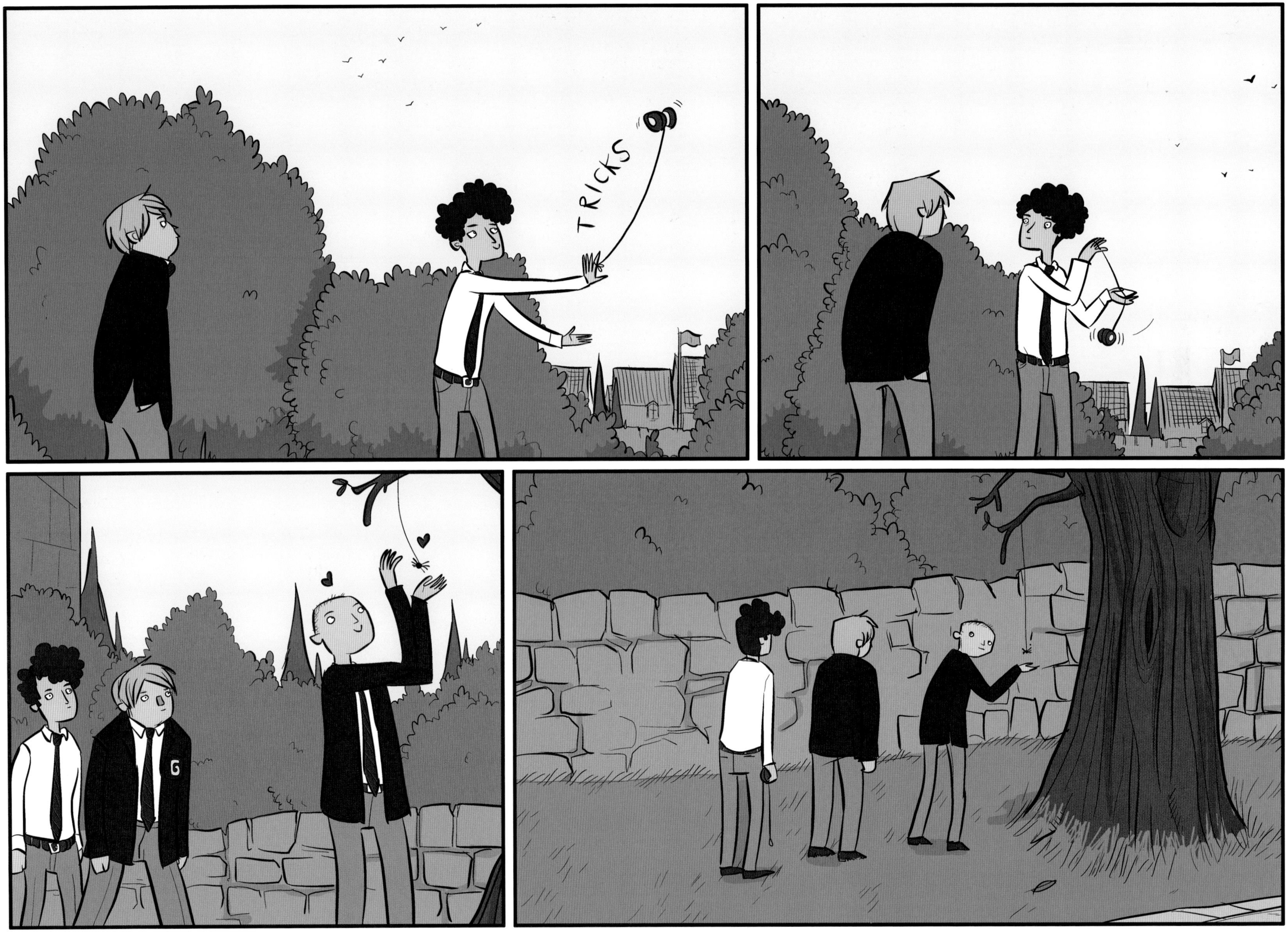
TRICKS

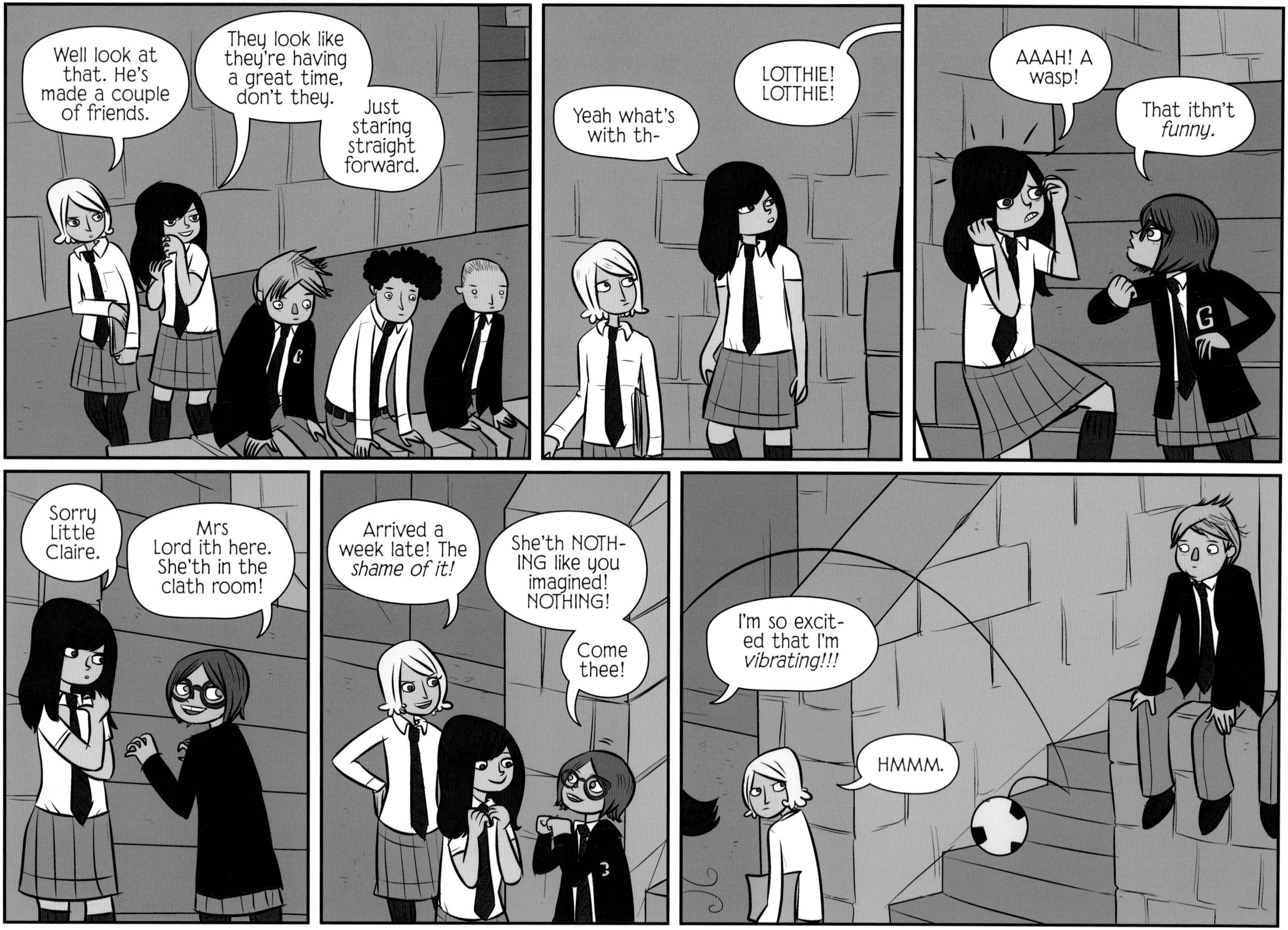
Well look at that. He's made a couple of friends.
They look like they're having a great time, don't they.
Just staring straight forward.
Yeah what's with th-
LOTTHIE! LOTTHIE!
AAAH! A wasp!
That ithn't *funny.*
Sorry Little Claire.
Mrs Lord ith here. She'th in the clath room!
Arrived a week late! The *shame of it!*
She'th NOTHING like you imagined! NOTHING!
Come thee!
I'm so excited that I'm *vibrating!!!*
HMMM.

The Case of the Lonely One

22

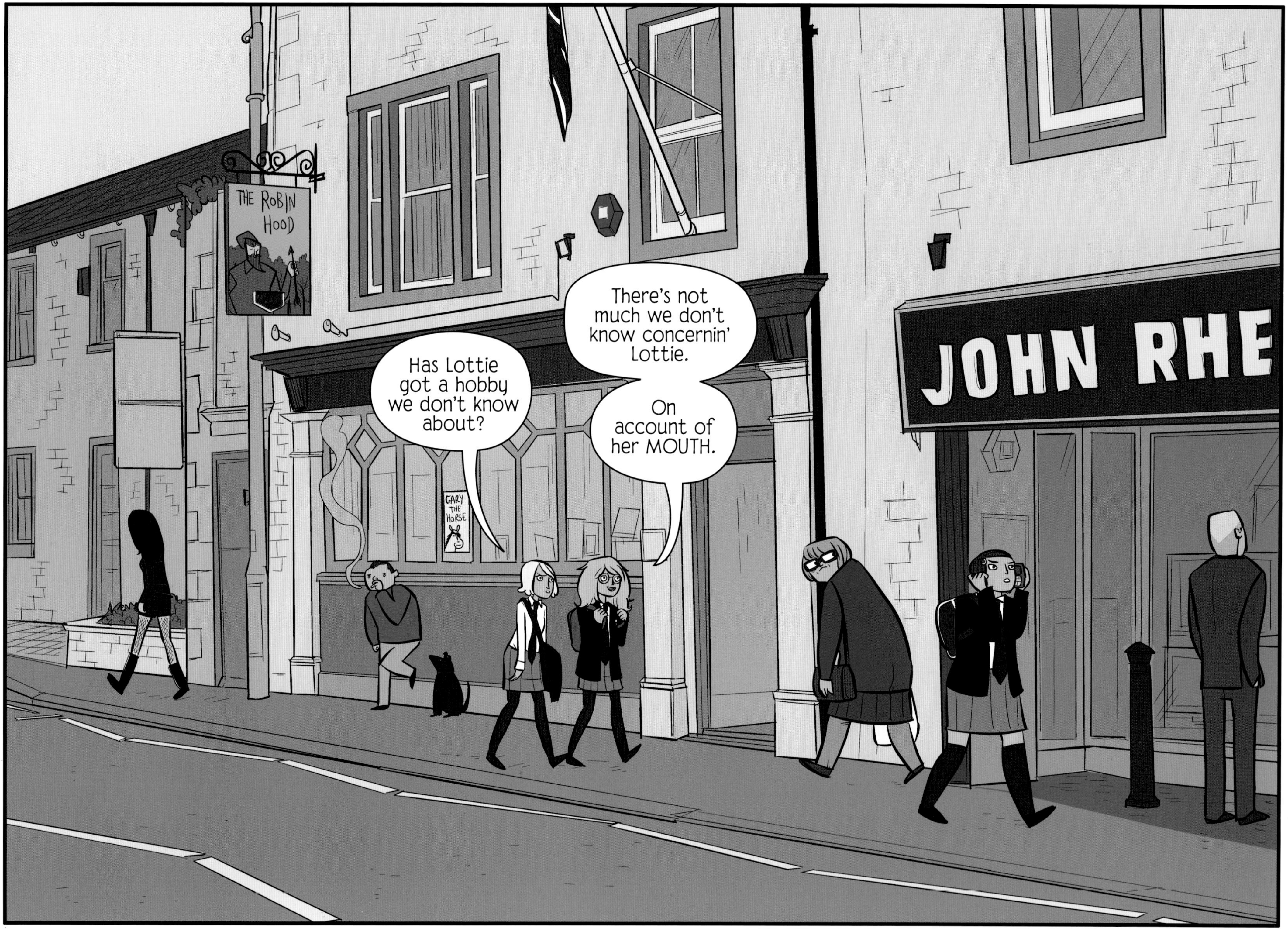
THE ROBIN HOOD
GARY THE HORSE
JOHN RHE
Has Lottie got a hobby we don't know about?
There's not much we don't know concernin' Lottie.
On account of her MOUTH.

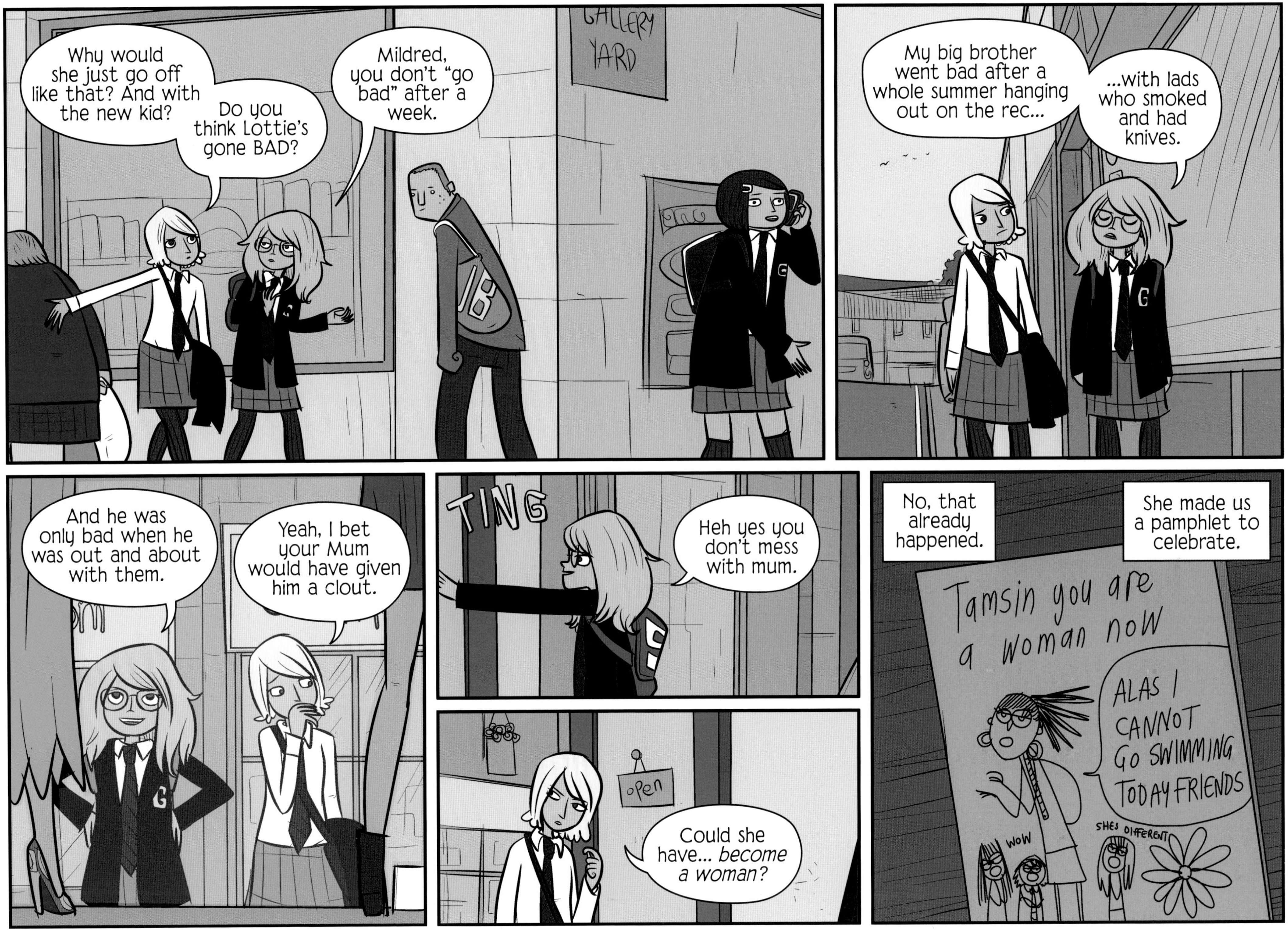
Why would she just go off like that? And with the new kid?
Do you think Lottie's gone BAD?
Mildred, you don't "go bad" after a week.
GALLERY YARD
My big brother went bad after a whole summer hanging out on the rec...
...with lads who smoked and had knives.
And he was only bad when he was out and about with them.
Yeah, I bet your Mum would have given him a clout.
TING
Heh yes you don't mess with mum.
open
Could she have... *become a woman?*
No, that already happened.
She made us a pamphlet to celebrate.
Tamsin you are a woman now
ALAS I CANNOT GO SWIMMING TODAY FRIENDS
WOW
SHES DIFFERENT

Bad Machinery, Volume Four

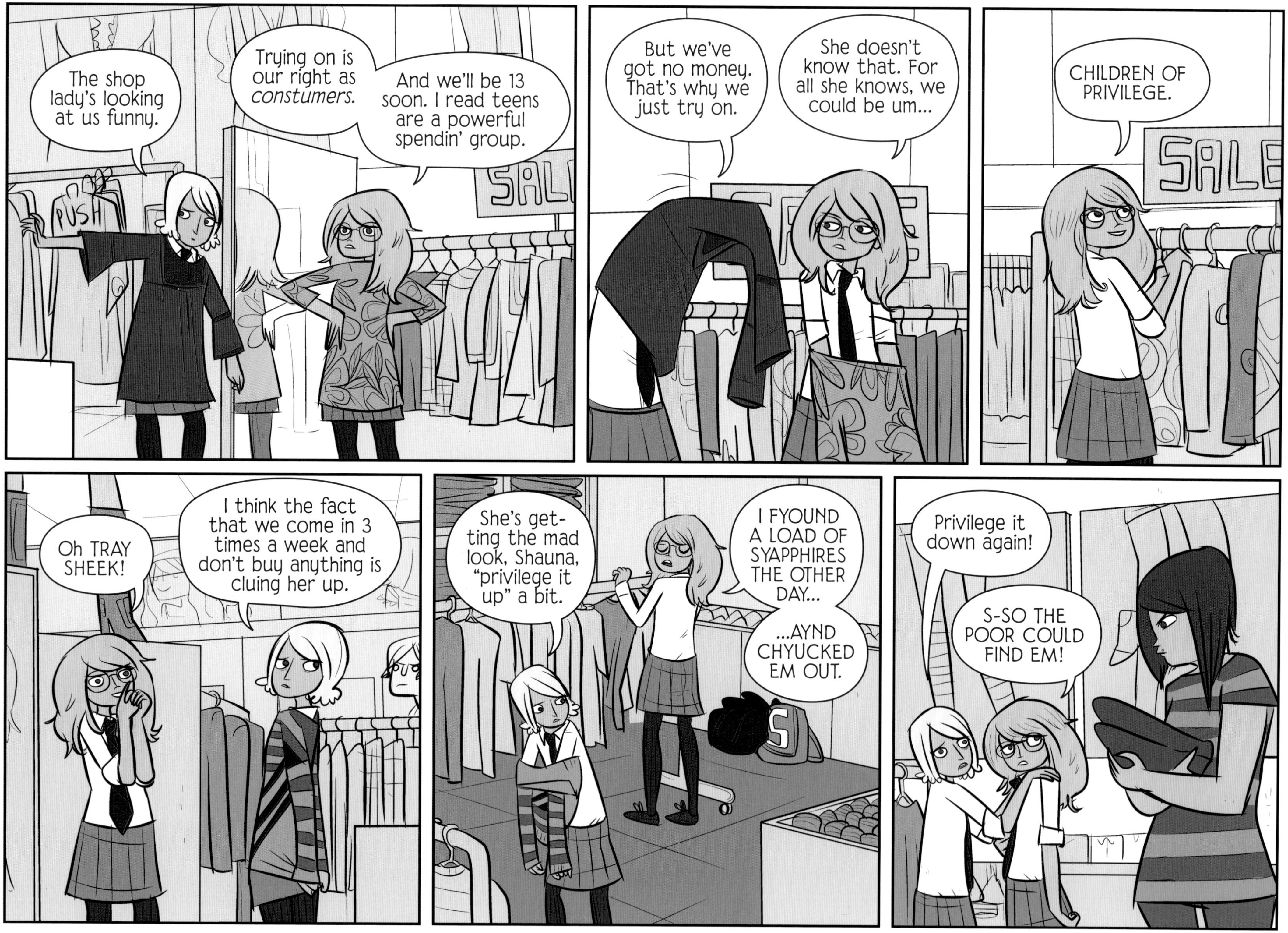
The shop lady's looking at us funny.
Trying on is our right as *constumers.*
And we'll be 13 soon. I read teens are a powerful spendin' group.
PUSH
SALE
But we've got no money. That's why we just try on.
She doesn't know that. For all she knows, we could be um...
CHILDREN OF PRIVILEGE.
SALE
Oh TRAY SHEEK!
I think the fact that we come in 3 times a week and don't buy anything is cluing her up.
She's getting the mad look, Shauna, "privilege it up" a bit.
I FYOUND A LOAD OF SYAPPHIRES THE OTHER DAY...
...AYND CHYUCKED EM OUT.
Privilege it down again!
S-SO THE POOR COULD FIND EM!

Psst! Look! Out in the wild!

Helloooo

Are you two behaving yourselves?

Hihihi yes!

Always, Mr Beckwith!

Mrs Beckwith's got me doing the shopping.

MRS BECKWITH!

Dang, what is your fascination with her?

She rode her bike through the school once

She always calls the headmaster "Chuffy"

She has the best hair AND TATTOOS

Er... yes. Those things are true. So how are you enjoying being in Mr Spink's class?

Permission to speak freely, sir?

TWEAK TWEAK

We suspect him of being mentile, sir

We think—maybe he needs a nice quiet hobby, sir.

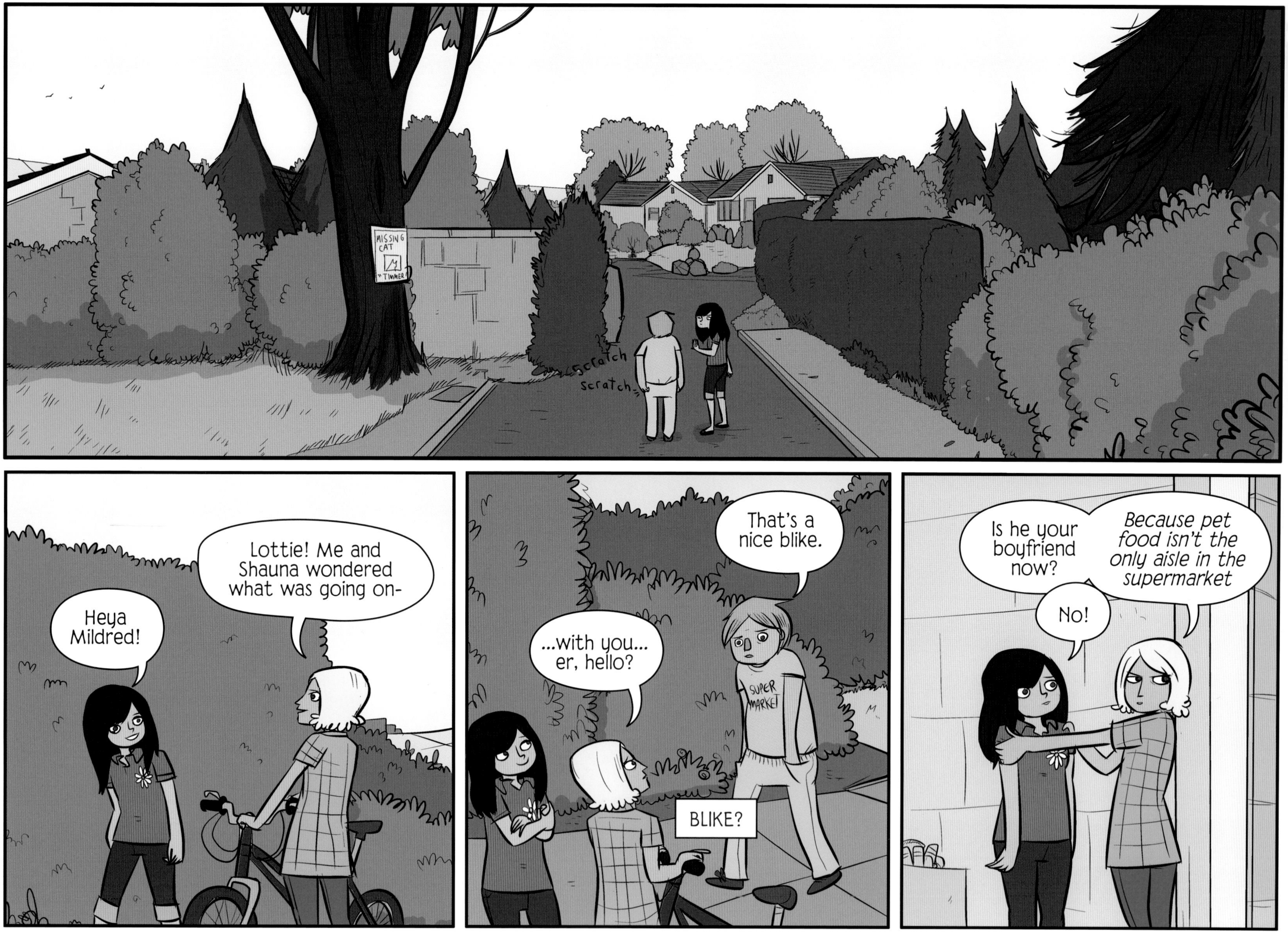
MISSING CAT
TIMMER
scratch
scratch
Heya Mildred!
Lottie! Me and Shauna wondered what was going on-
...with you... er, hello?
That's a nice blike.
SUPER MARKET
BLIKE?
Is he your boyfriend now?
No!
Because pet food isn't the only aisle in the supermarket

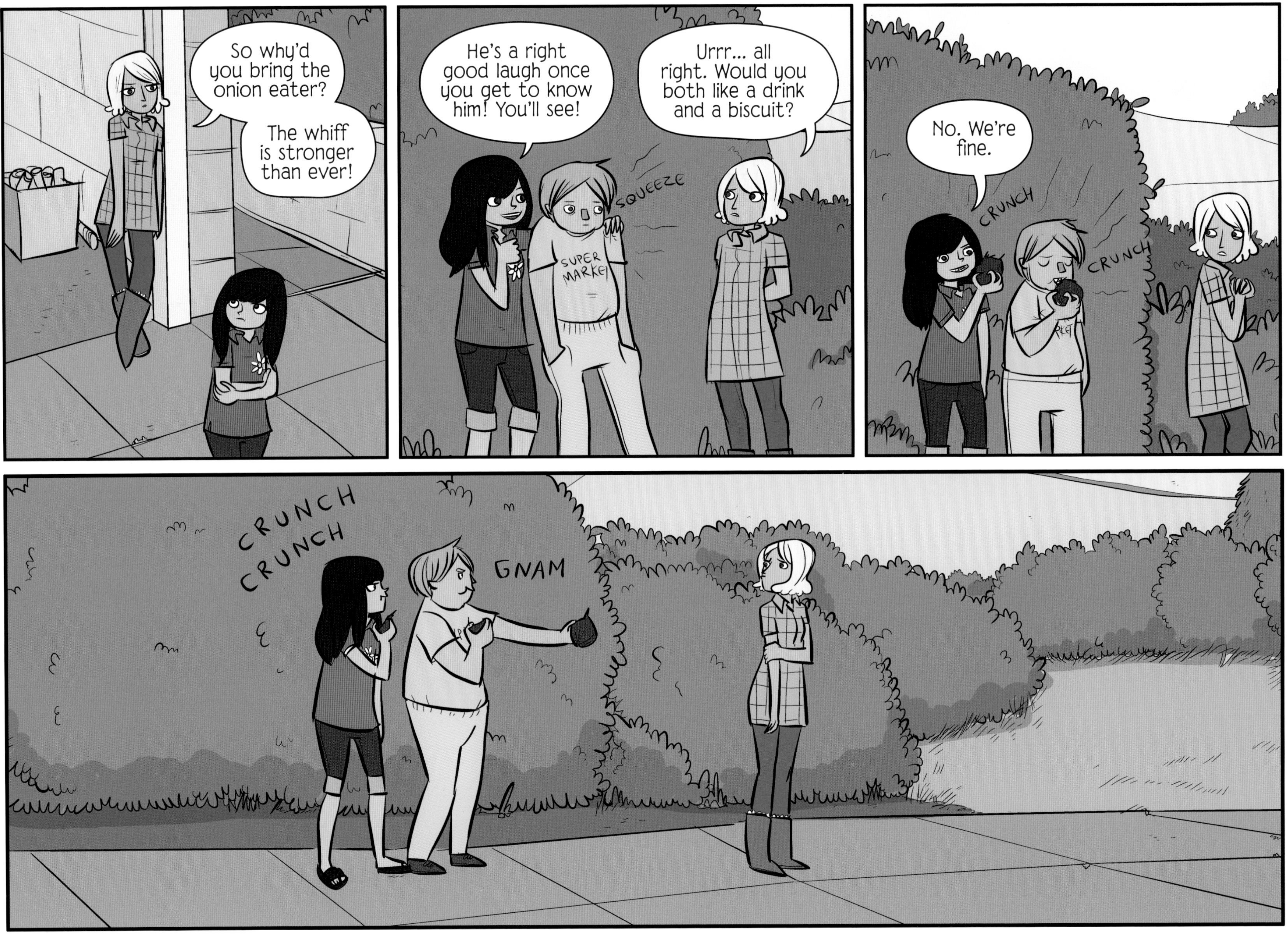
So why'd you bring the onion eater?
The whiff is stronger than ever!
He's a right good laugh once you get to know him! You'll see!
SQUEEZE
Urrr... all right. Would you both like a drink and a biscuit?
SUPER MARKET
No. We're fine.
CRUNCH
CRUNCH
CRUNCH
CRUNCH
GNAM

The Case of the Lonely One

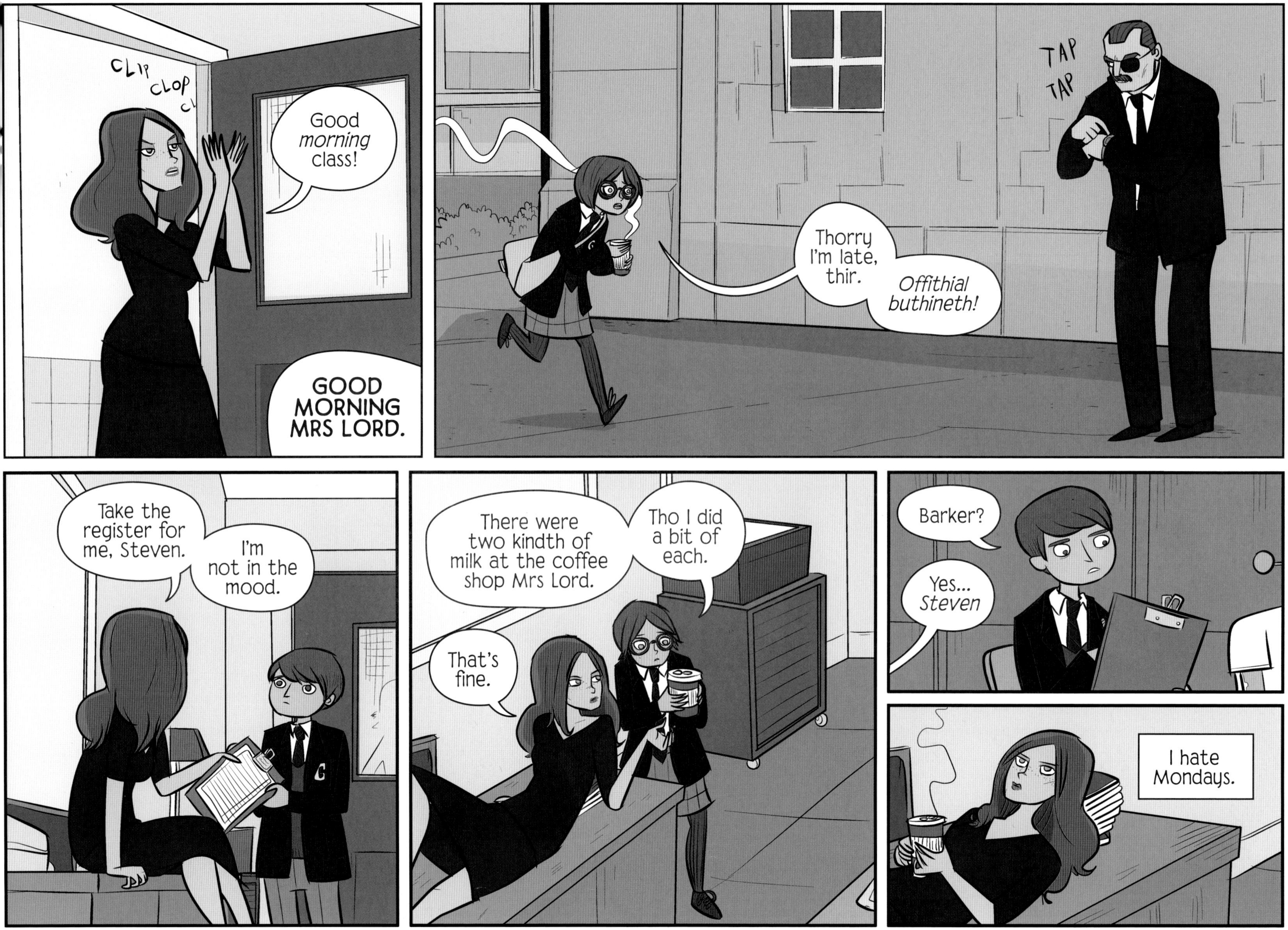
CLIP CLOP CL
Good *morning* class!
GOOD MORNING MRS LORD.
TAP TAP
Thorry I'm late, thir.
Offithial buthineth!
Take the register for me, Steven.
I'm not in the mood.
There were two kindth of milk at the coffee shop Mrs Lord.
Tho I did a bit of each.
That's fine.
Barker?
Yes... *Steven*
I hate Mondays.

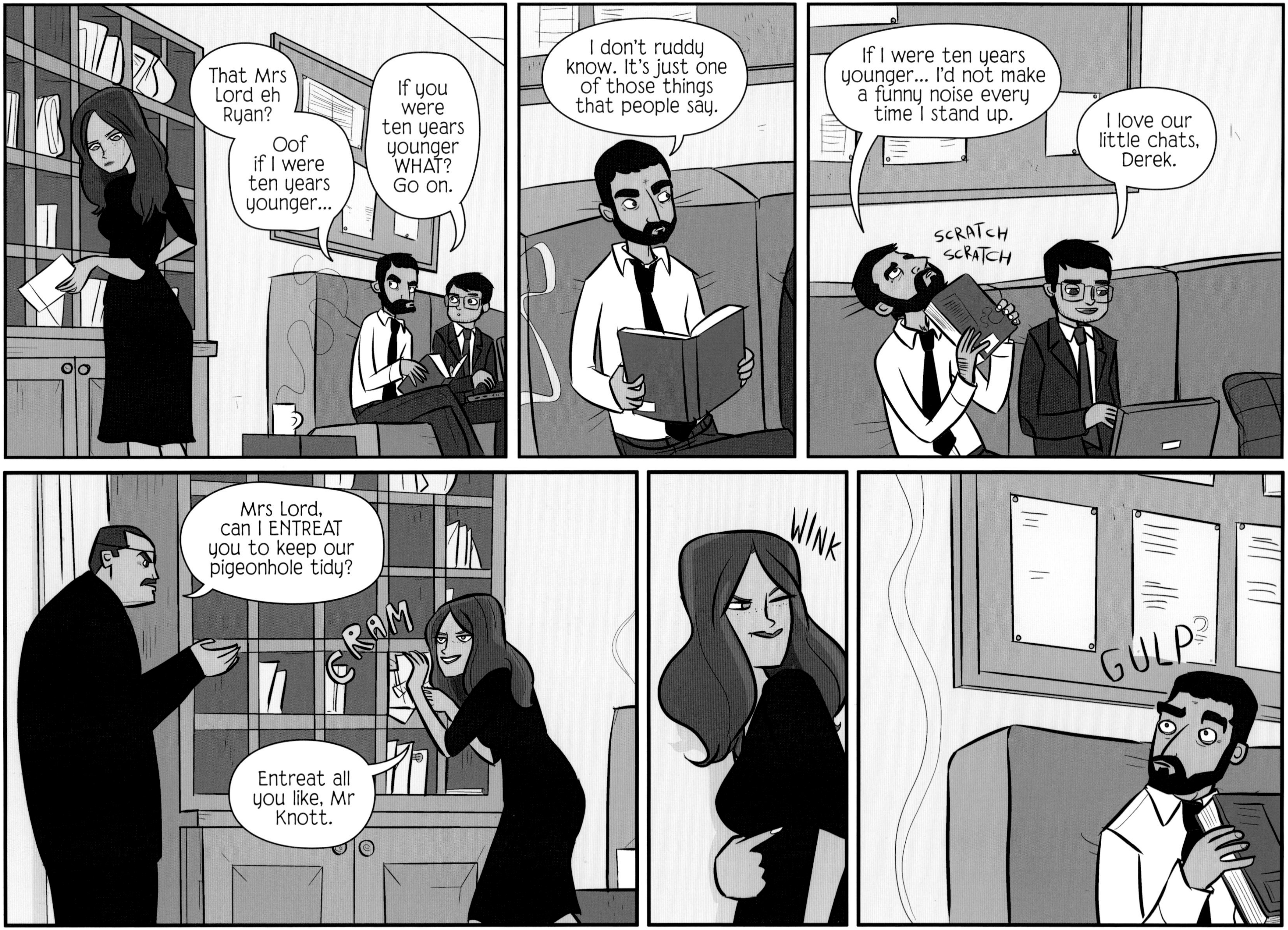
That Mrs Lord eh Ryan?
Oof if I were ten years younger...
If you were ten years younger WHAT? Go on.
I don't ruddy know. It's just one of those things that people say.
If I were ten years younger... I'd not make a funny noise every time I stand up.
SCRATCH SCRATCH
I love our little chats, Derek.
Mrs Lord, can I ENTREAT you to keep our pigeonhole tidy?
CRAM
Entreat all you like, Mr Knott.
WINK
GULP

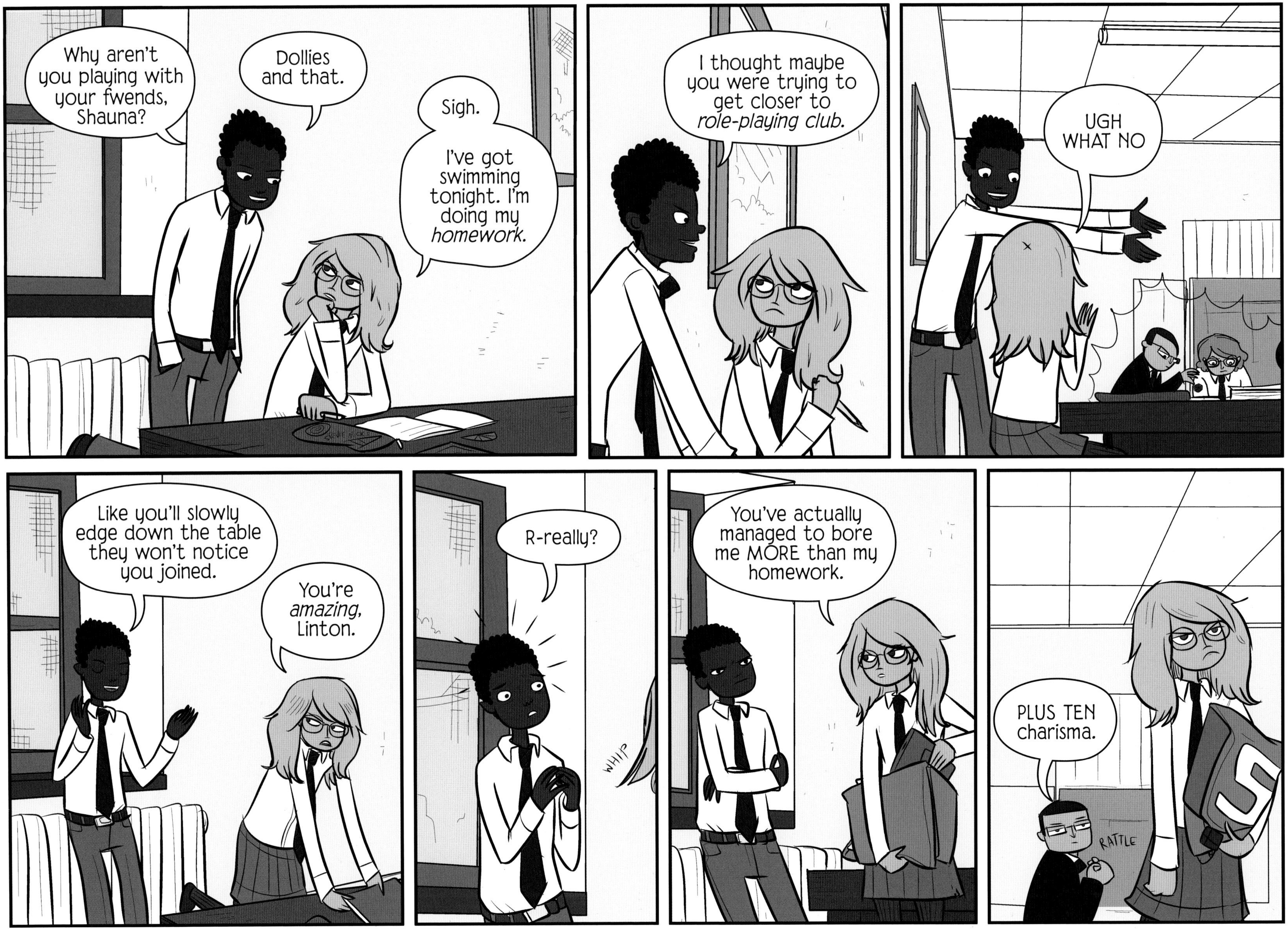
Why aren't you playing with your fwends, Shauna?
Dollies and that.
Sigh.
I've got swimming tonight. I'm doing my *homework*.
I thought maybe you were trying to get closer to *role-playing club*.
UGH WHAT NO
Like you'll slowly edge down the table they won't notice you joined.
You're *amazing*, Linton.
R-really?
WHIP
You've actually managed to bore me MORE than my homework.
PLUS TEN charisma.
RATTLE

Just keep an eye on Mildred, she's been quiet the last couple of days.

They're growing up. Suddenly they have to keep EVERY-THING secret.

When they were noisy, at least you always knew what they were up to.

He's a bit *wrong*.

So what do you want to play?

Tom, I'm really not sure about this new friend of hers.

I don't know. I'm going to the toilet. You two decide.

You're the guest, you choose, Lem.

OW OW I've got something in my eye!!

Don't rub it, let me look!

You'll like me when you get to know me, Sonny...

I'm a right... good... laugh.

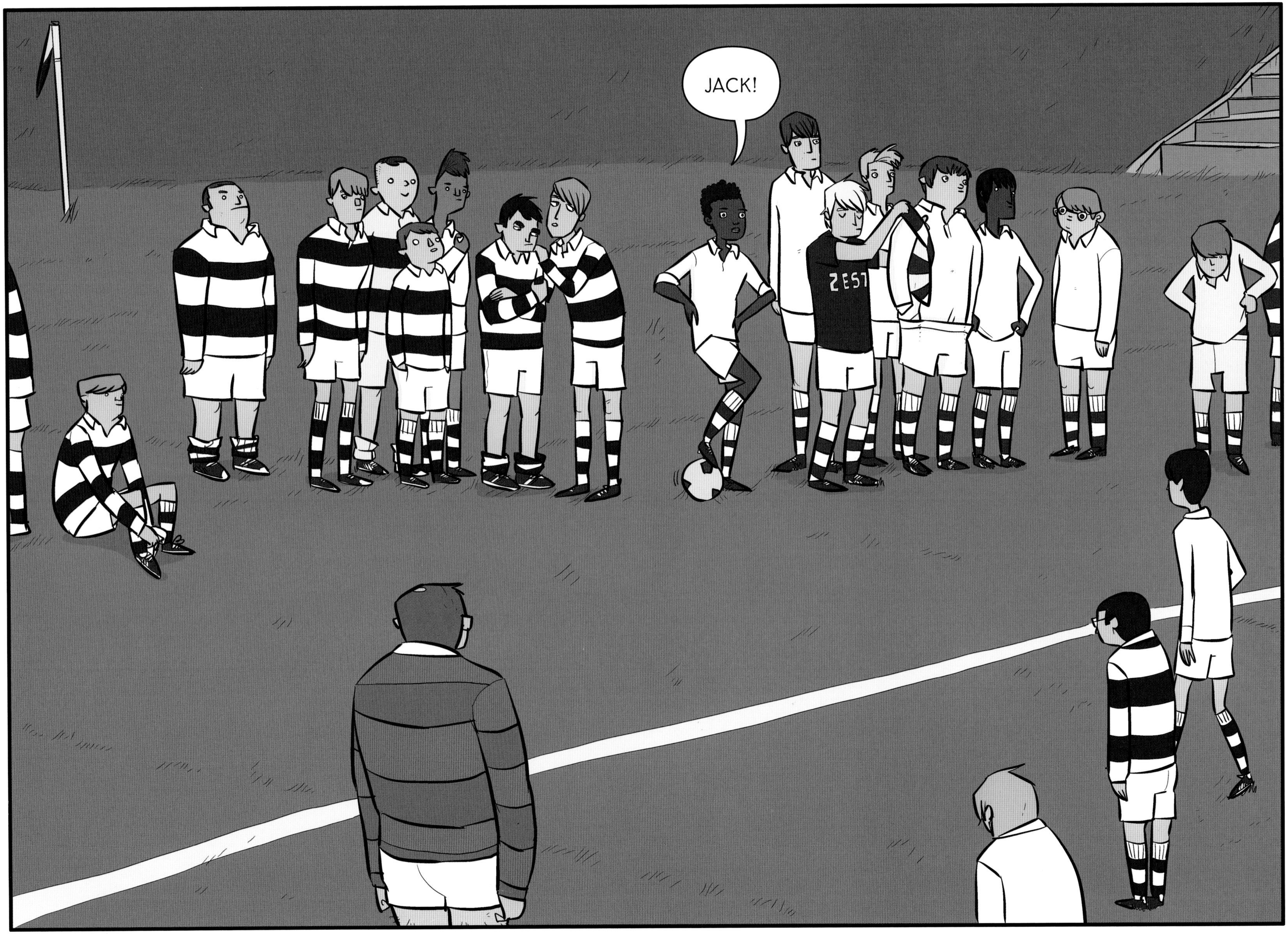
JACK!

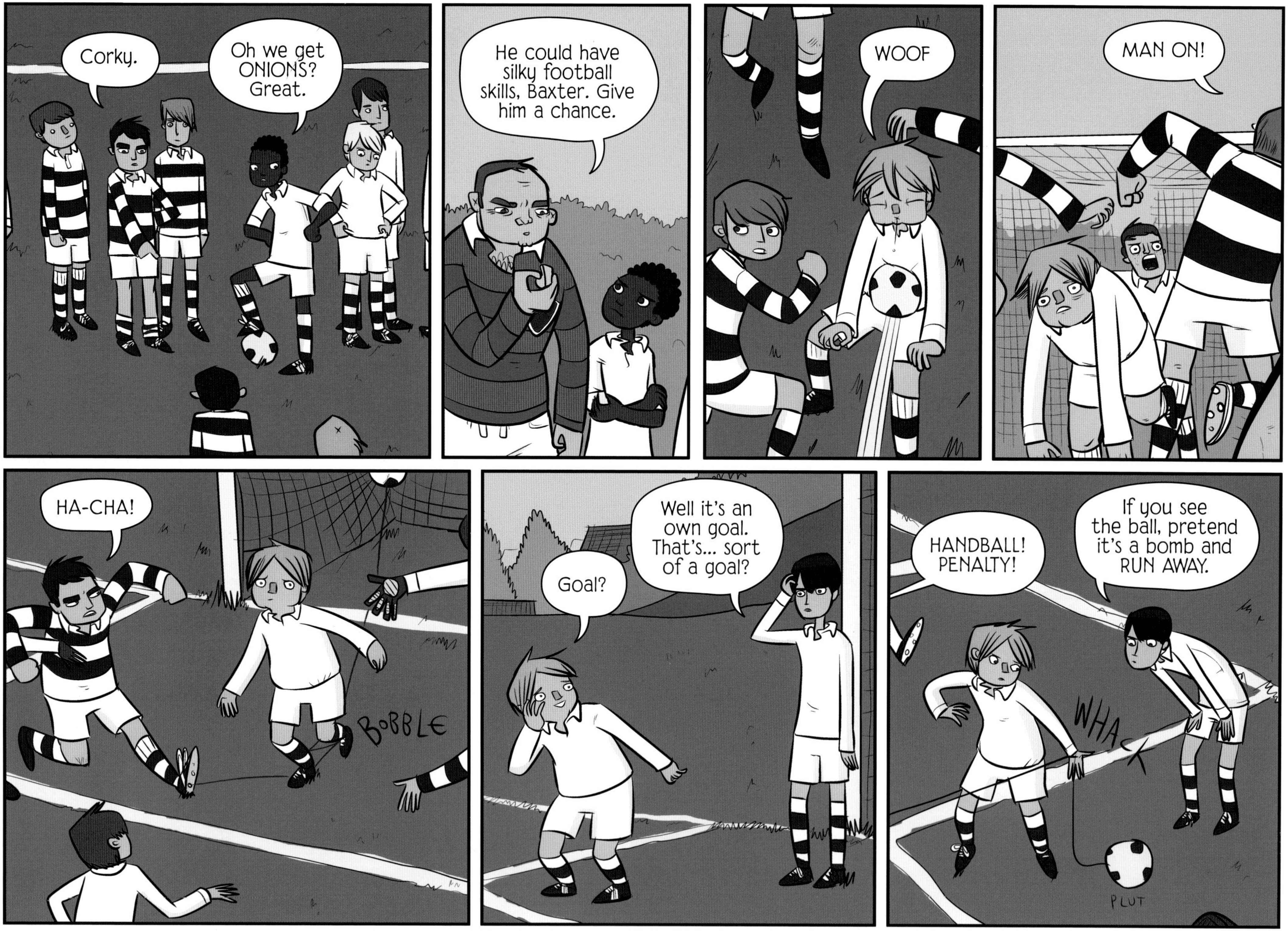
Corky.
Oh we get ONIONS? Great.
He could have silky football skills, Baxter. Give him a chance.
WOOF
MAN ON!
HA-CHA!
BOBBLE
Goal?
Well it's an own goal. That's... sort of a goal?
HANDBALL! PENALTY!
If you see the ball, pretend it's a bomb and RUN AWAY.
WHACK
PLUT

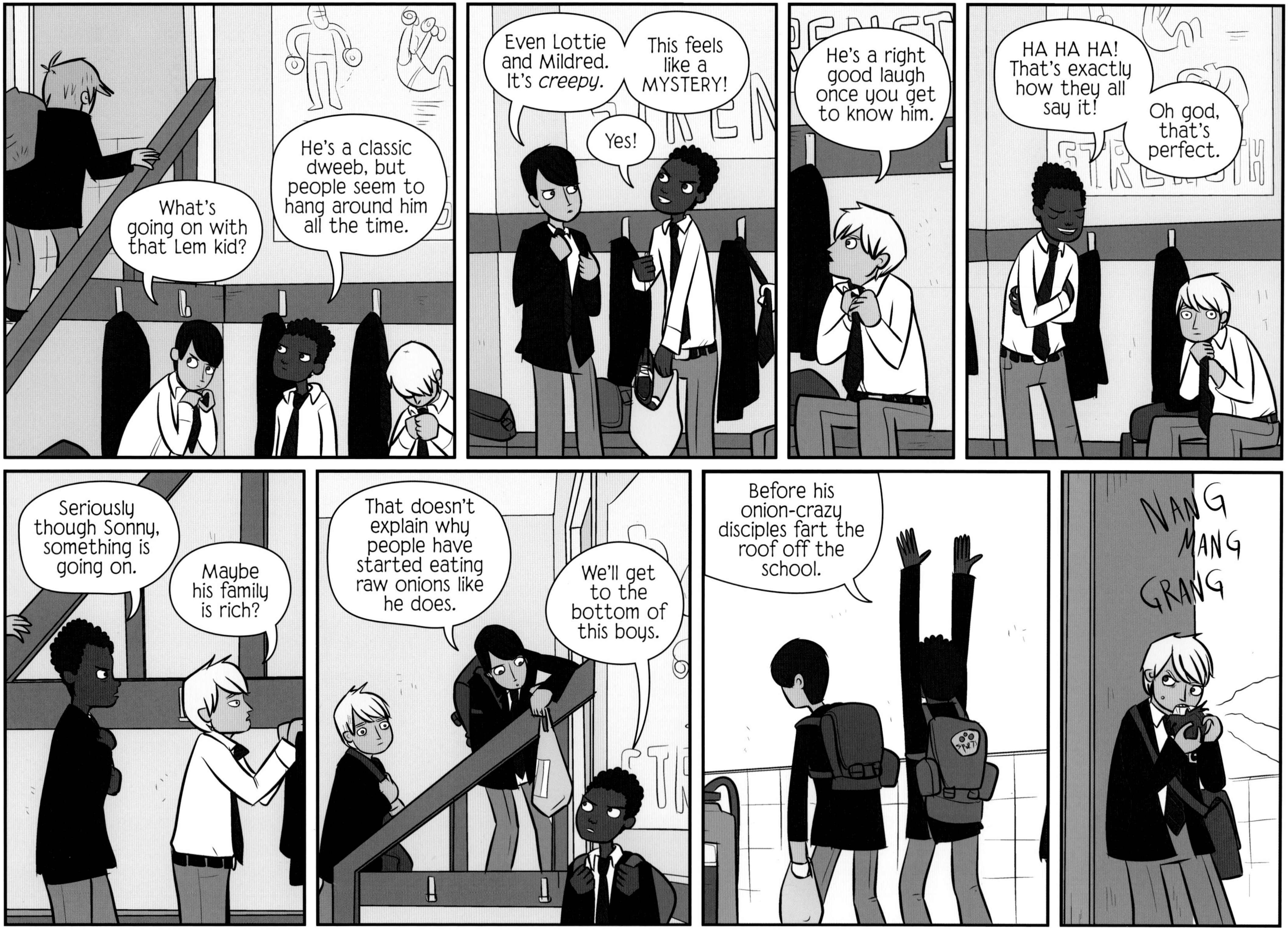
What's going on with that Lem kid?
He's a classic dweeb, but people seem to hang around him all the time.
Even Lottie and Mildred. It's *creepy*.
This feels like a MYSTERY!
Yes!
He's a right good laugh once you get to know him.
HA HA HA! That's exactly how they all say it!
Oh god, that's perfect.
Seriously though Sonny, something is going on.
Maybe his family is rich?
That doesn't explain why people have started eating raw onions like he does.
We'll get to the bottom of this boys.
Before his onion-crazy disciples fart the roof off the school.
NANG
MANG
GRANG

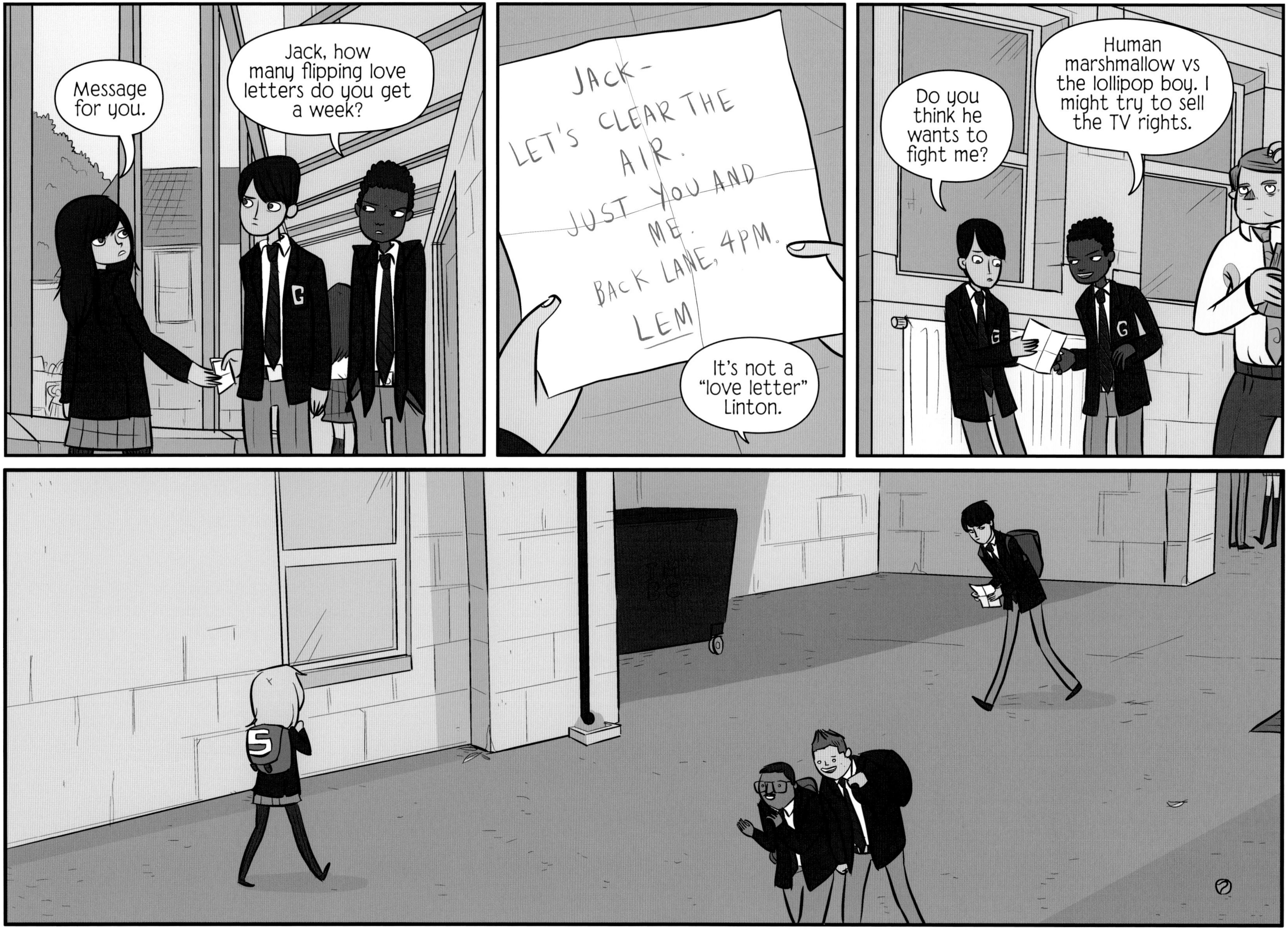

Message for you.
Jack, how many flipping love letters do you get a week?
JACK -
LET'S CLEAR THE AIR.
JUST YOU AND ME.
BACK LANE, 4PM.
LEM
It's not a "love letter" Linton.
Do you think he wants to fight me?
Human marshmallow vs the lollipop boy. I might try to sell the TV rights.

Bad Machinery, Volume Four

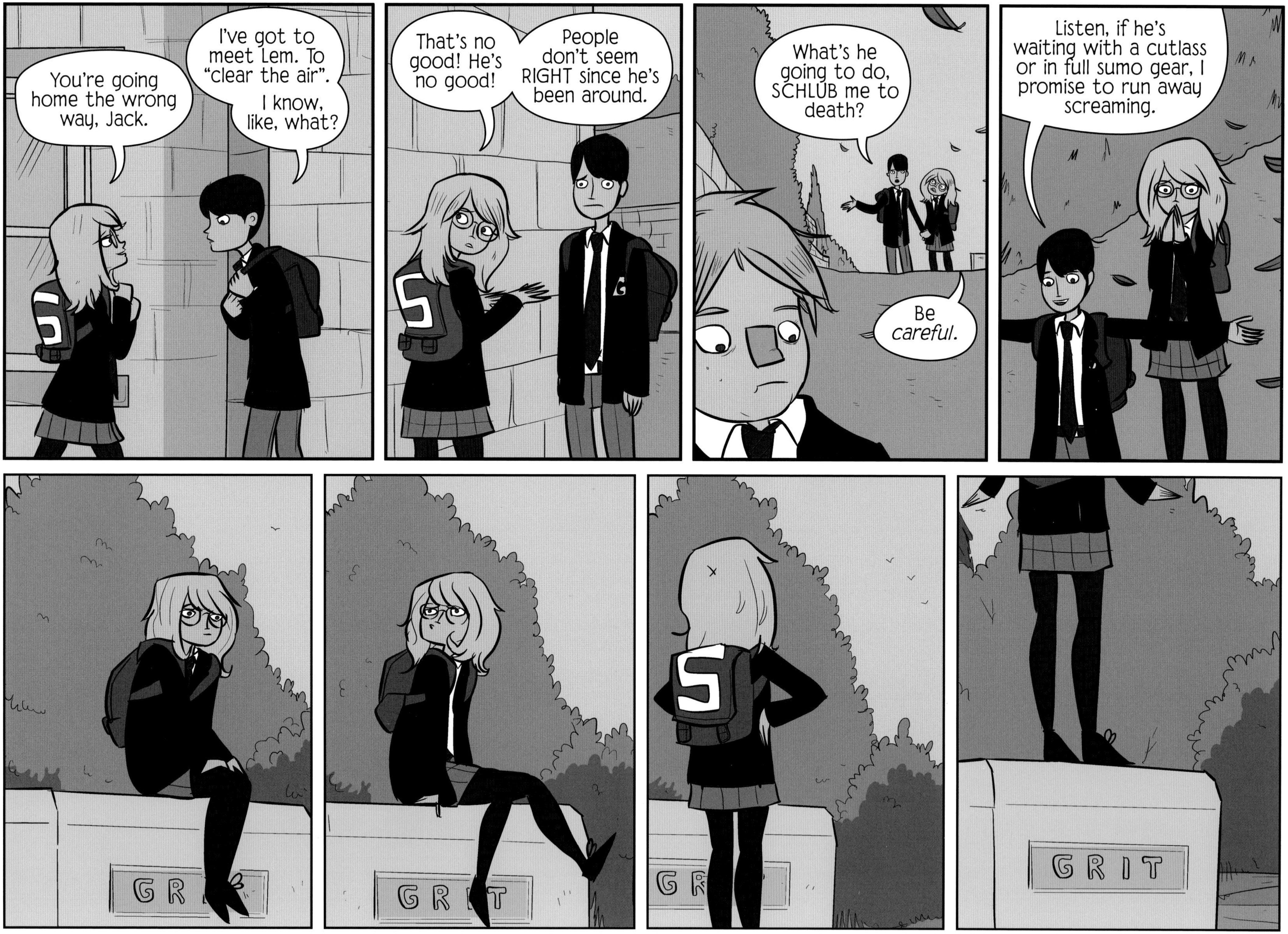
You're going home the wrong way, Jack.
I've got to meet Lem. To "clear the air".
I know, like, what?
That's no good! He's no good!
People don't seem RIGHT since he's been around.
What's he going to do, SCHLUB me to death?
Be *careful.*
Listen, if he's waiting with a cutlass or in full sumo gear, I promise to run away screaming.
GRIT

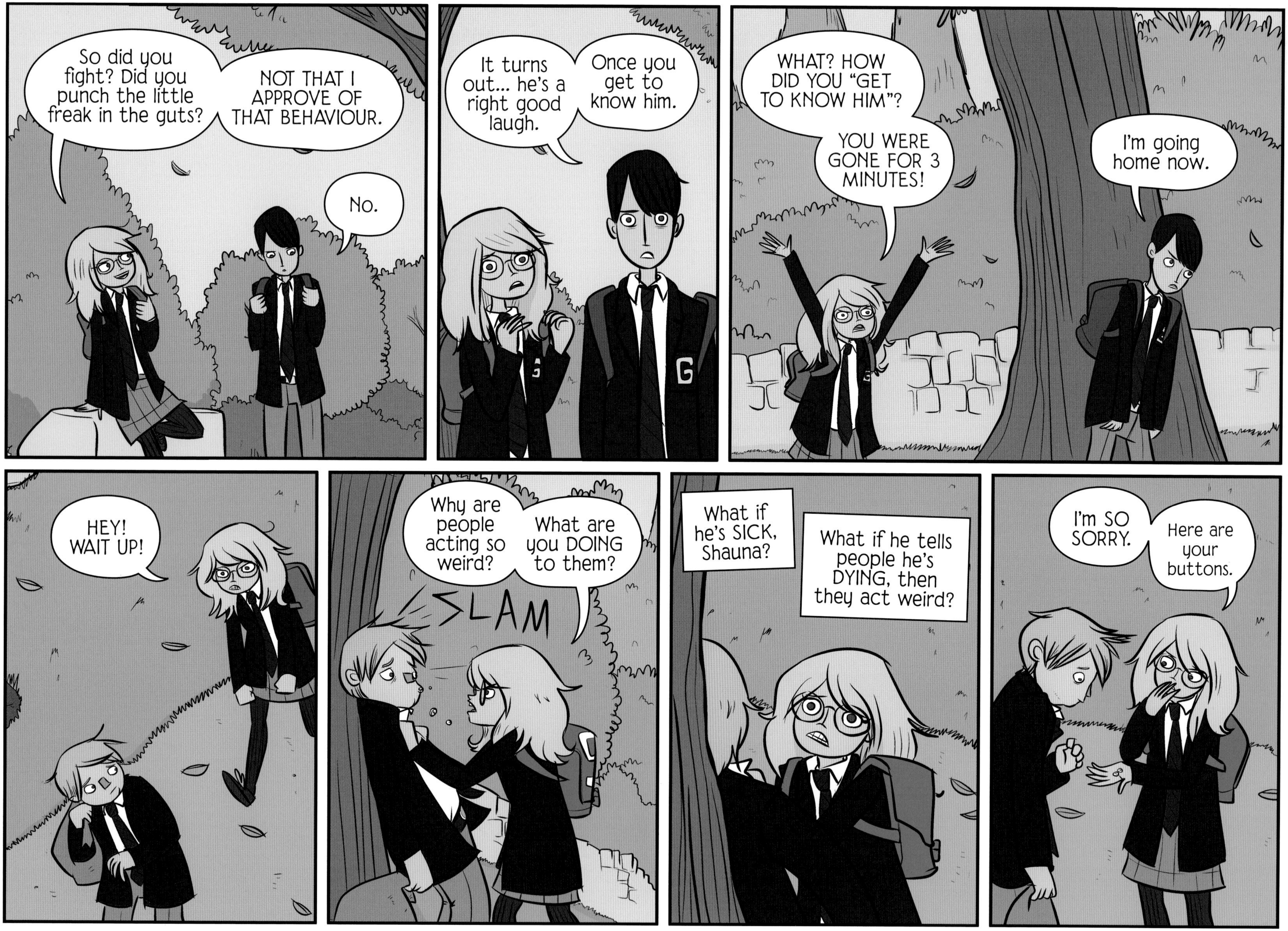
So did you fight? Did you punch the little freak in the guts?
NOT THAT I APPROVE OF THAT BEHAVIOUR.
No.
It turns out... he's a right good laugh.
Once you get to know him.
WHAT? HOW DID YOU "GET TO KNOW HIM"?
YOU WERE GONE FOR 3 MINUTES!
I'm going home now.
HEY! WAIT UP!
Why are people acting so weird?
What are you DOING to them?
SLAM
What if he's SICK, Shauna?
What if he tells people he's DYING, then they act weird?
I'm SO SORRY.
Here are your buttons.

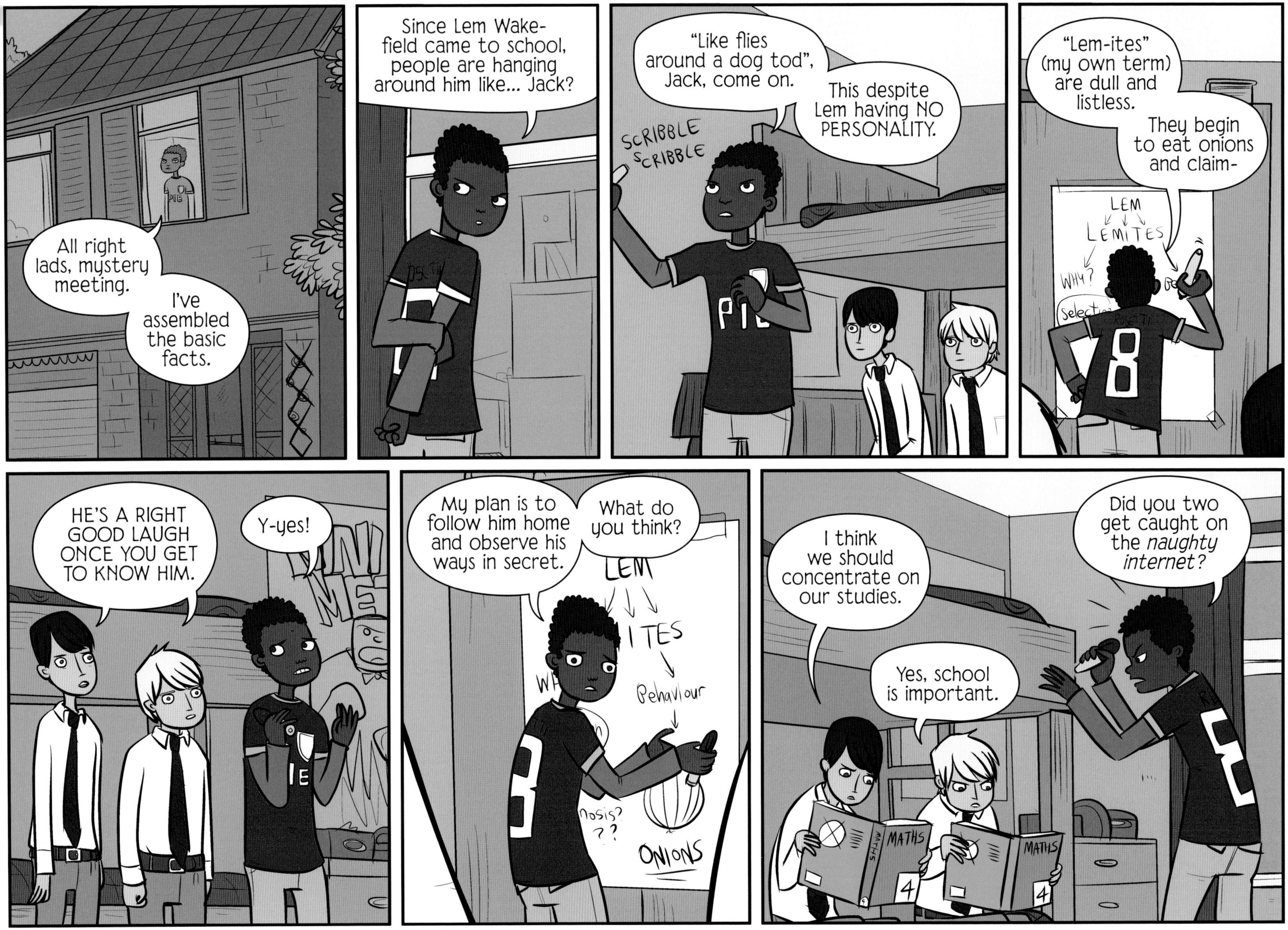
All right lads, mystery meeting.
I've assembled the basic facts.
Since Lem Wakefield came to school, people are hanging around him like... Jack?
"Like flies around a dog tod", Jack, come on.
SCRIBBLE SCRIBBLE
This despite Lem having NO PERSONALITY.
"Lem-ites" (my own term) are dull and listless.
They begin to eat onions and claim-
LEM
LEMITES
WHY?
HE'S A RIGHT GOOD LAUGH ONCE YOU GET TO KNOW HIM.
Y-yes!
My plan is to follow him home and observe his ways in secret.
What do you think?
LEM
ITES
Behaviour
ONIONS
I think we should concentrate on our studies.
Yes, school is important.
Did you two get caught on the *naughty internet?*
MATHS
MATHS

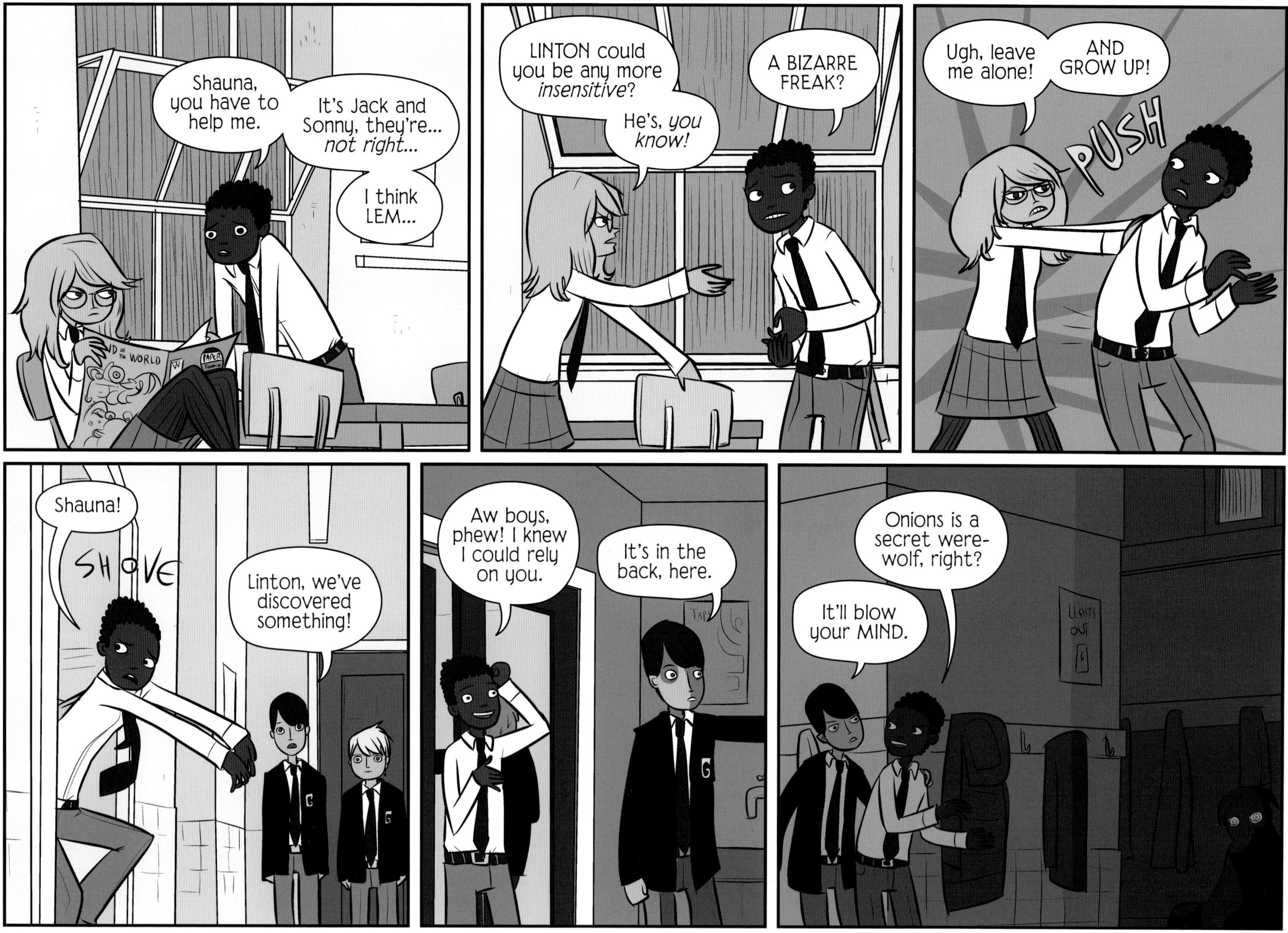
Shauna, you have to help me.
It's Jack and Sonny, they're... *not right*...
I think LEM...
LINTON could you be any more *insensitive*?
He's, *you know*!
A BIZARRE FREAK?
Ugh, leave me alone!
AND GROW UP!
PUSH
Shauna!
SHOVE
Linton, we've discovered something!
Aw boys, phew! I knew I could rely on you.
It's in the back, here.
Onions is a secret were-wolf, right?
It'll blow your MIND.

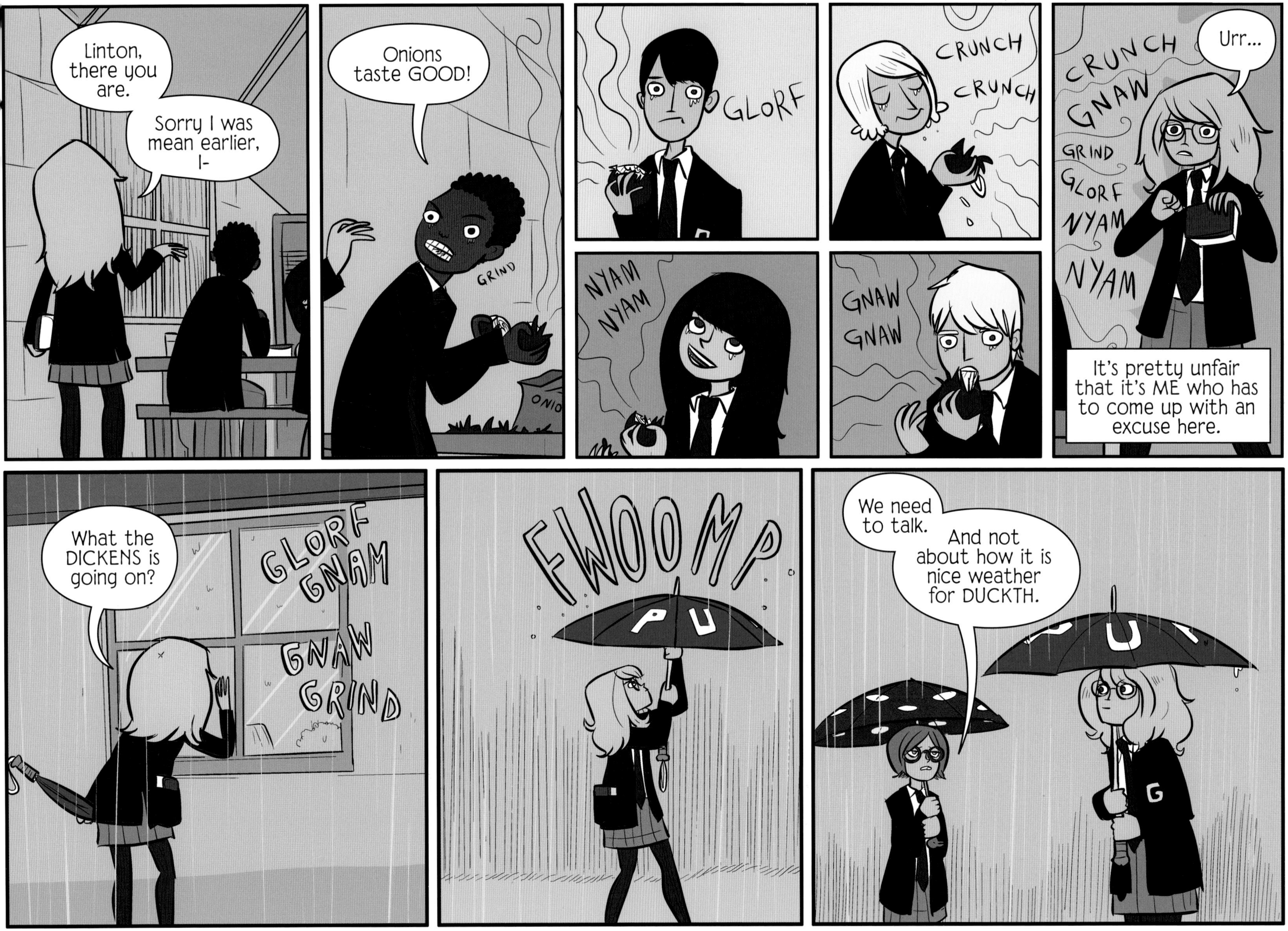
Linton, there you are.
Sorry I was mean earlier, I-
Onions taste GOOD!
GRIND
GLORF
CRUNCH
CRUNCH
NYAM NYAM
GNAW GNAW
CRUNCH GNAW GRIND GLORF NYAM NYAM
Urr...
It's pretty unfair that it's ME who has to come up with an excuse here.
What the DICKENS is going on?
GLORF GNAM
GNAW GRIND
FWOOMP
We need to talk.
And not about how it is nice weather for DUCKTH.

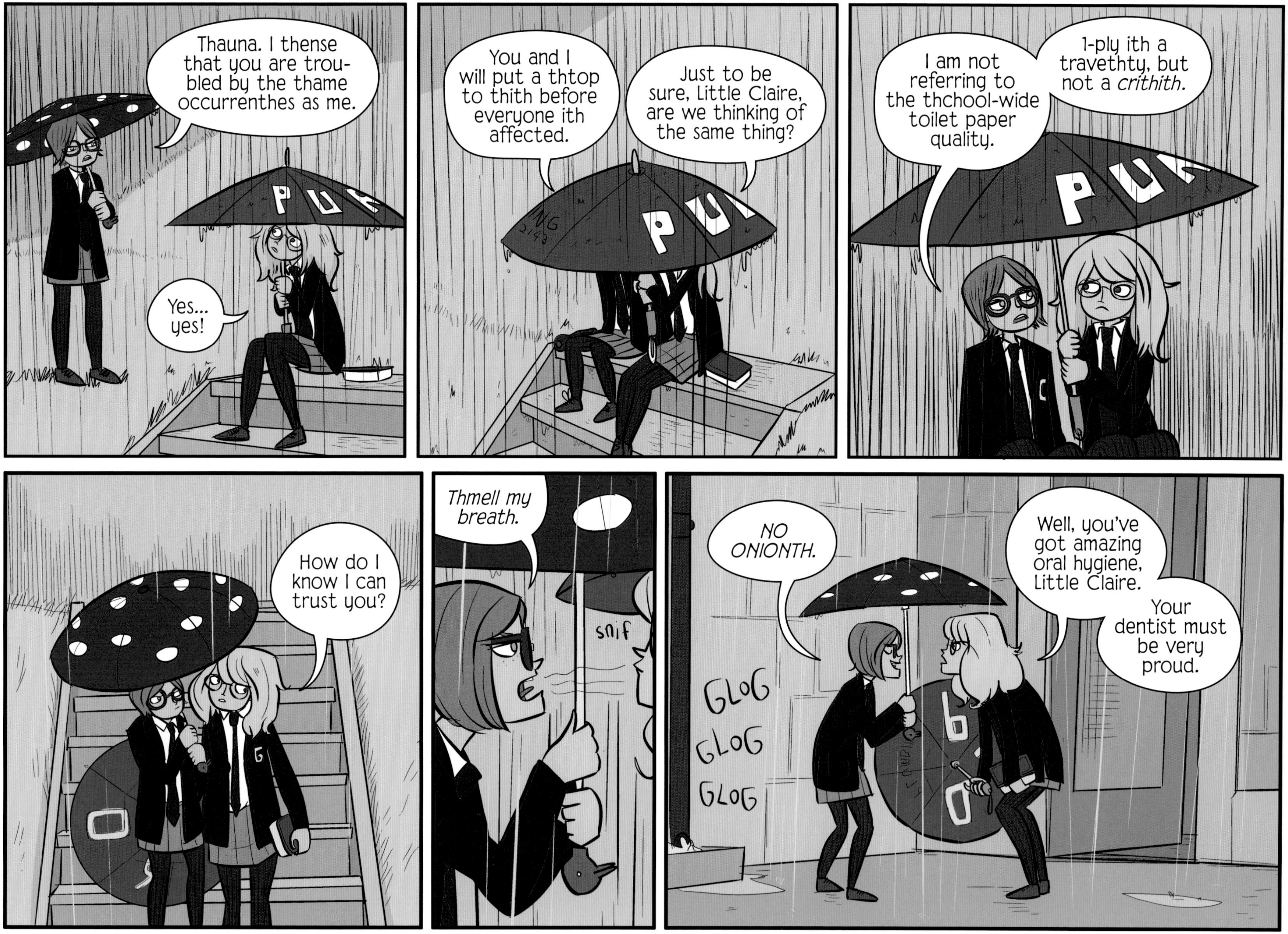
Thauna. I thense that you are troubled by the thame occurrenthes as me.
Yes... yes!
You and I will put a thtop to thith before everyone ith affected.
Just to be sure, Little Claire, are we thinking of the same thing?
I am not referring to the thchool-wide toilet paper quality.
1-ply ith a travethty, but not a *crithith.*
How do I know I can trust you?
Thmell my breath.
snif
NO ONIONTH.
Well, you've got amazing oral hygiene, Little Claire.
Your dentist must be very proud.
GLOG
GLOG
GLOG

The Case of the Lonely One

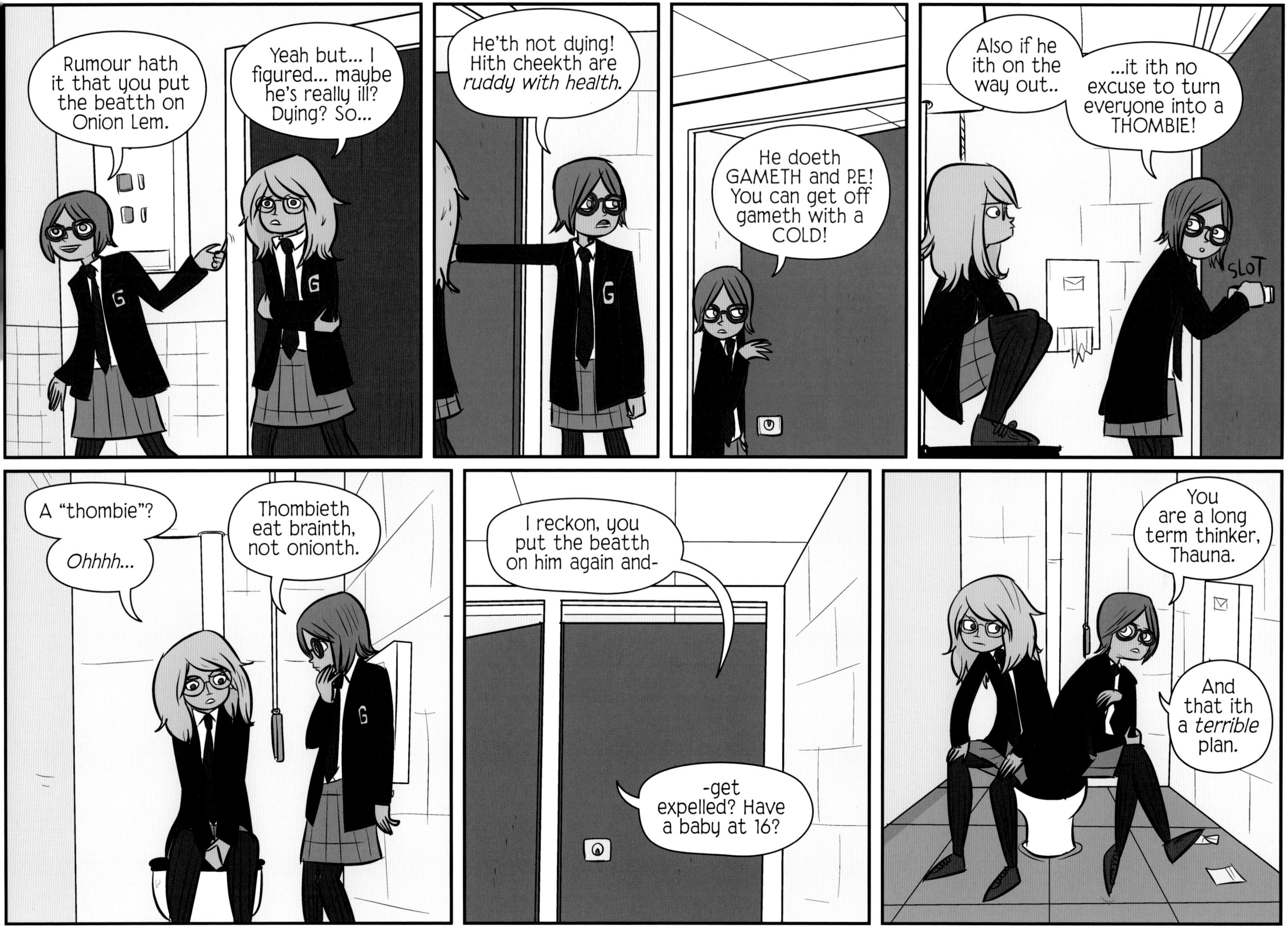
Rumour hath it that you put the beatth on Onion Lem.
Yeah but... I figured... maybe he's really ill? Dying? So...
He'th not dying! Hith cheekth are *ruddy with health.*
He doeth GAMETH and P.E! You can get off gameth with a COLD!
Also if he ith on the way out..
...it ith no excuse to turn everyone into a THOMBIE!
SLOT
A "thombie"?
Ohhhh...
Thombieth eat brainth, not onionth.
I reckon, you put the beatth on him again and-
-get expelled? Have a baby at 16?
You are a long term thinker, Thauna.
And that ith a *terrible* plan.

Bad Machinery, Volume Four

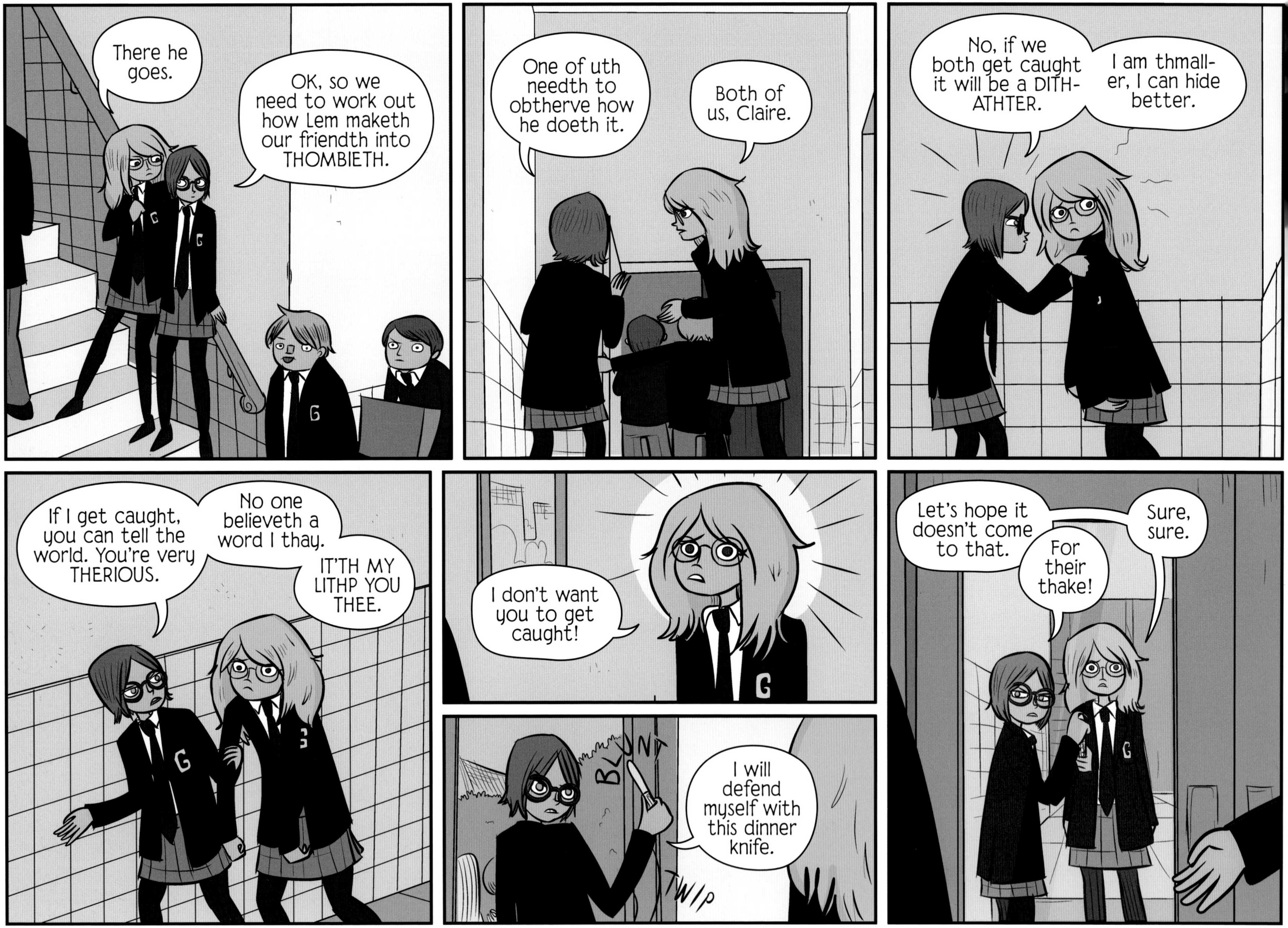
There he goes.
OK, so we need to work out how Lem maketh our friendth into THOMBIETH.
One of uth needth to obtherve how he doeth it.
Both of us, Claire.
No, if we both get caught it will be a DITH-ATHTER.
I am thmall-er, I can hide better.
If I get caught, you can tell the world. You're very THERIOUS.
No one believeth a word I thay.
IT'TH MY LITHP YOU THEE.
I don't want you to get caught!
BLUNT
I will defend myself with this dinner knife.
TWIP
Let's hope it doesn't come to that.
Sure, sure.
For their thake!

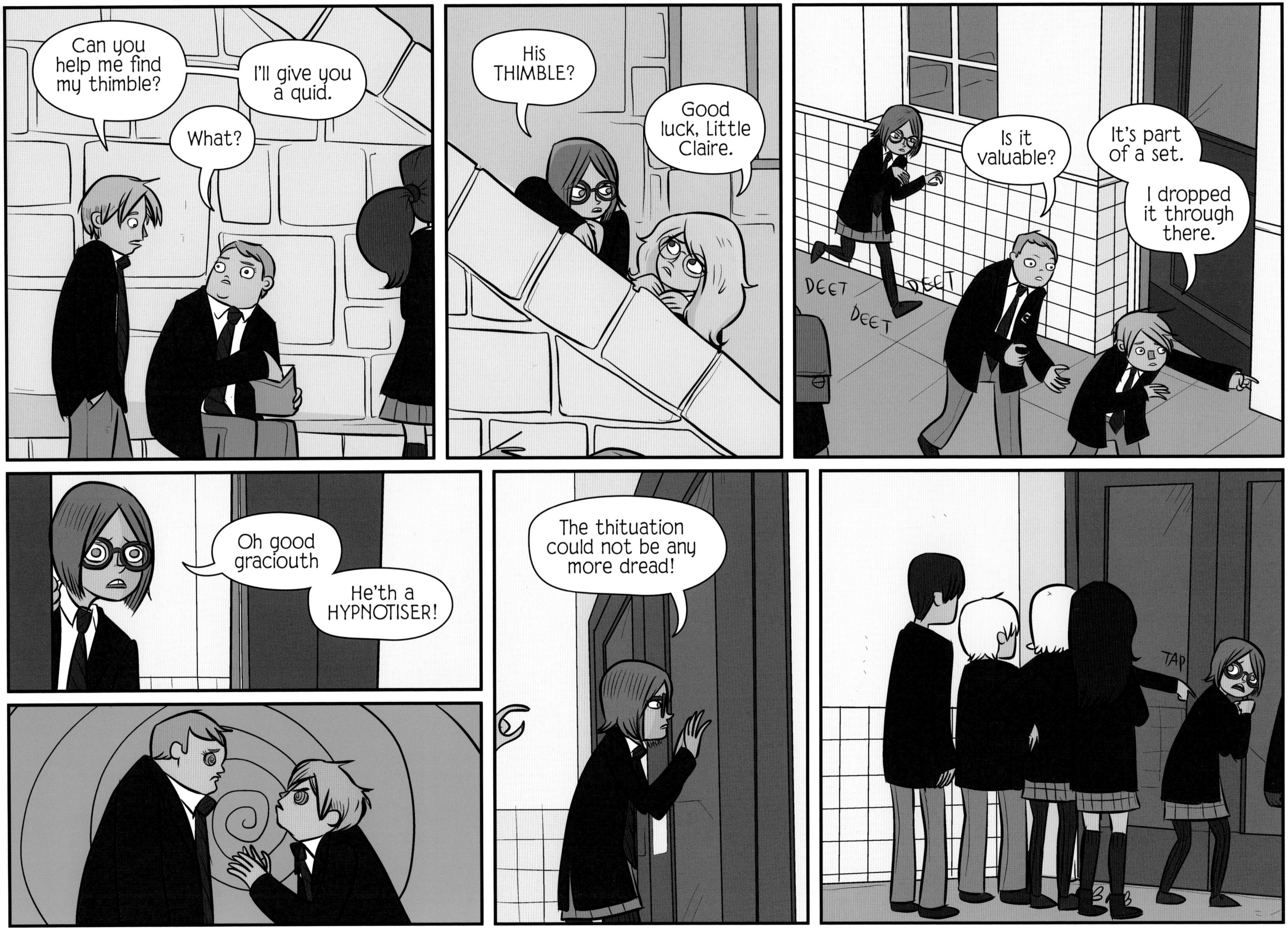
Can you help me find my thimble?
What?
I'll give you a quid.
His THIMBLE?
Good luck, Little Claire.
DEET
DEET
DEET
Is it valuable?
It's part of a set.
I dropped it through there.
Oh good graciouth
He'th a HYPNOTISER!
The thituation could not be any more dread!
TAP

The Case of the Lonely One

50

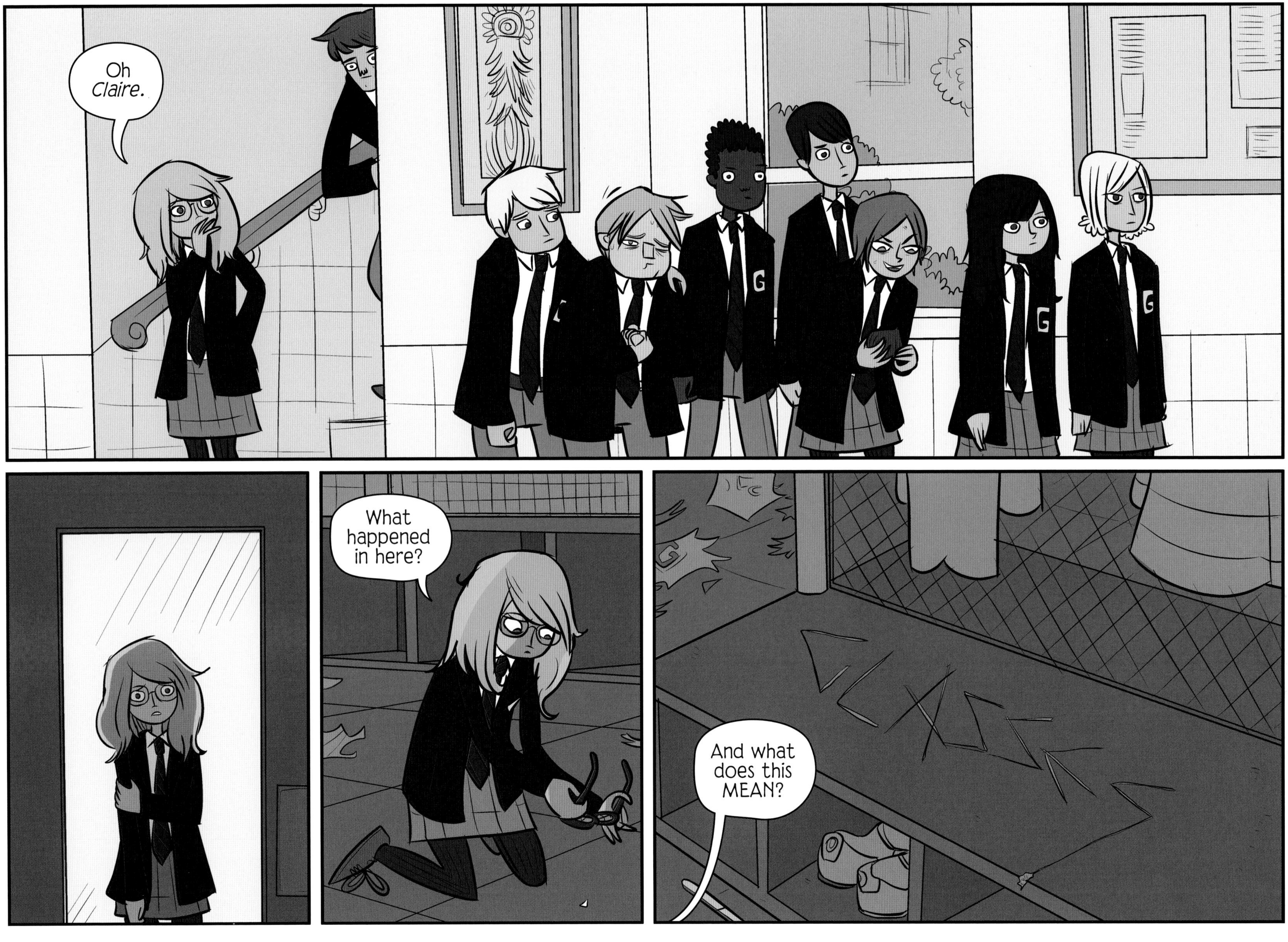
Oh Claire.
What happened in here?
And what does this MEAN?

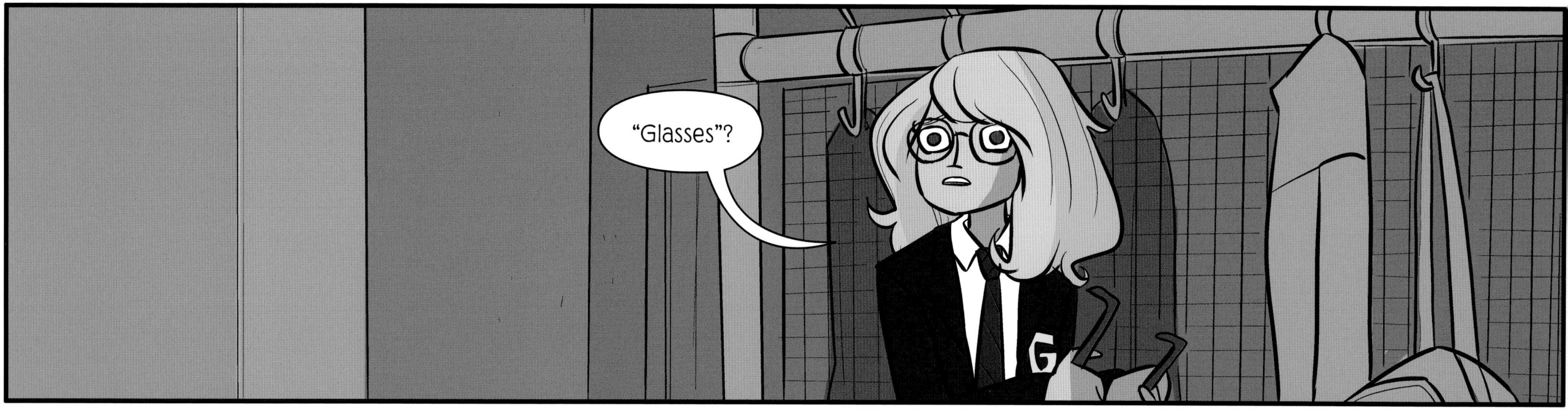
"Glasses"?

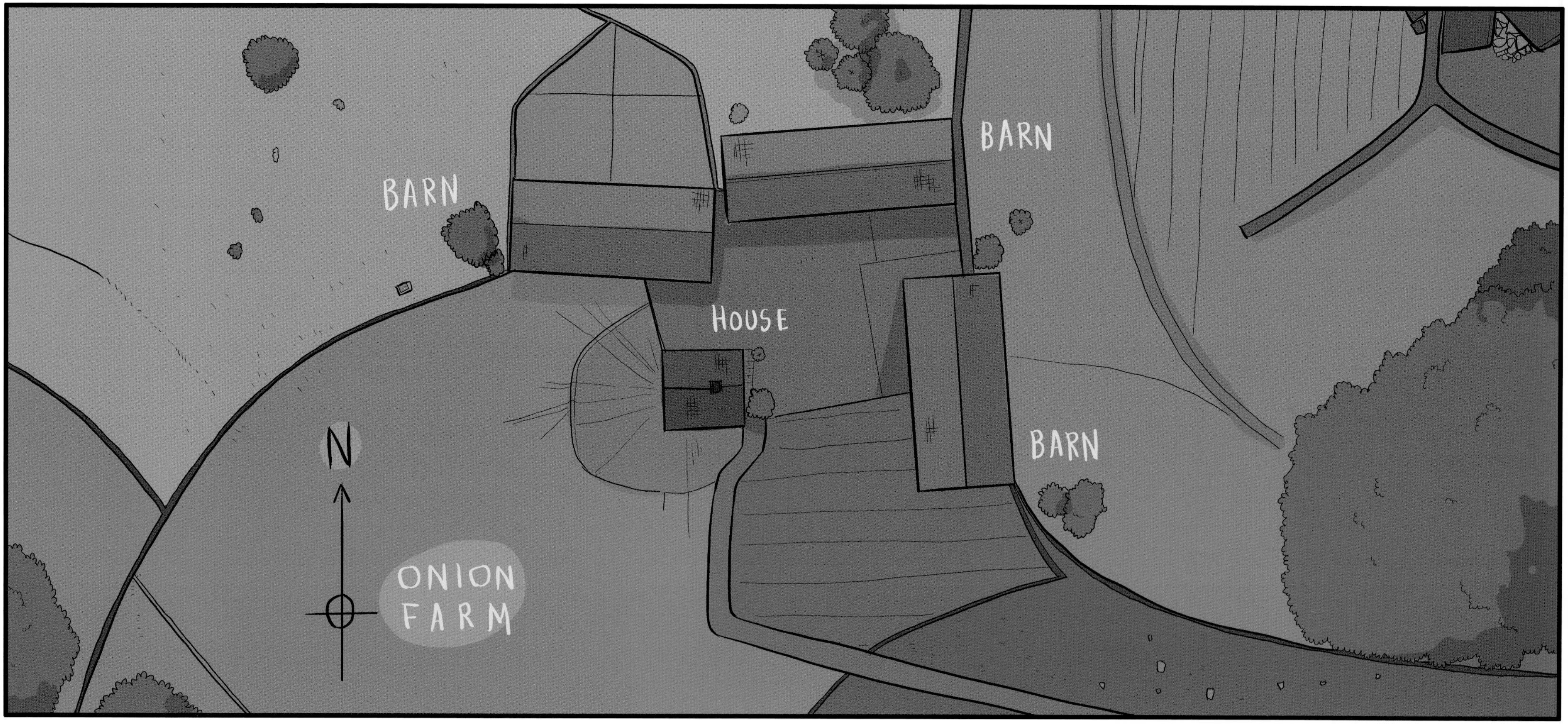
BARN
BARN
HOUSE
BARN
N
ONION FARM

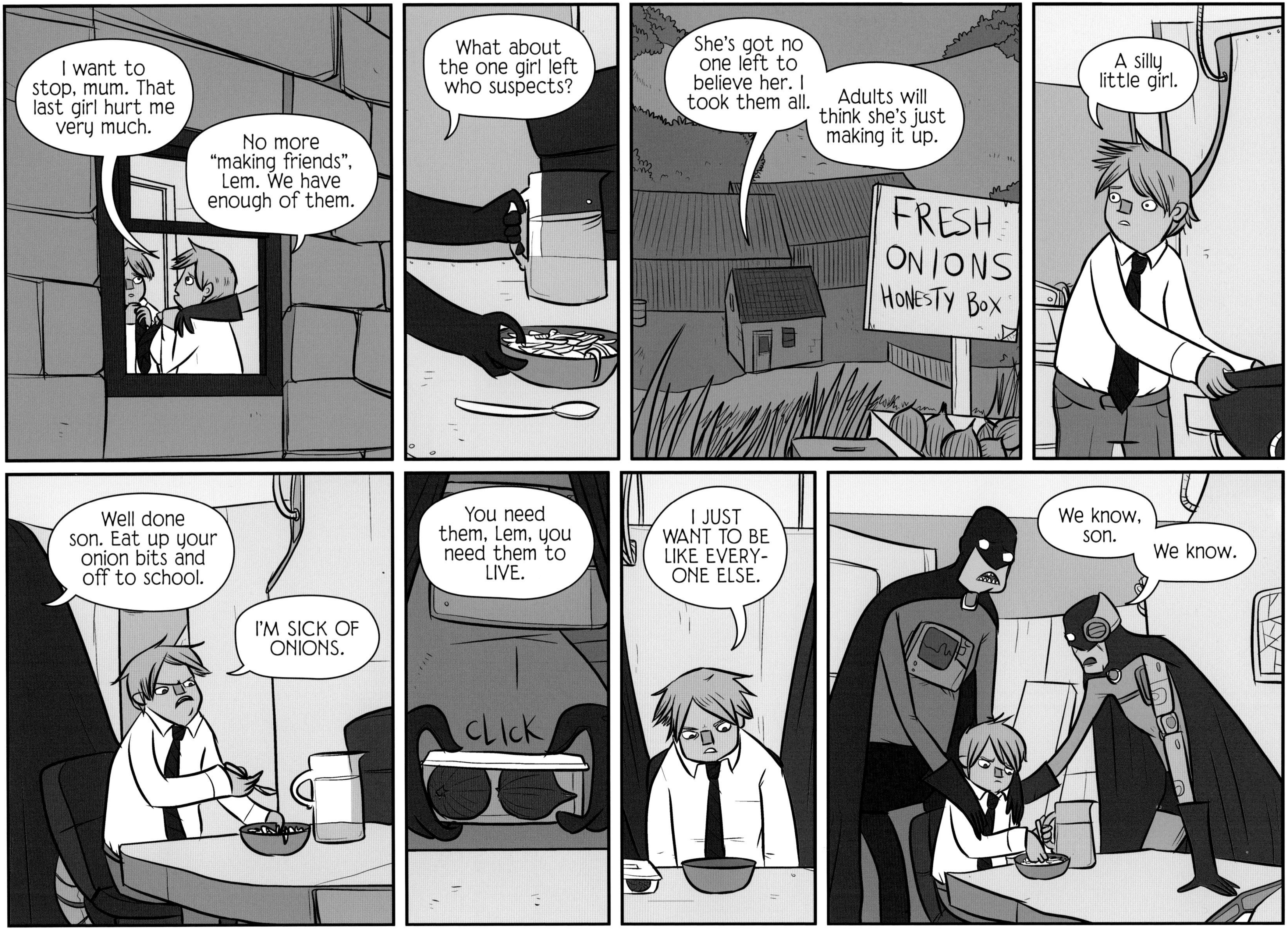
I want to stop, mum. That last girl hurt me very much.
No more "making friends", Lem. We have enough of them.
What about the one girl left who suspects?
She's got no one left to believe her. I took them all.
Adults will think she's just making it up.
FRESH ONIONS HONESTY BOX
A silly little girl.
Well done son. Eat up your onion bits and off to school.
I'M SICK OF ONIONS.
You need them, Lem, you need them to LIVE.
CLICK
I JUST WANT TO BE LIKE EVERY-ONE ELSE.
We know, son.
We know.

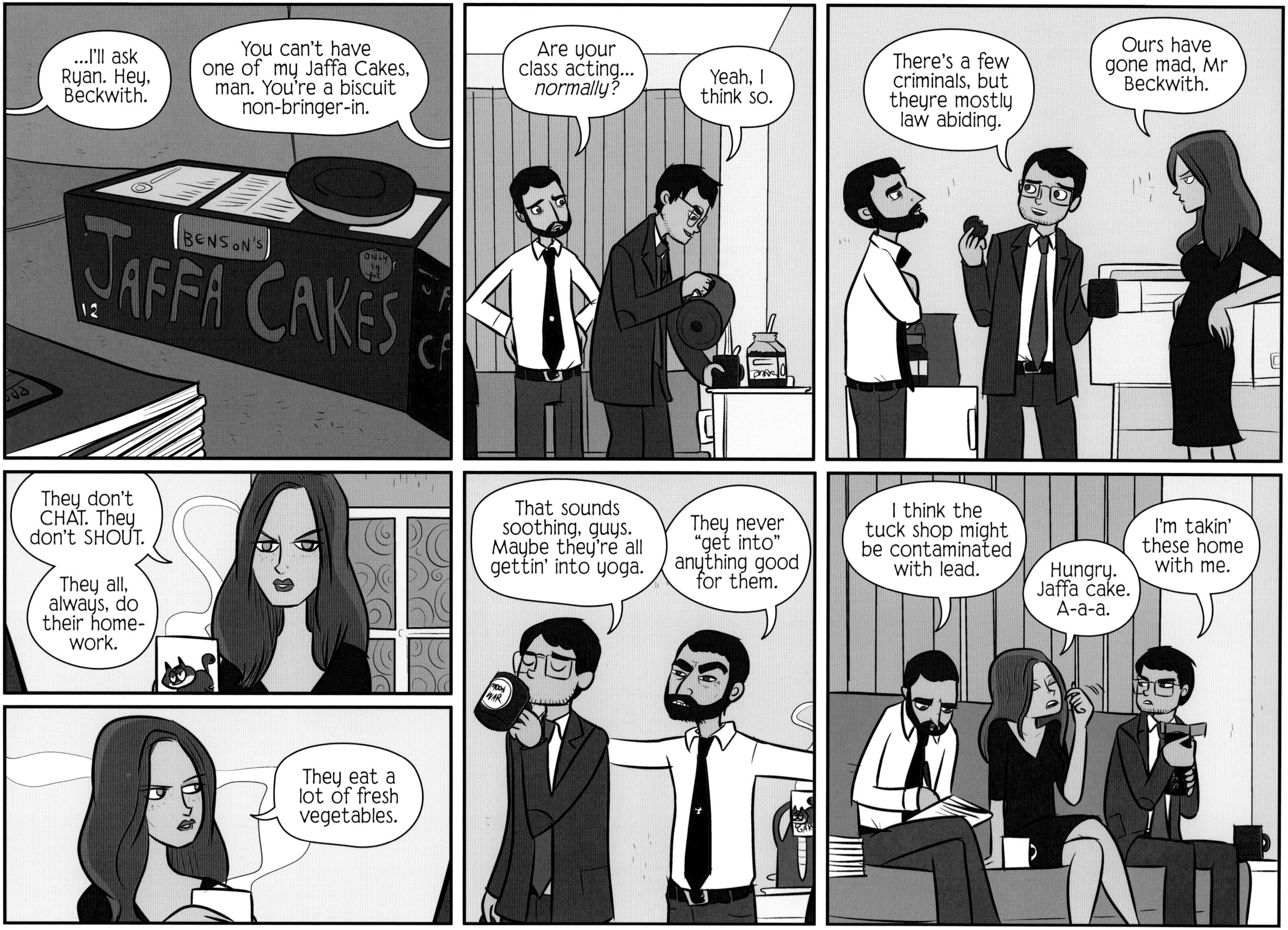
...I'll ask Ryan. Hey, Beckwith.
You can't have one of my Jaffa Cakes, man. You're a biscuit non-bringer-in.
BENSON'S
JAFFA CAKES
Are your class acting... *normally*?
Yeah, I think so.
There's a few criminals, but theyre mostly law abiding.
Ours have gone mad, Mr Beckwith.
They don't CHAT. They don't SHOUT.
They all, always, do their home-work.
They eat a lot of fresh vegetables.
That sounds soothing, guys. Maybe they're all gettin' into yoga.
They never "get into" anything good for them.
I think the tuck shop might be contaminated with lead.
Hungry. Jaffa cake. A-a-a.
I'm takin' these home with me.

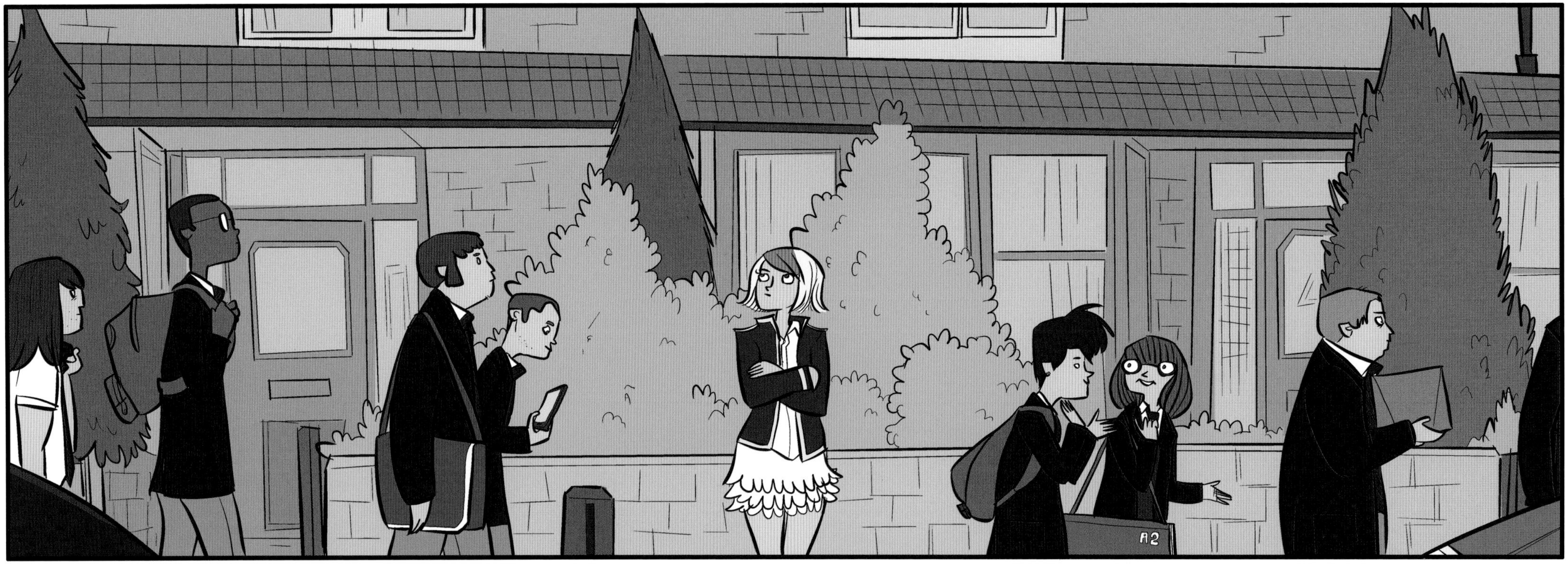

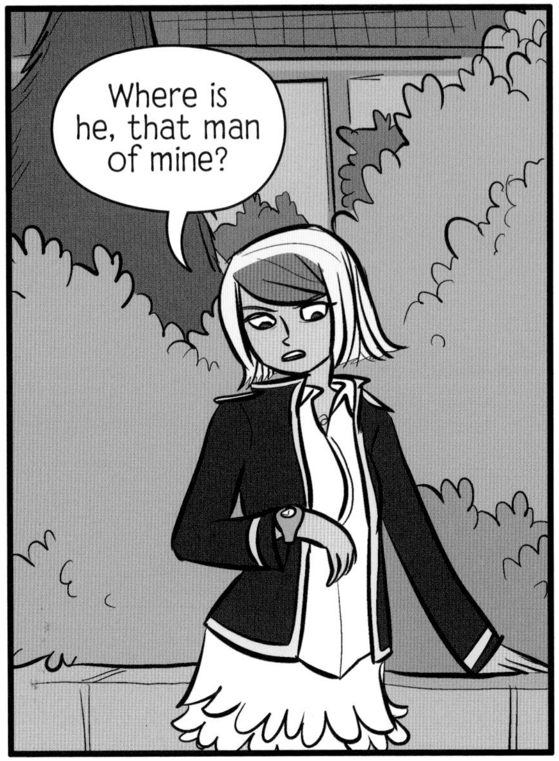
Where is he, that man of mine?

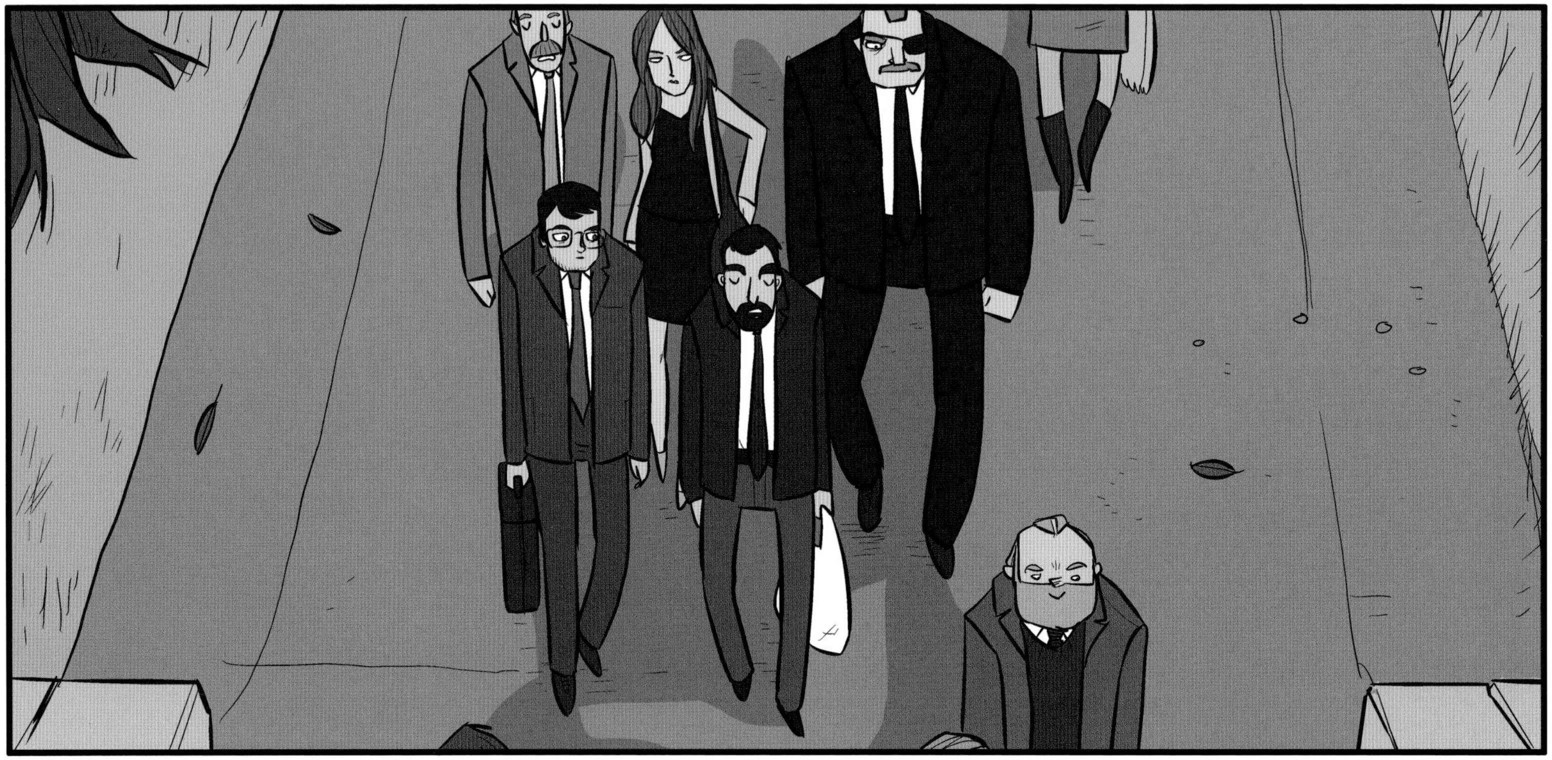

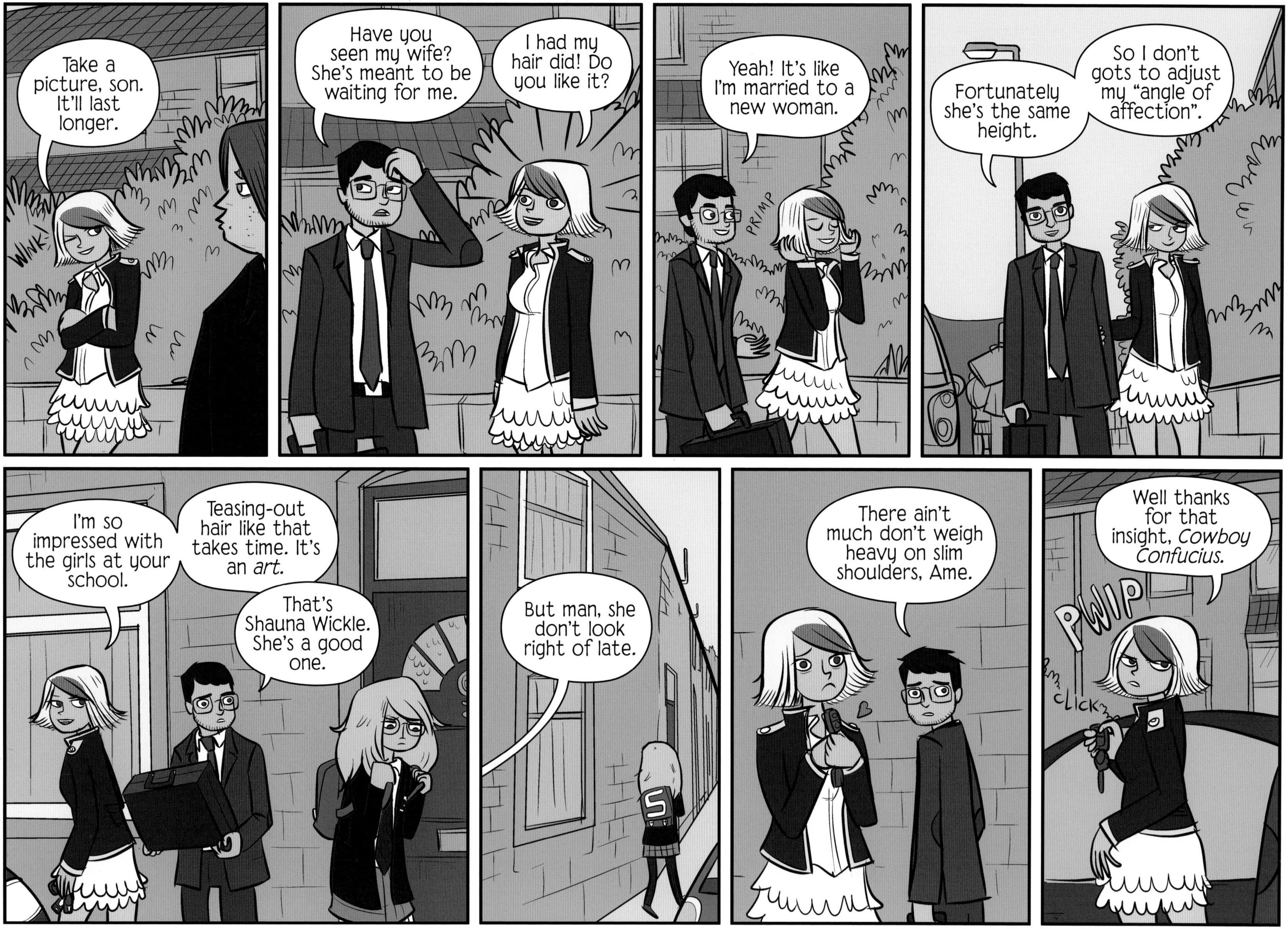
Take a picture, son. It'll last longer.
WINK
Have you seen my wife? She's meant to be waiting for me.
I had my hair did! Do you like it?
Yeah! It's like I'm married to a new woman.
PRIMP
Fortunately she's the same height.
So I don't gots to adjust my "angle of affection".
I'm so impressed with the girls at your school.
Teasing-out hair like that takes time. It's an *art*.
That's Shauna Wickle. She's a good one.
But man, she don't look right of late.
There ain't much don't weigh heavy on slim shoulders, Ame.
Well thanks for that insight, *Cowboy Confucius*.
PWIP
CLICK

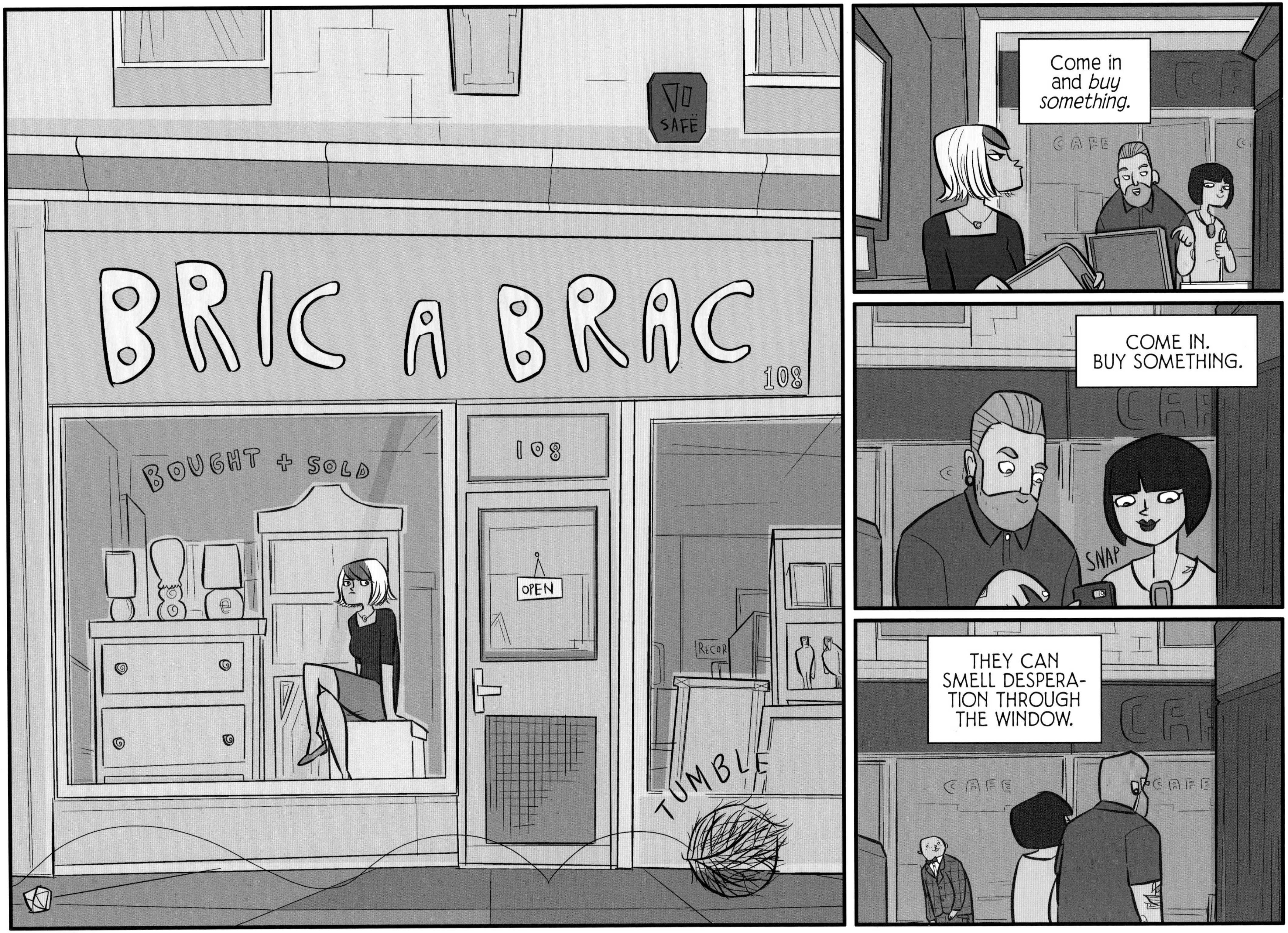
SAFË
BRIC A BRAC
108
BOUGHT + SOLD
108
OPEN
RECOR
TUMBLE
Come in and *buy something.*
CAFE
COME IN. BUY SOMETHING.
SNAP
THEY CAN SMELL DESPERA-TION THROUGH THE WINDOW.
CAFE
CAFE

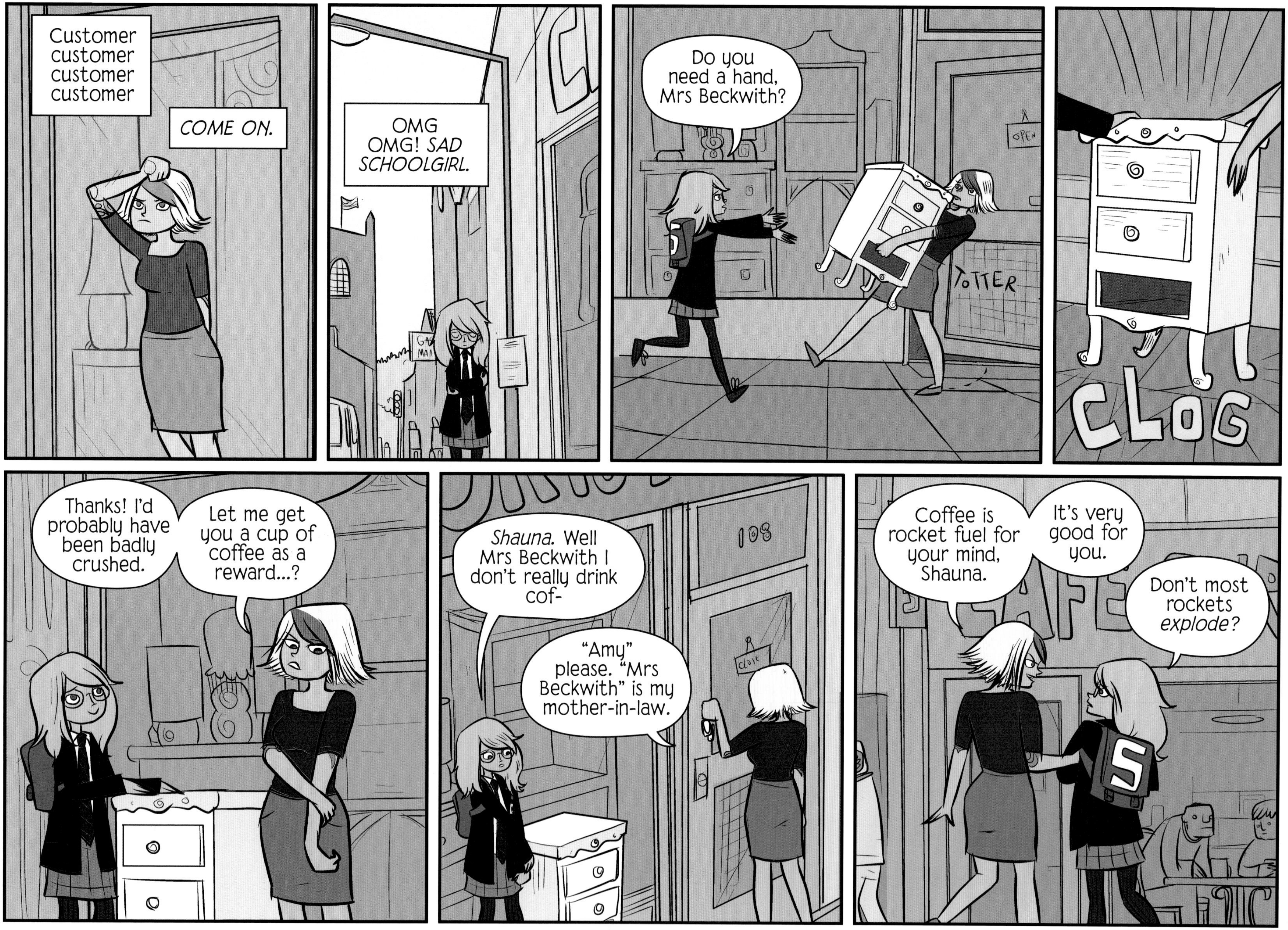

Customer customer customer customer customer
COME ON.
OMG OMG! *SAD SCHOOLGIRL.*
Do you need a hand, Mrs Beckwith?
TOTTER
CLOG
Thanks! I'd probably have been badly crushed.
Let me get you a cup of coffee as a reward...?
Shauna. Well Mrs Beckwith I don't really drink cof-
"Amy" please. "Mrs Beckwith" is my mother-in-law.
Coffee is rocket fuel for your mind, Shauna.
It's very good for you.
Don't most rockets *explode?*

The Case of the Lonely One

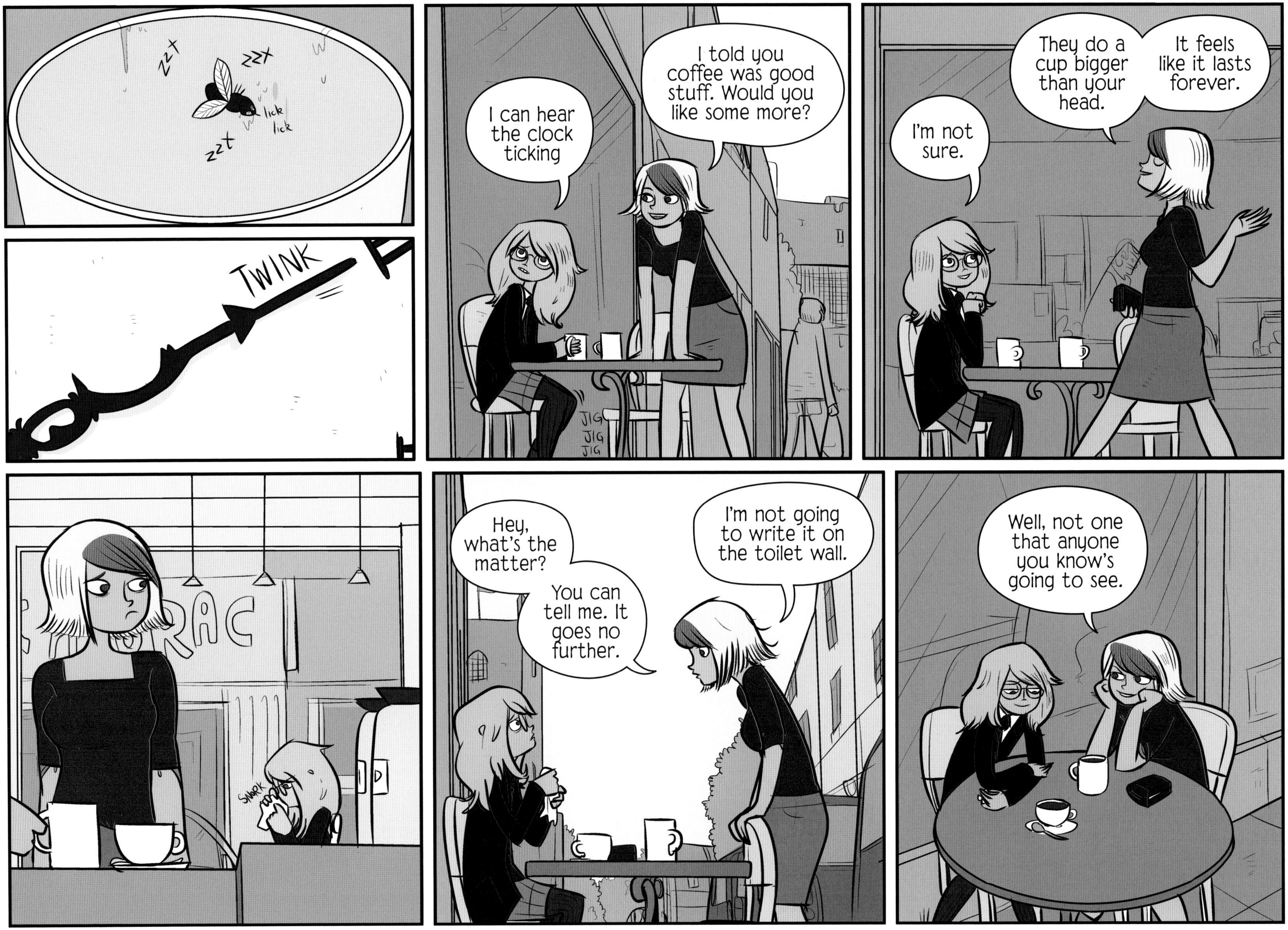

zzt
zzt
zzt
lick
lick
TWINK
I can hear the clock ticking
I told you coffee was good stuff. Would you like some more?
JIG
JIG
JIG
I'm not sure.
They do a cup bigger than your head.
It feels like it lasts forever.
SNARK
Hey, what's the matter?
You can tell me. It goes no further.
I'm not going to write it on the toilet wall.
Well, not one that anyone you know's going to see.

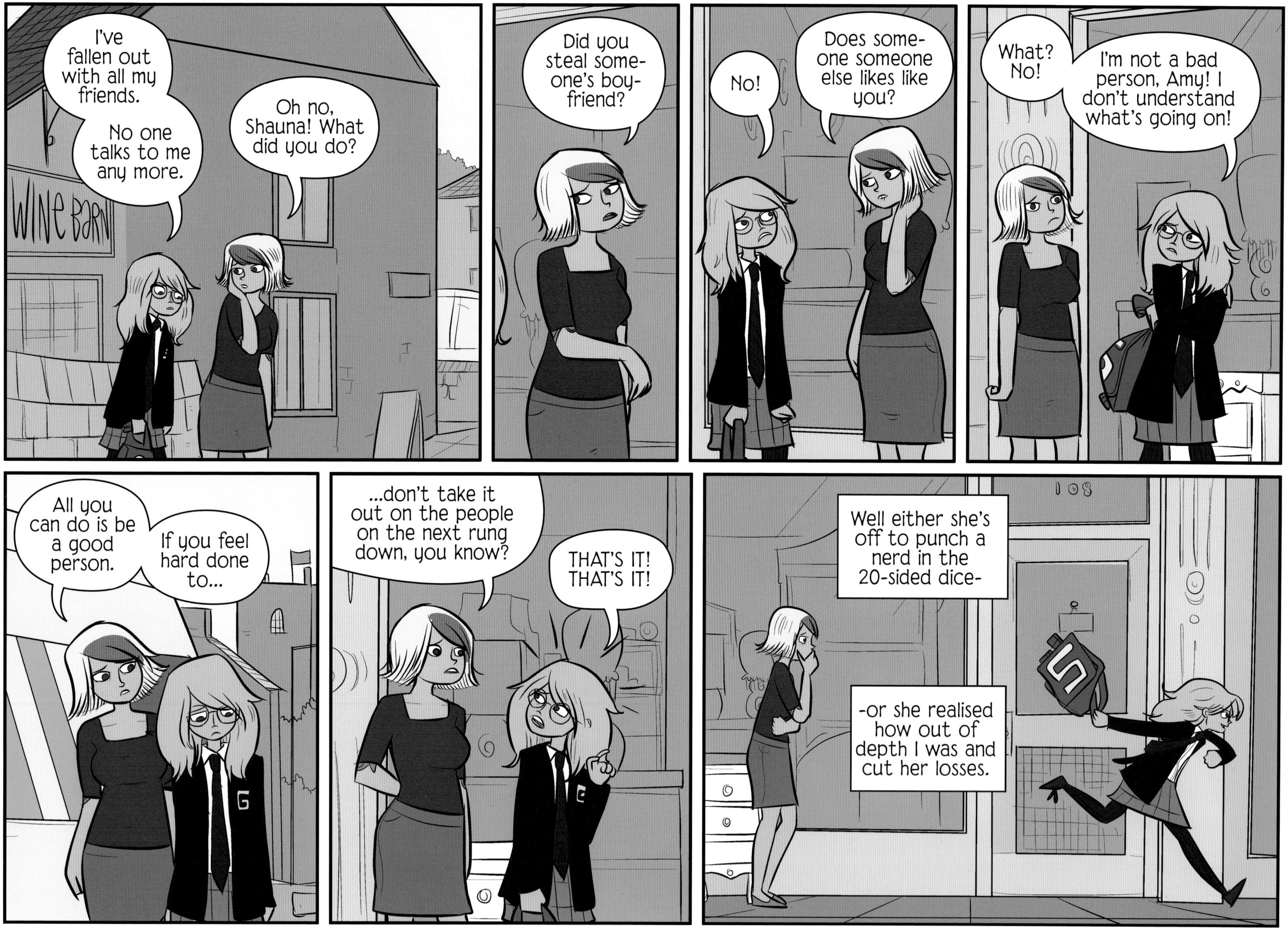

I've fallen out with all my friends.
No one talks to me any more.
Oh no, Shauna! What did you do?
WINE BARN
Did you steal someone's boyfriend?
No!
Does someone someone else likes like you?
What? No!
I'm not a bad person, Amy! I don't understand what's going on!
All you can do is be a good person.
If you feel hard done to...
...don't take it out on the people on the next rung down, you know?
THAT'S IT! THAT'S IT!
108
Well either she's off to punch a nerd in the 20-sided dice-
-or she realised how out of depth I was and cut her losses.

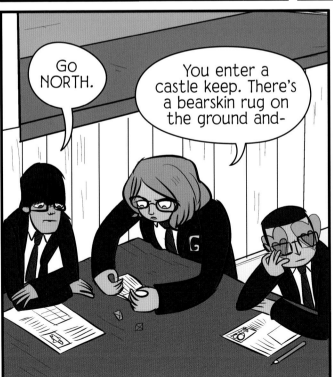

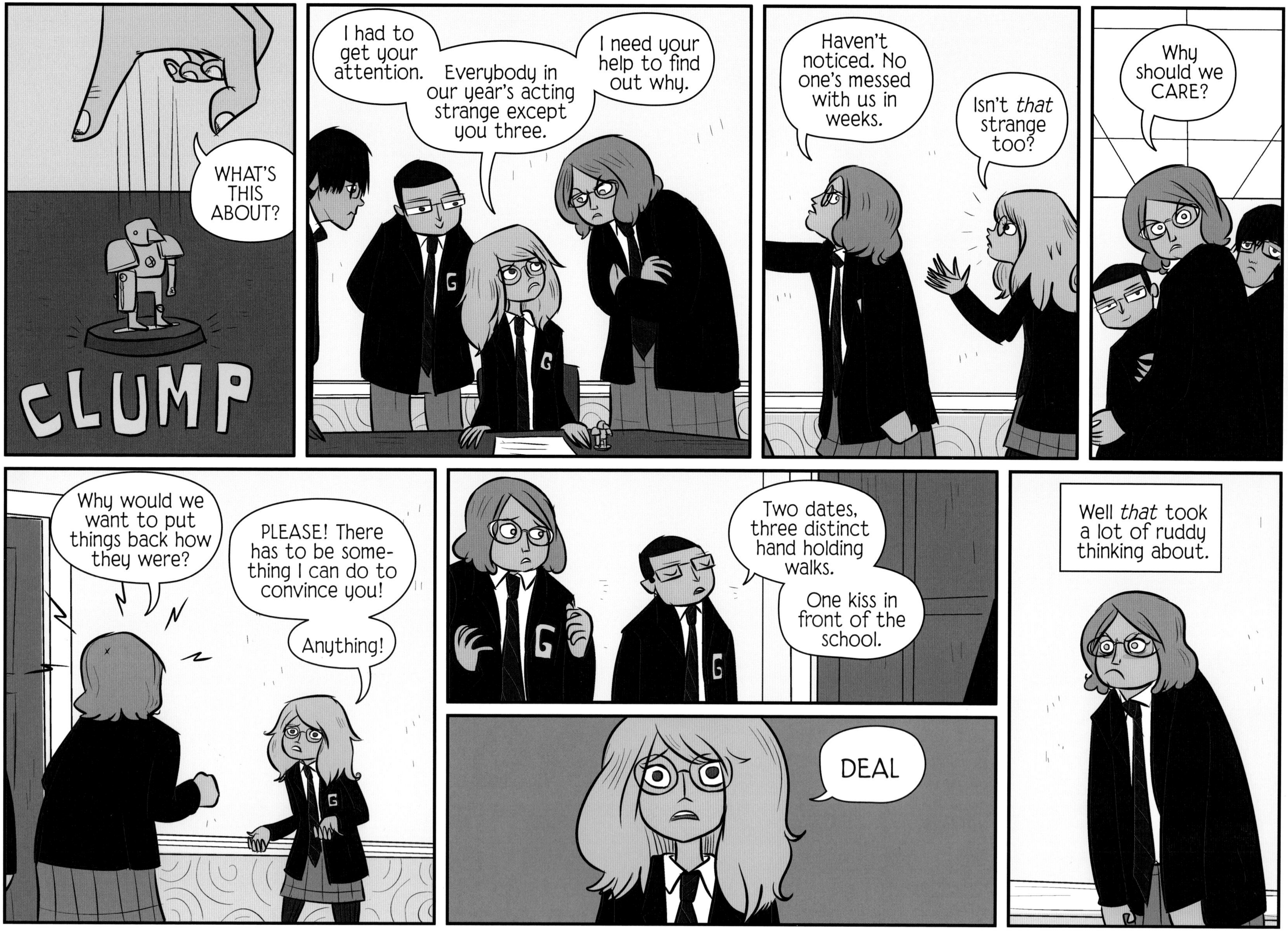
WHAT'S THIS ABOUT?
CLUMP
I had to get your attention.
Everybody in our year's acting strange except you three.
I need your help to find out why.
Haven't noticed. No one's messed with us in weeks.
Isn't *that* strange too?
Why should we CARE?
Why would we want to put things back how they were?
PLEASE! There has to be some-thing I can do to convince you!
Anything!
Two dates, three distinct hand holding walks.
One kiss in front of the school.
DEAL
Well *that* took a lot of ruddy thinking about.

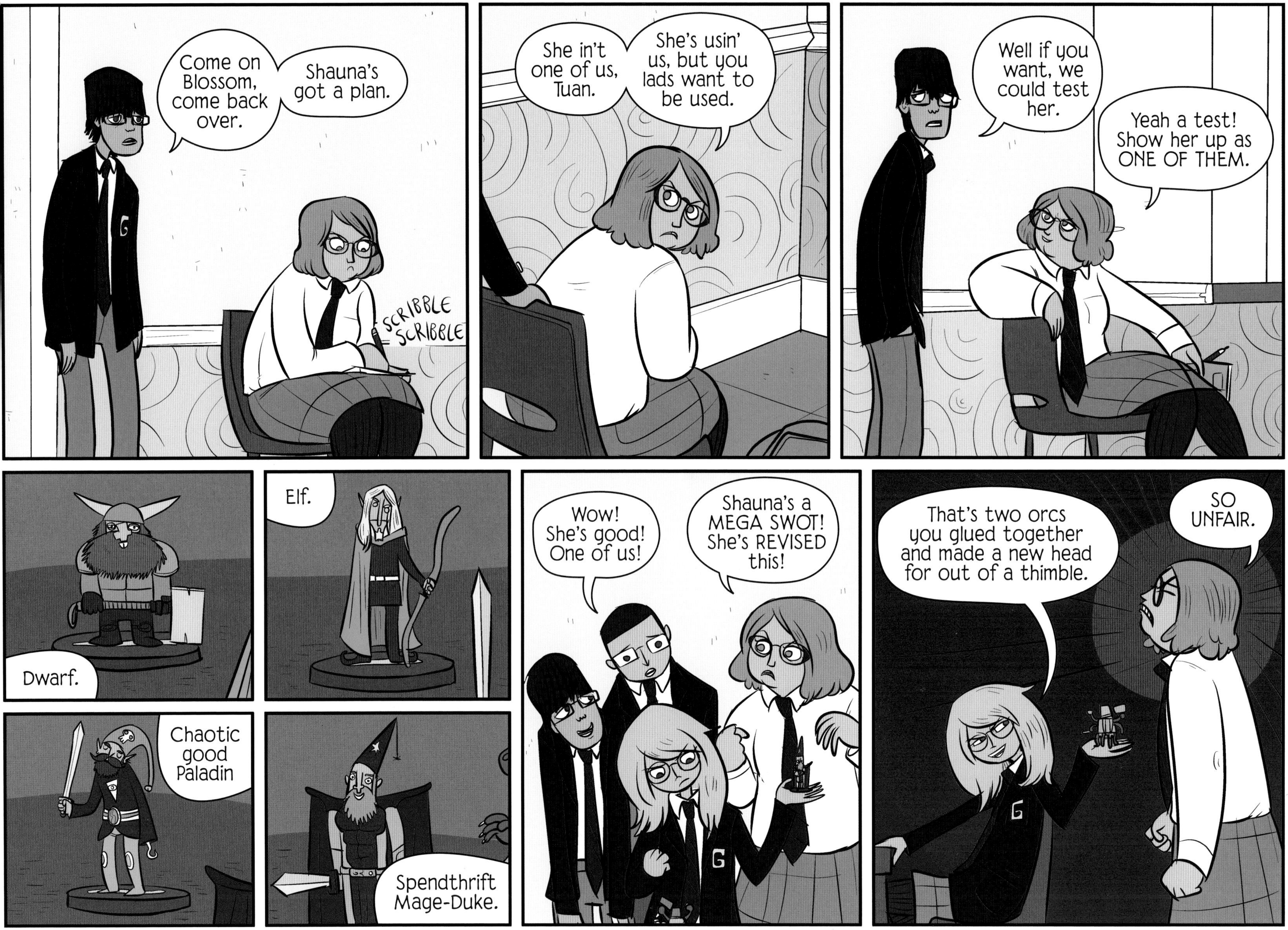
Come on Blossom, come back over.
Shauna's got a plan.
SCRIBBLE SCRIBBLE
She in't one of us, Tuan.
She's usin' us, but you lads want to be used.
Well if you want, we could test her.
Yeah a test! Show her up as ONE OF THEM.
Dwarf.
Elf.
Chaotic good Paladin
Spendthrift Mage-Duke.
Wow! She's good! One of us!
Shauna's a MEGA SWOT! She's REVISED this!
That's two orcs you glued together and made a new head for out of a thimble.
SO UNFAIR.

Bad Machinery, Volume Four

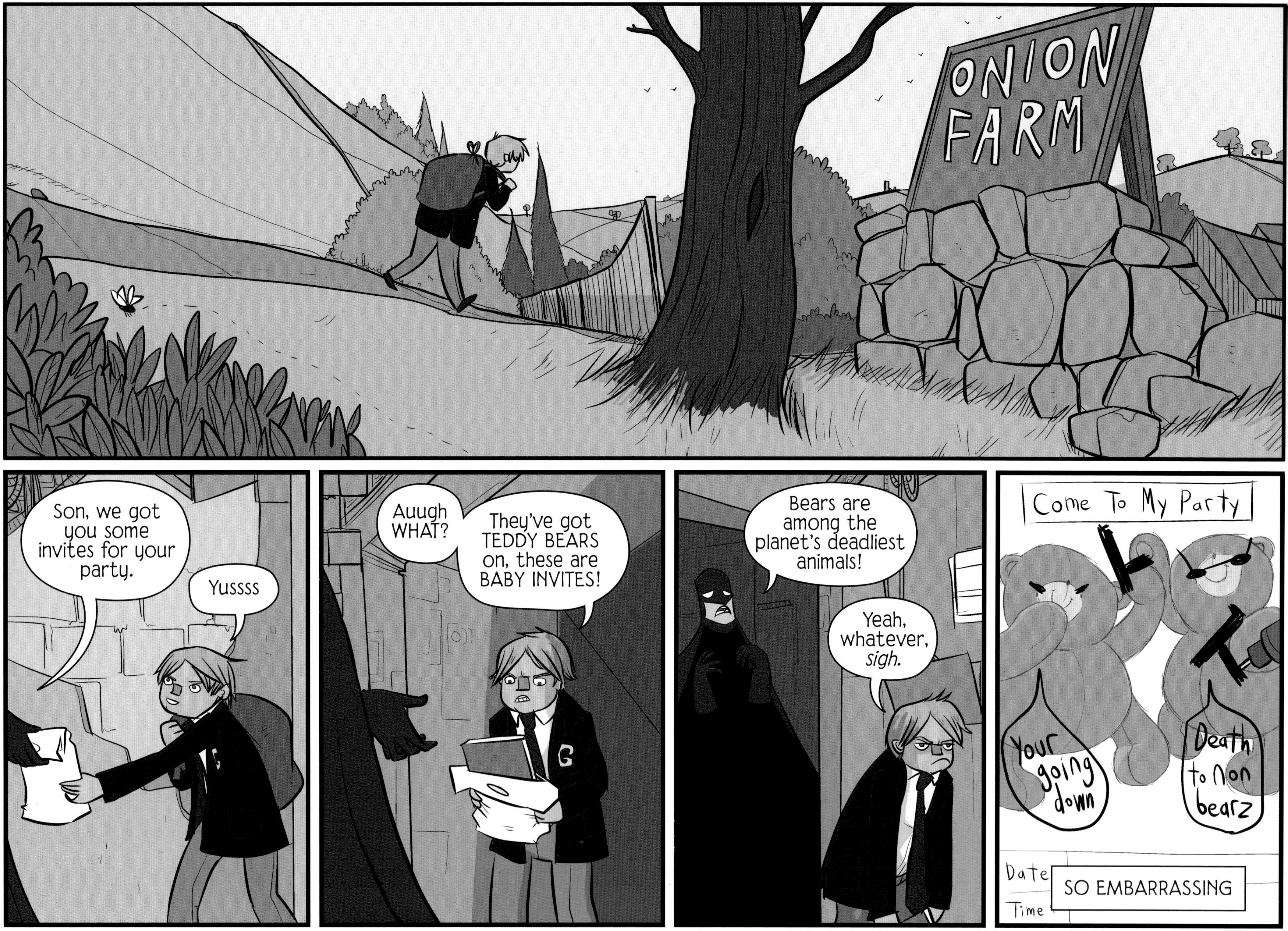
ONION FARM
Son, we got you some invites for your party.
Yussss
Auugh WHAT?
They've got TEDDY BEARS on, these are BABY INVITES!
Bears are among the planet's deadliest animals!
Yeah, whatever, *sigh.*
Come To My Party
Your going down
Death to non bearz
Date
Time
SO EMBARRASSING

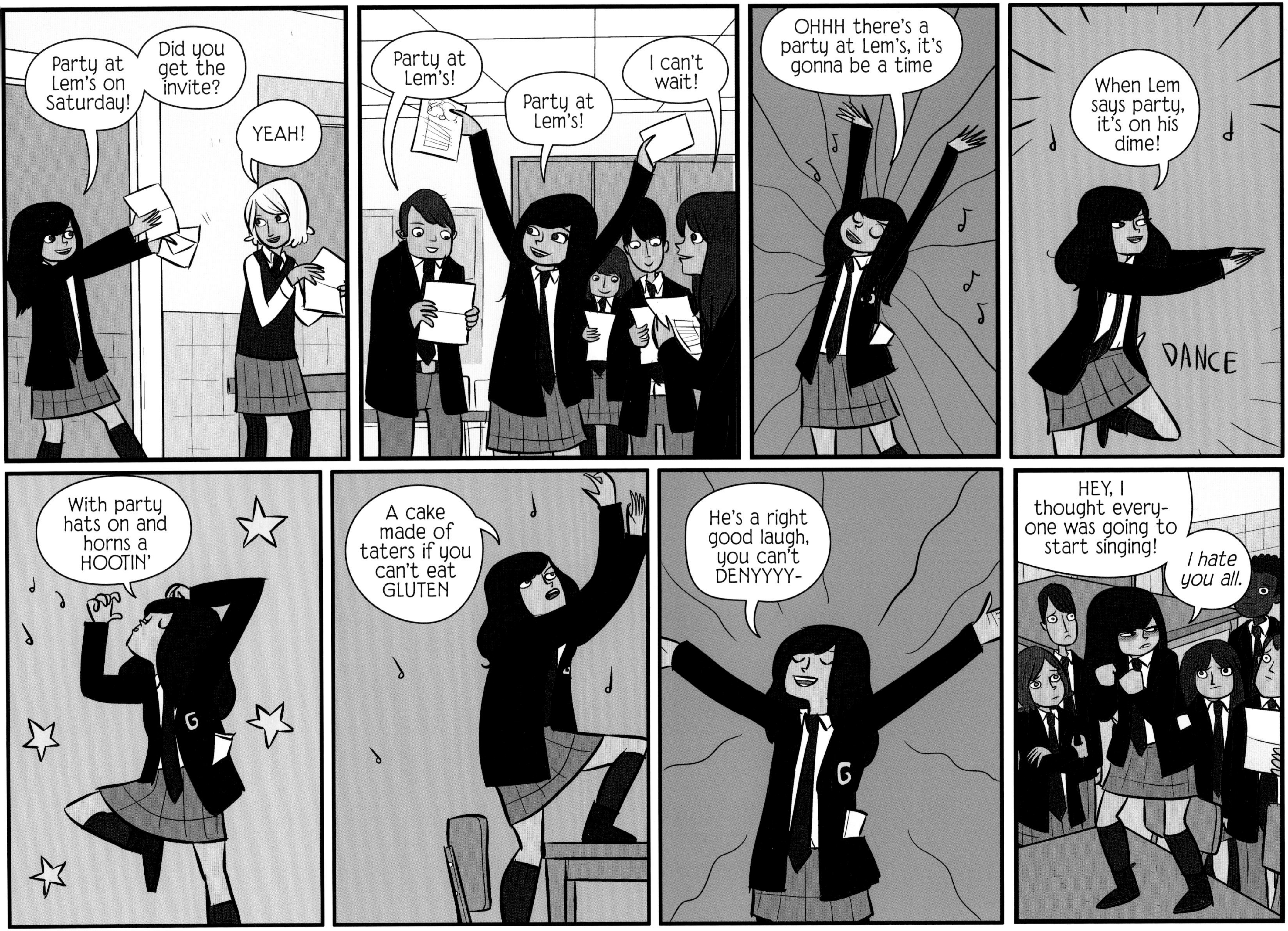
Party at Lem's on Saturday!
Did you get the invite?
YEAH!
Party at Lem's!
Party at Lem's!
I can't wait!
OHHH there's a party at Lem's, it's gonna be a time
When Lem says party, it's on his dime!
DANCE
With party hats on and horns a HOOTIN'
A cake made of taters if you can't eat GLUTEN
He's a right good laugh, you can't DENYYYY-
HEY, I thought every-one was going to start singing!
I hate you all.

Bad Machinery, Volume Four

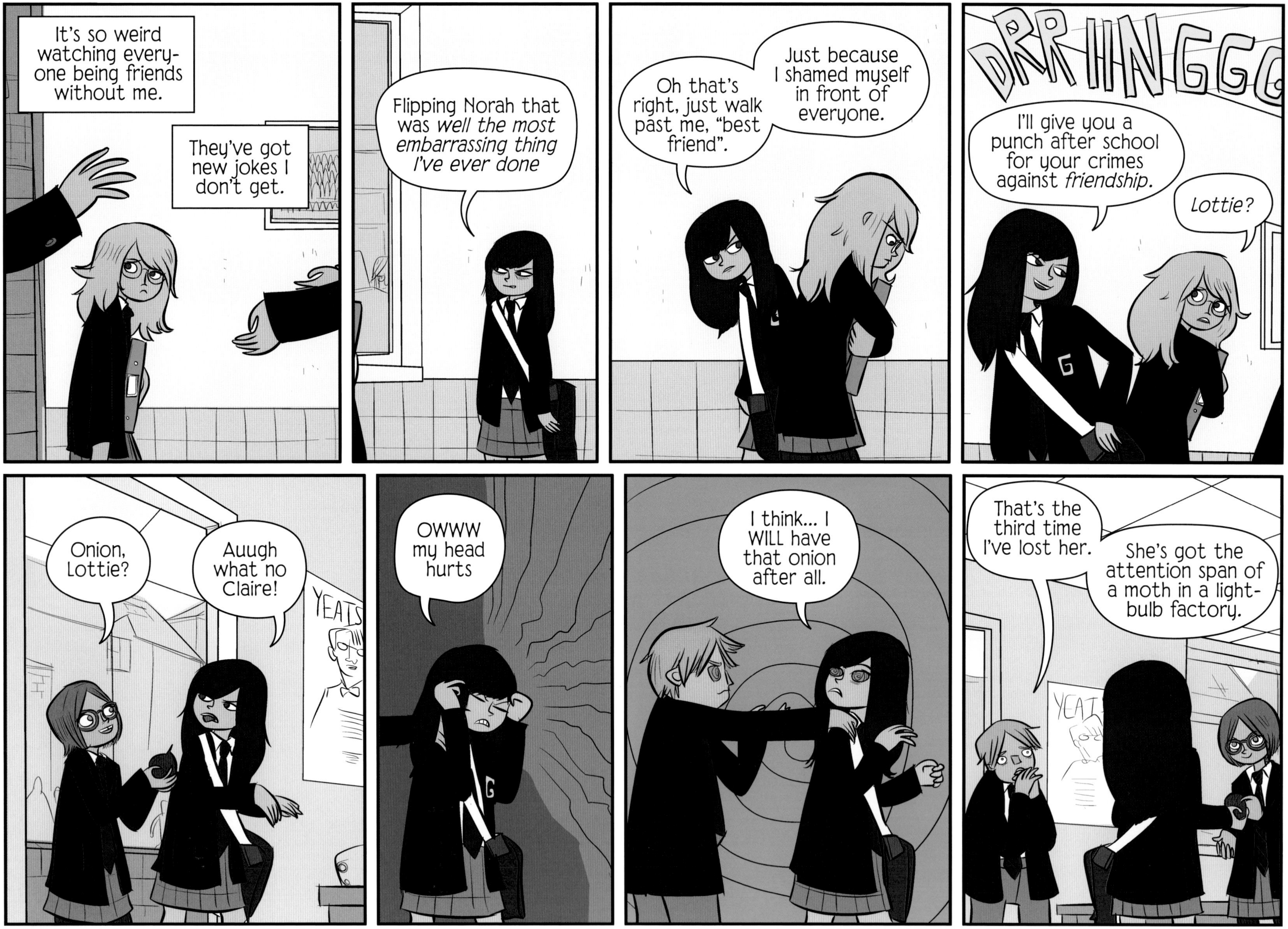
It's so weird watching every-one being friends without me.
They've got new jokes I don't get.
Flipping Norah that was *well the most embarrassing thing I've ever done*
Oh that's right, just walk past me, "best friend".
Just because I shamed myself in front of everyone.
DRRIINGGG
I'll give you a punch after school for your crimes against *friendship*.
Lottie?
Onion, Lottie?
Auugh what no Claire!
YEATS
OWWW my head hurts
I think... I WILL have that onion after all.
That's the third time I've lost her.
She's got the attention span of a moth in a light-bulb factory.

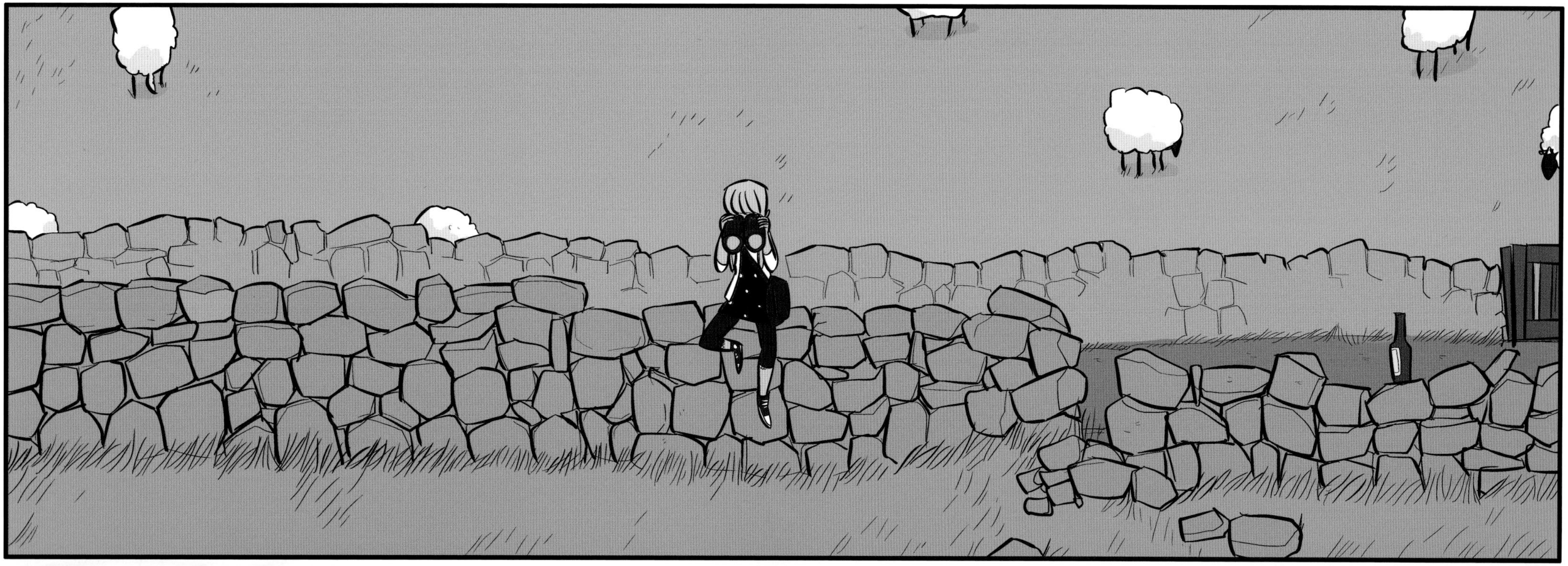

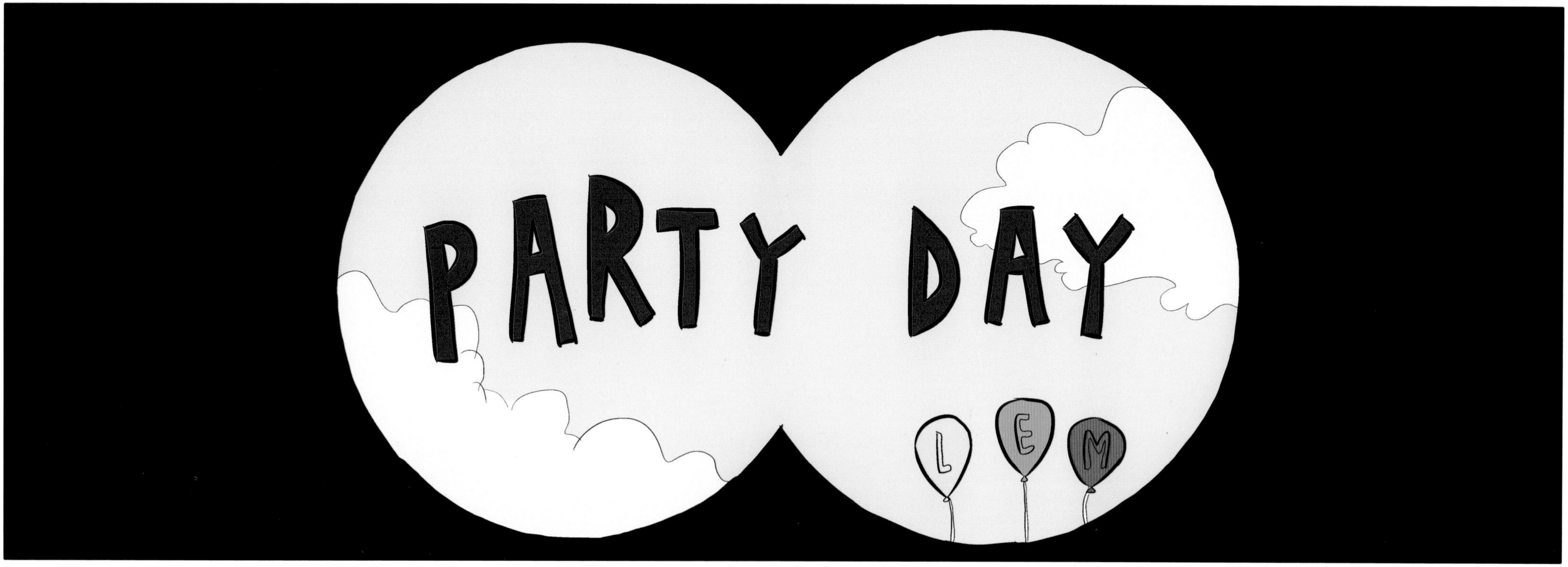
PARTY DAY
L E M

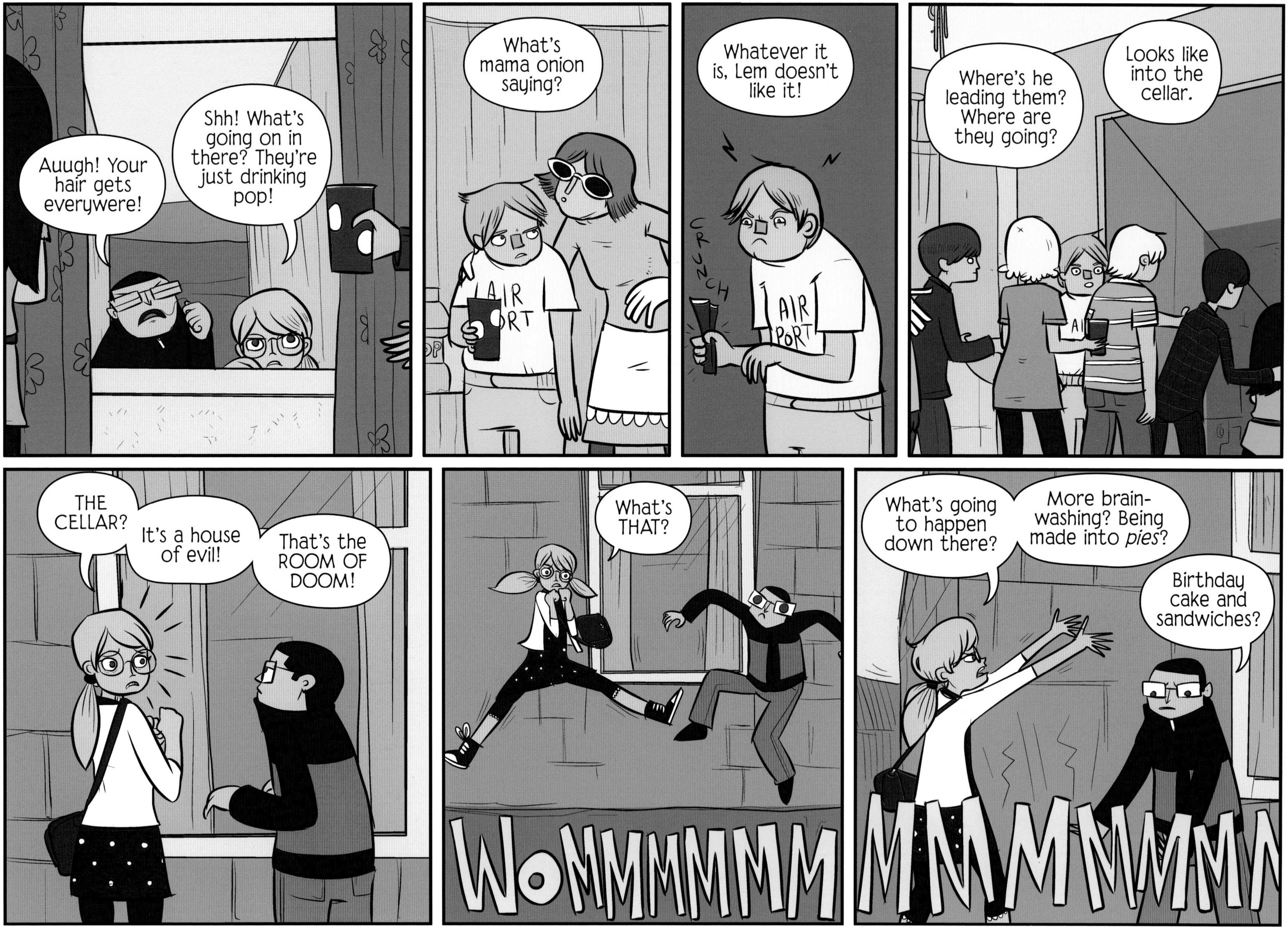
Auugh! Your hair gets everywere!
Shh! What's going on in there? They're just drinking pop!
What's mama onion saying?
Whatever it is, Lem doesn't like it!
CRUNCH
AIR PORT
Where's he leading them? Where are they going?
Looks like into the cellar.
THE CELLAR?
It's a house of evil!
That's the ROOM OF DOOM!
What's THAT?
What's going to happen down there?
More brain-washing? Being made into *pies*?
Birthday cake and sandwiches?
WOMMMMMMMMMMMMMMM

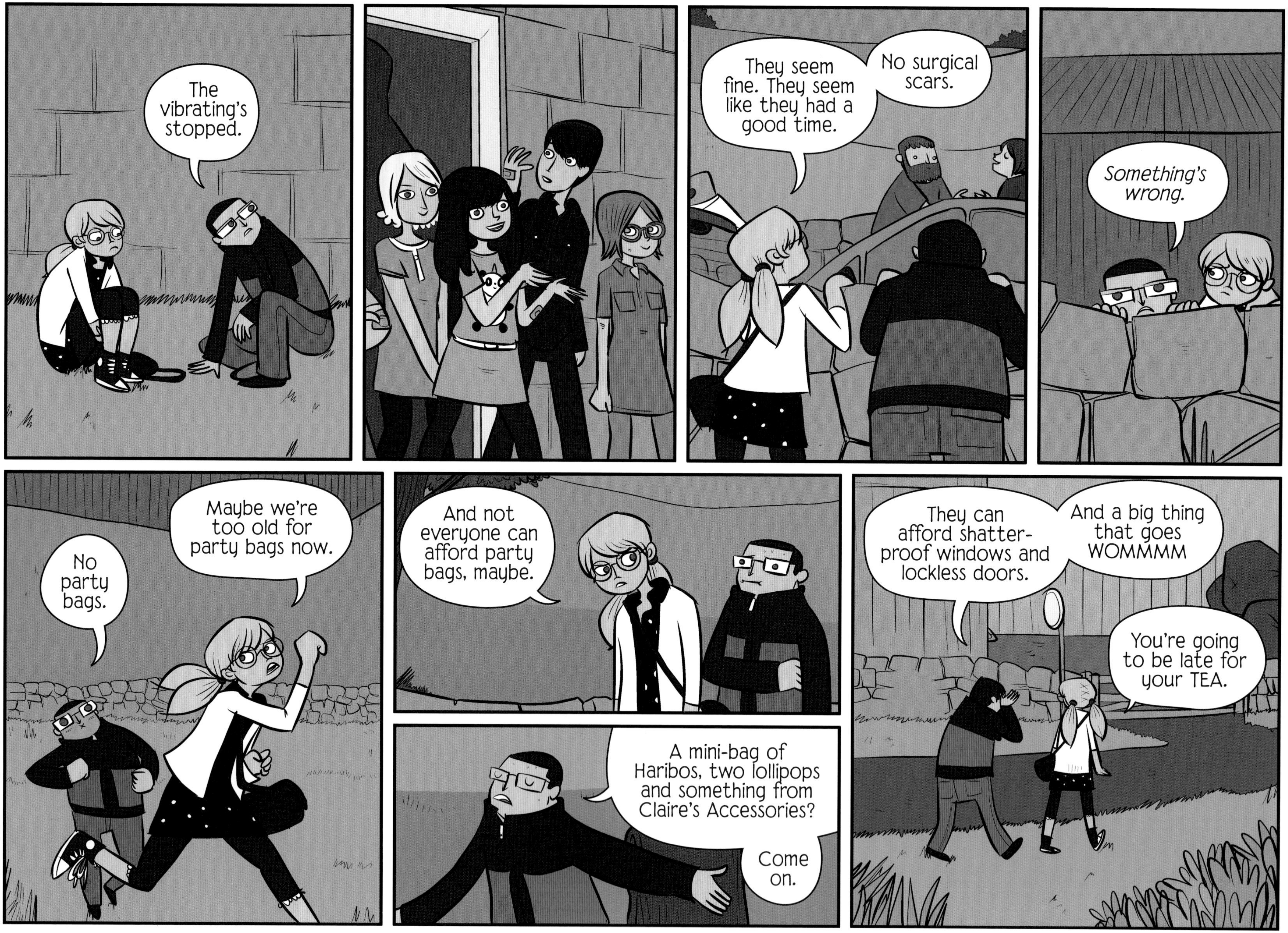

The vibrating's stopped.
They seem fine. They seem like they had a good time.
No surgical scars.
Something's wrong.
No party bags.
Maybe we're too old for party bags now.
And not everyone can afford party bags, maybe.
A mini-bag of Haribos, two lollipops and something from Claire's Accessories?
Come on.
They can afford shatter-proof windows and lockless doors.
And a big thing that goes WOMMMM
You're going to be late for your TEA.

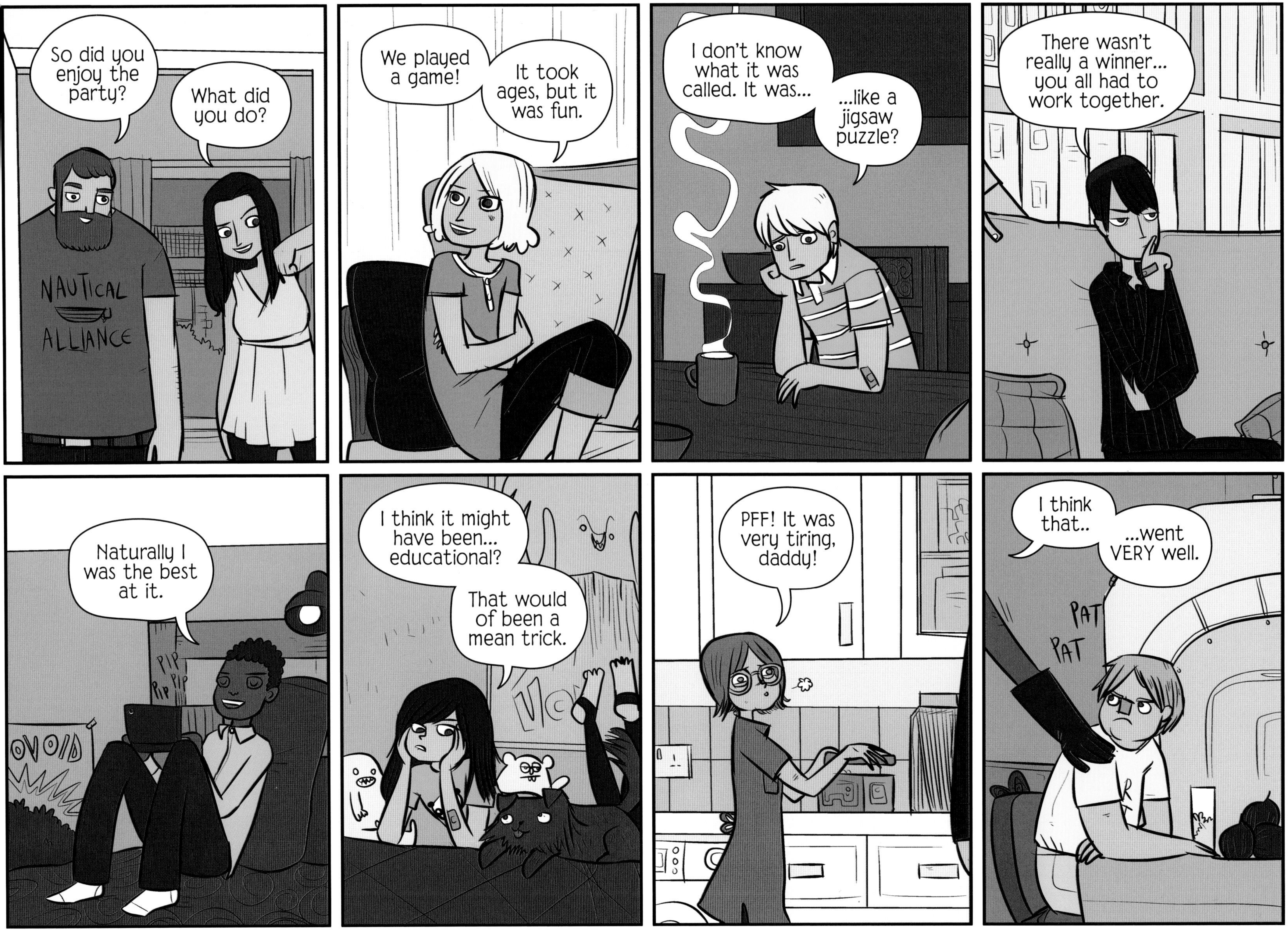
So did you enjoy the party?
What did you do?
NAUTICAL ALLIANCE
We played a game!
It took ages, but it was fun.
I don't know what it was called. It was...
...like a jigsaw puzzle?
There wasn't really a winner... you all had to work together.
Naturally I was the best at it.
PIP PIP PIP
OVOID
I think it might have been... educational?
That would of been a mean trick.
PFF! It was very tiring, daddy!
I think that..
...went VERY well.
PAT PAT

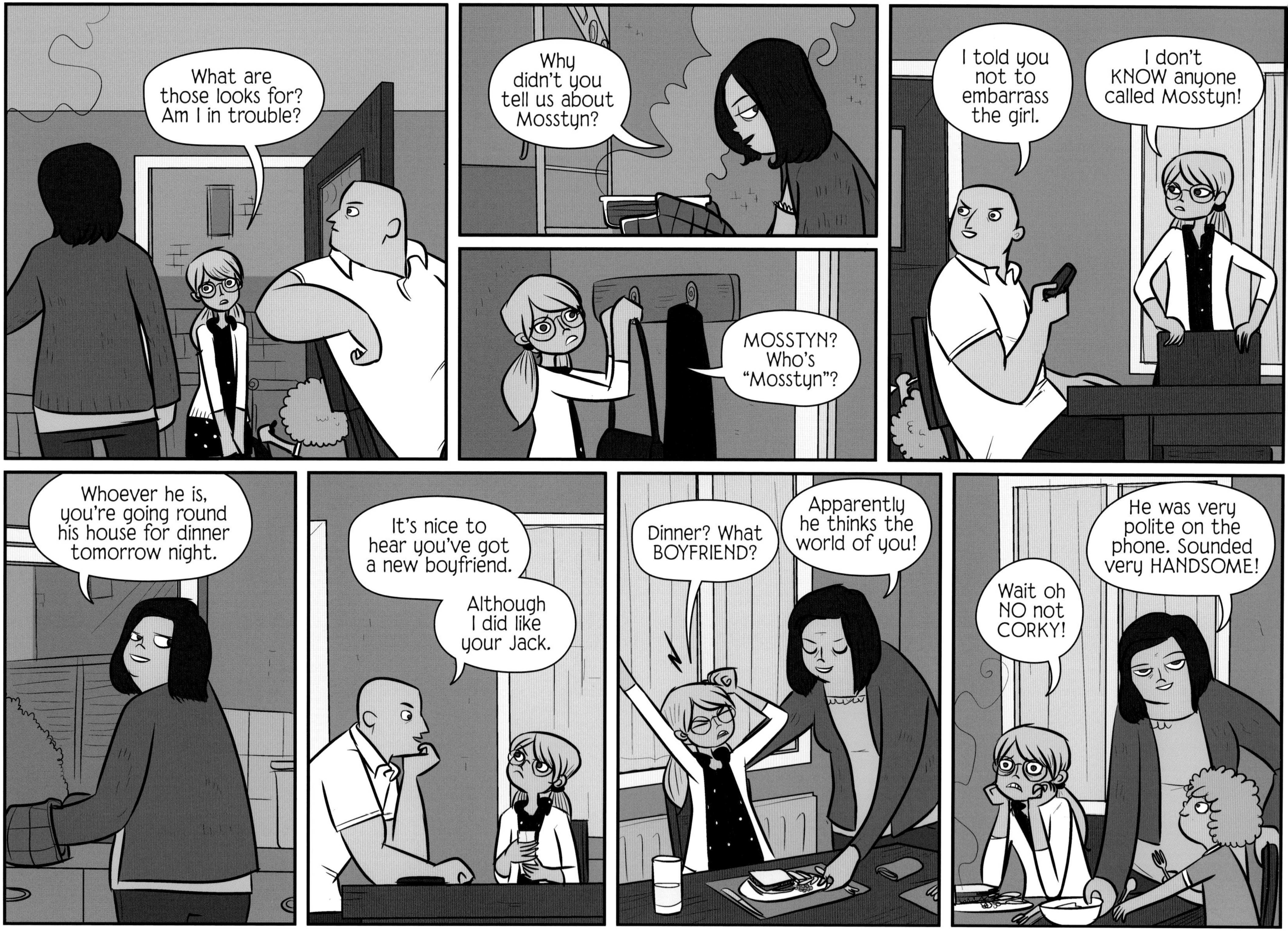
What are those looks for? Am I in trouble?
Why didn't you tell us about Mosstyn?
MOSSTYN? Who's "Mosstyn"?
I told you not to embarrass the girl.
I don't KNOW anyone called Mosstyn!
Whoever he is, you're going round his house for dinner tomorrow night.
It's nice to hear you've got a new boyfriend.
Although I did like your Jack.
Dinner? What BOYFRIEND?
Apparently he thinks the world of you!
He was very polite on the phone. Sounded very HANDSOME!
Wait oh NO not CORKY!

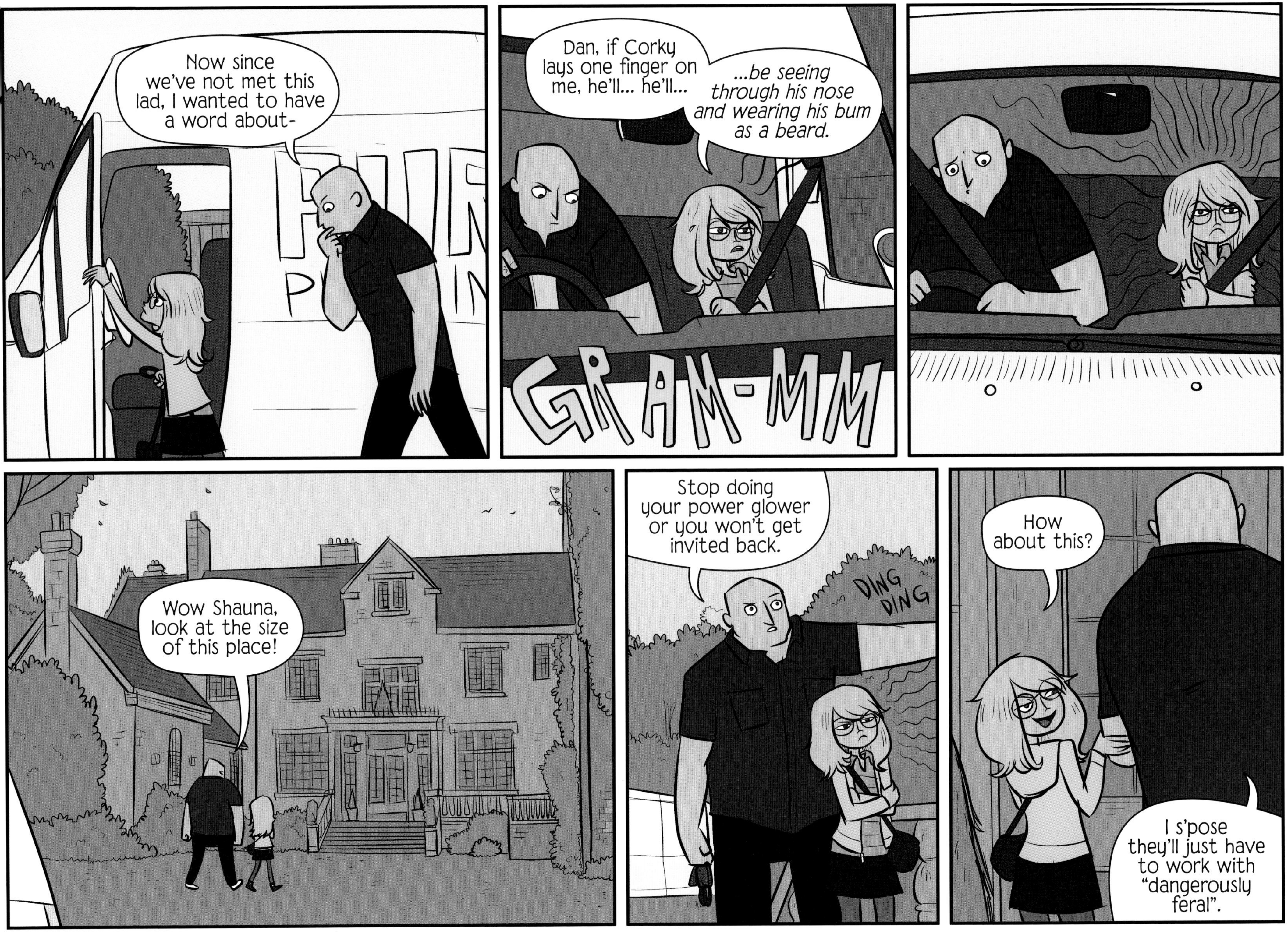
Now since we've not met this lad, I wanted to have a word about-
Dan, if Corky lays one finger on me, he'll... he'll...
...be seeing through his nose and wearing his bum as a beard.
GRAM-MM
Wow Shauna, look at the size of this place!
Stop doing your power glower or you won't get invited back.
DING DING
How about this?
I s'pose they'll just have to work with "dangerously feral".

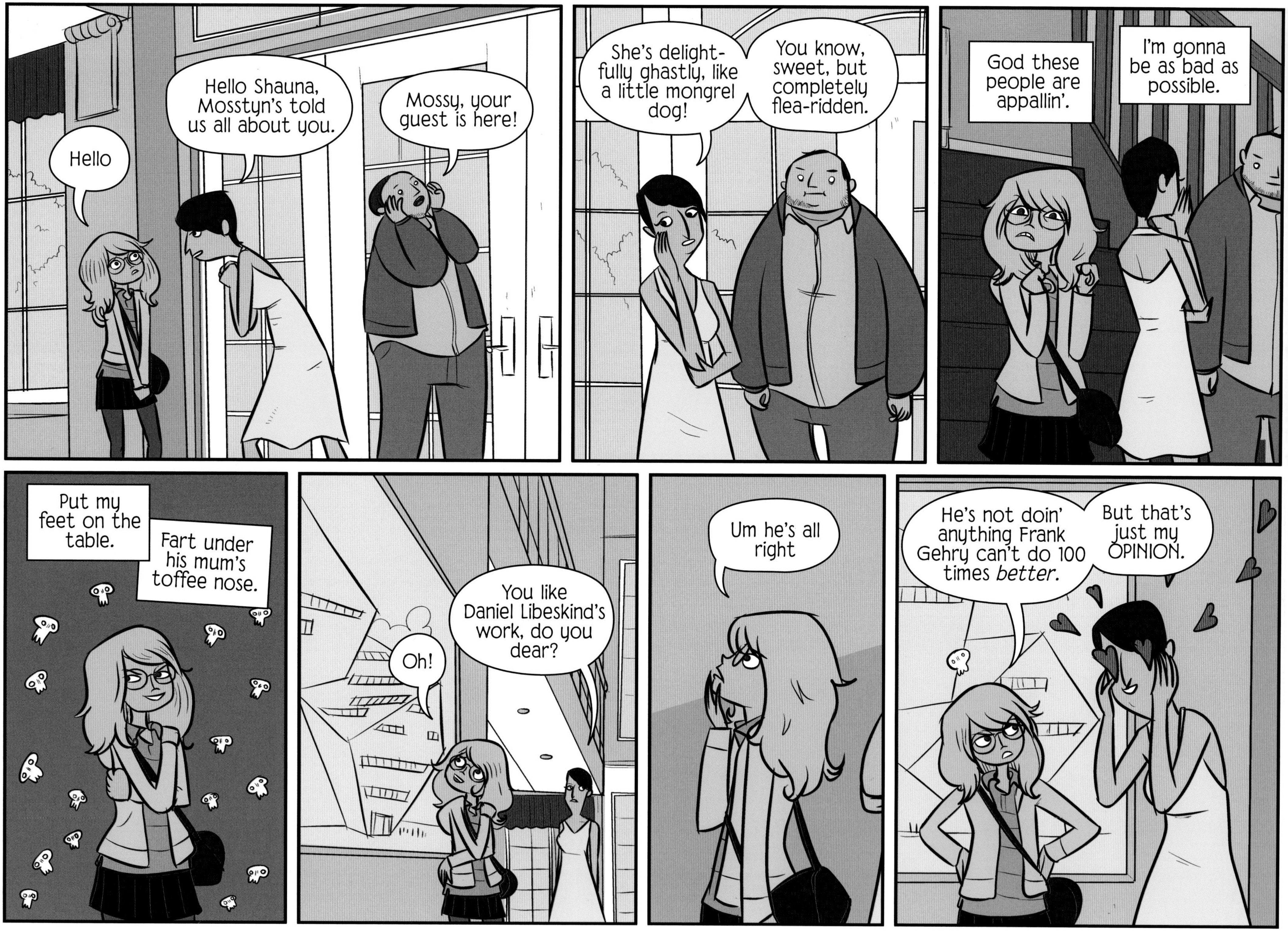
Hello
Hello Shauna, Mosstyn's told us all about you.
Mossy, your guest is here!
She's delightfully ghastly, like a little mongrel dog!
You know, sweet, but completely flea-ridden.
God these people are appallin'.
I'm gonna be as bad as possible.
Put my feet on the table.
Fart under his mum's toffee nose.
Oh!
You like Daniel Libeskind's work, do you dear?
Um he's all right
He's not doin' anything Frank Gehry can't do 100 times *better.*
But that's just my OPINION.

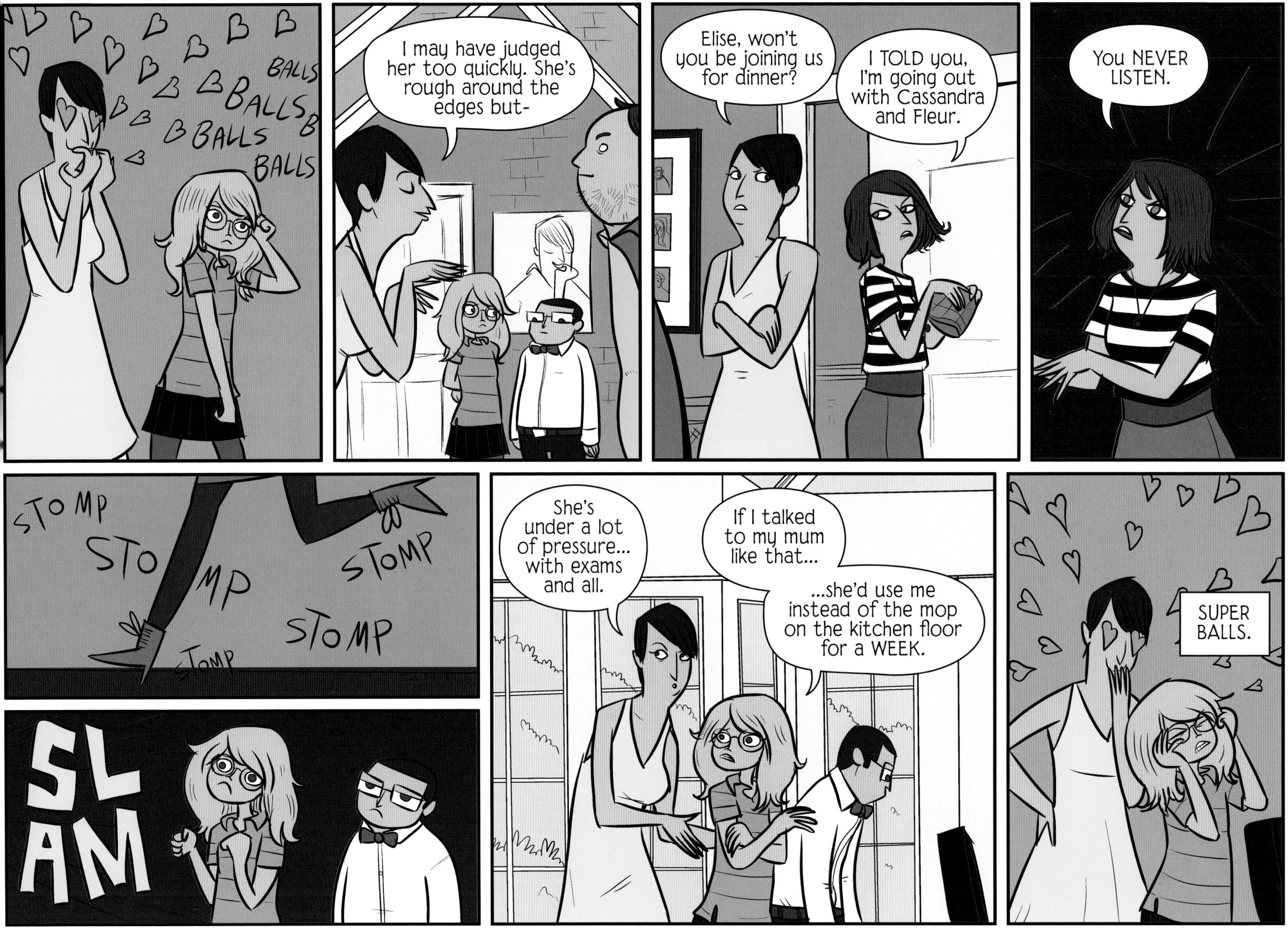
BALLS
BALLS
BALLS
BALLS
I may have judged her too quickly. She's rough around the edges but-
Elise, won't you be joining us for dinner?
I TOLD you, I'm going out with Cassandra and Fleur.
You NEVER LISTEN.
STOMP
STOMP
STOMP
STOMP
STOMP
SLAM
She's under a lot of pressure... with exams and all.
If I talked to my mum like that...
...she'd use me instead of the mop on the kitchen floor for a WEEK.
SUPER BALLS.

Bad Machinery, Volume Four

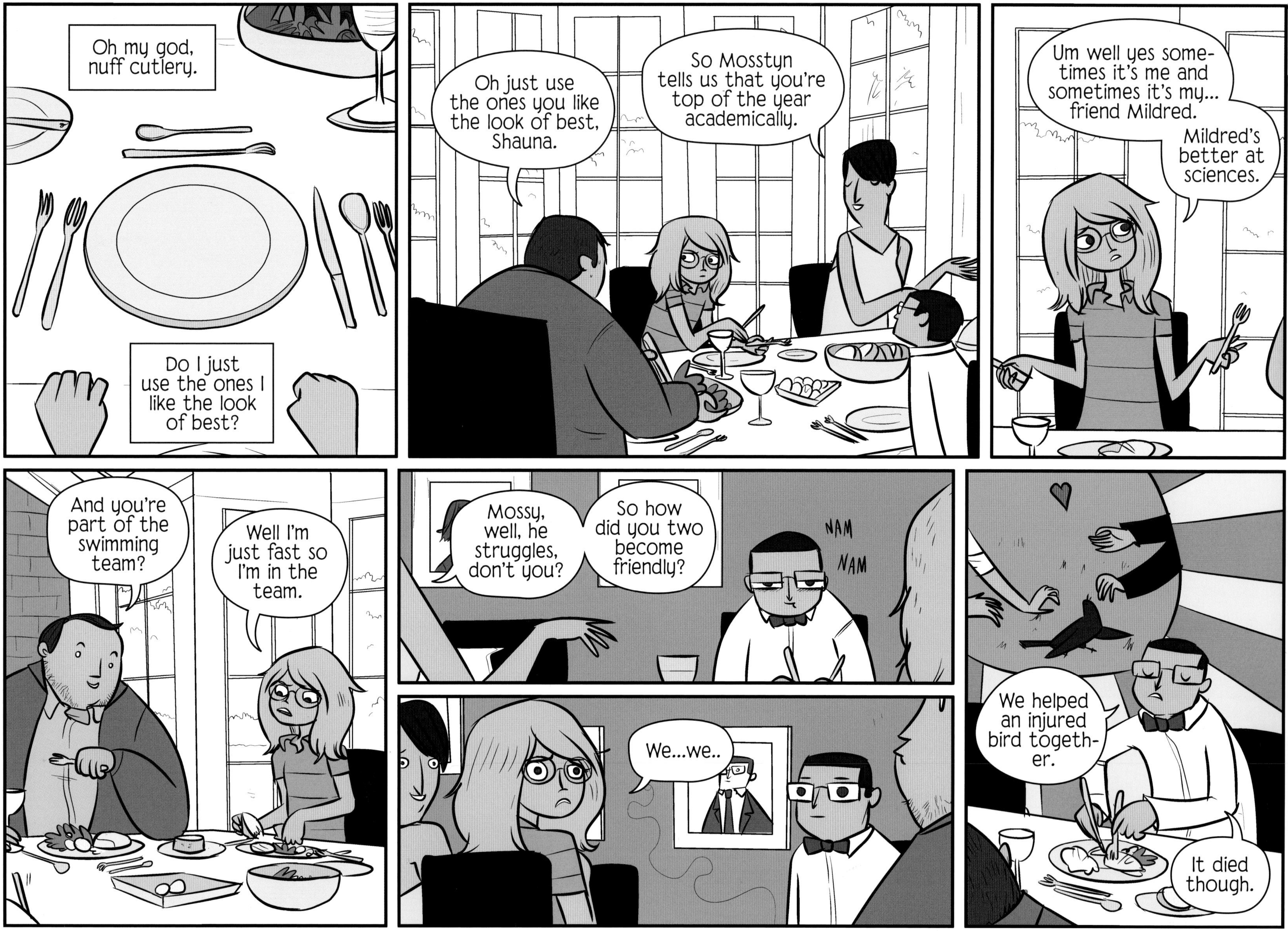
Oh my god, nuff cutlery.
Do I just use the ones I like the look of best?
Oh just use the ones you like the look of best, Shauna.
So Mosstyn tells us that you're top of the year academically.
Um well yes some-times it's me and sometimes it's my... friend Mildred.
Mildred's better at sciences.
And you're part of the swimming team?
Well I'm just fast so I'm in the team.
Mossy, well, he struggles, don't you?
So how did you two become friendly?
NAM
NAM
We...we..
We helped an injured bird togeth-er.
It died though.

ON YOUR FEET CORKY! I haven't finished with you.

Wheeze

PERFECT

STEP HOP

STEP

No he can't come to the phone right now.

He's dancing with his girlfriend.

BIP BEEP YEAH

Okay.

Shauna, now that we're going out-

Corky we are NOT GOING OUT.

STEP STEP HOP HOP STEP

This is one date off your deal.

Three hand holds, one date, one pash left.

I don't *fancy* you.

Associates.

Play your cards right, you might make it to *colleague.*

Are we... friends?

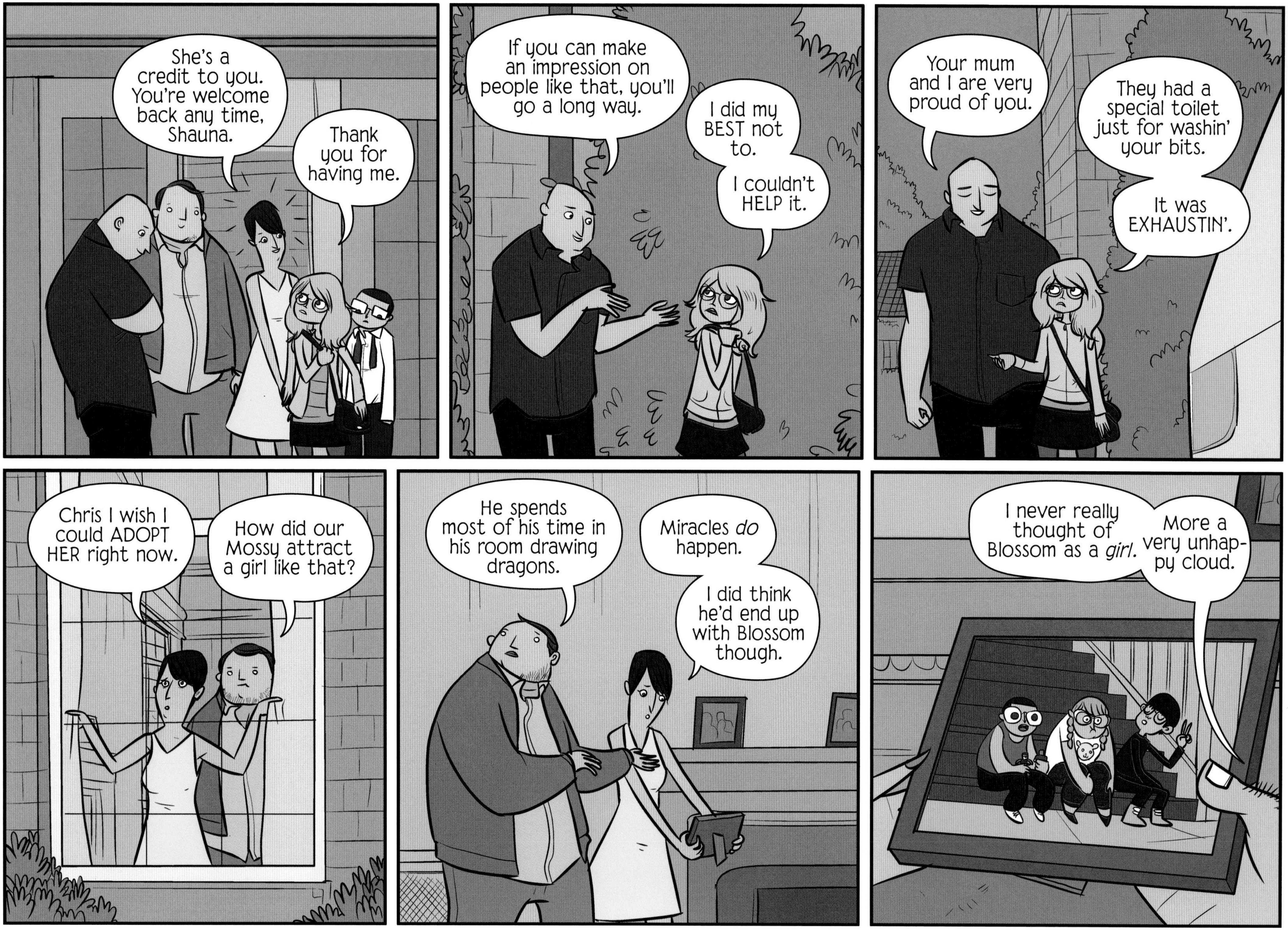
She's a credit to you. You're welcome back any time, Shauna.
Thank you for having me.
If you can make an impression on people like that, you'll go a long way.
I did my BEST not to.
I couldn't HELP it.
Your mum and I are very proud of you.
They had a special toilet just for washin' your bits.
It was EXHAUSTIN'.
Chris I wish I could ADOPT HER right now.
How did our Mossy attract a girl like that?
He spends most of his time in his room drawing dragons.
Miracles *do* happen.
I did think he'd end up with Blossom though.
I never really thought of Blossom as a *girl.*
More a very unhap-py cloud.

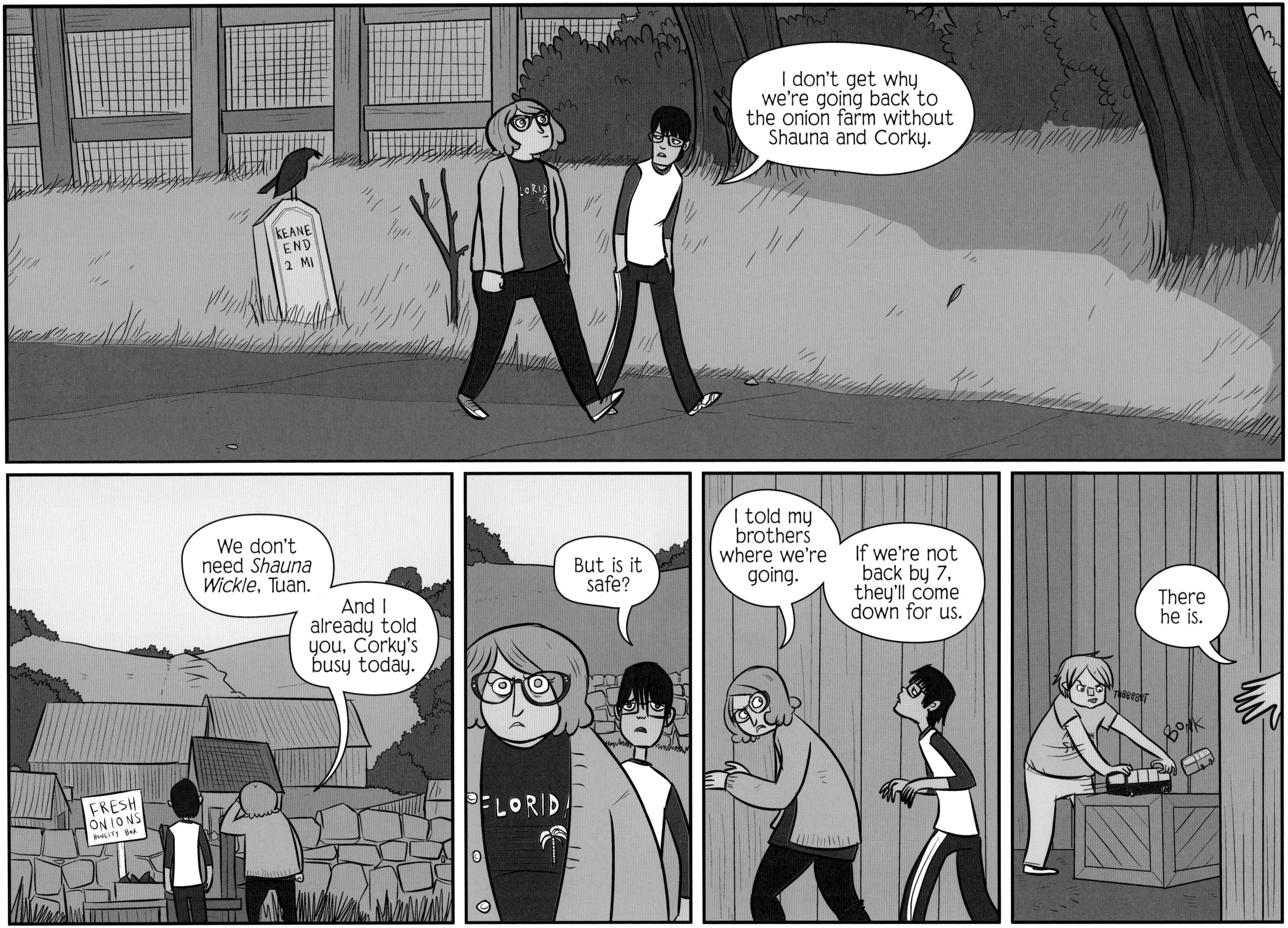
KEANE END 2 MI
I don't get why we're going back to the onion farm without Shauna and Corky.
We don't need *Shauna Wickle*, Tuan.
And I already told you, Corky's busy today.
FRESH ONIONS
HONESTY BOX
But is it safe?
FLORIDA
I told my brothers where we're going.
If we're not back by 7, they'll come down for us.
There he is.
BONK

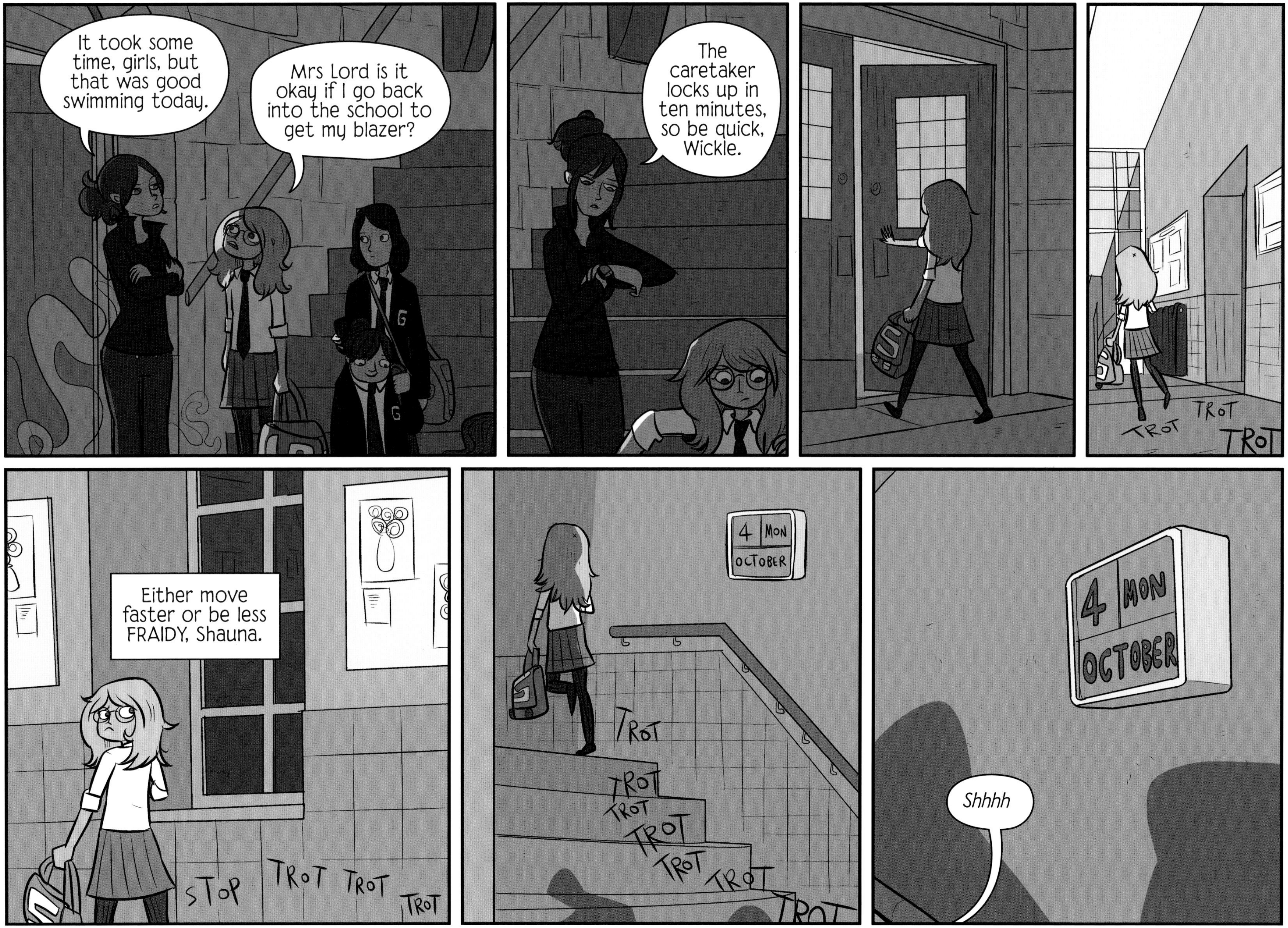

It took some time, girls, but that was good swimming today.
Mrs Lord is it okay if I go back into the school to get my blazer?
The caretaker locks up in ten minutes, so be quick, Wickle.
TROT TROT TROT
Either move faster or be less FRAIDY, Shauna.
STOP TROT TROT TROT
4 MON OCTOBER
TROT TROT TROT TROT TROT TROT TROT
4 MON OCTOBER
Shhhh

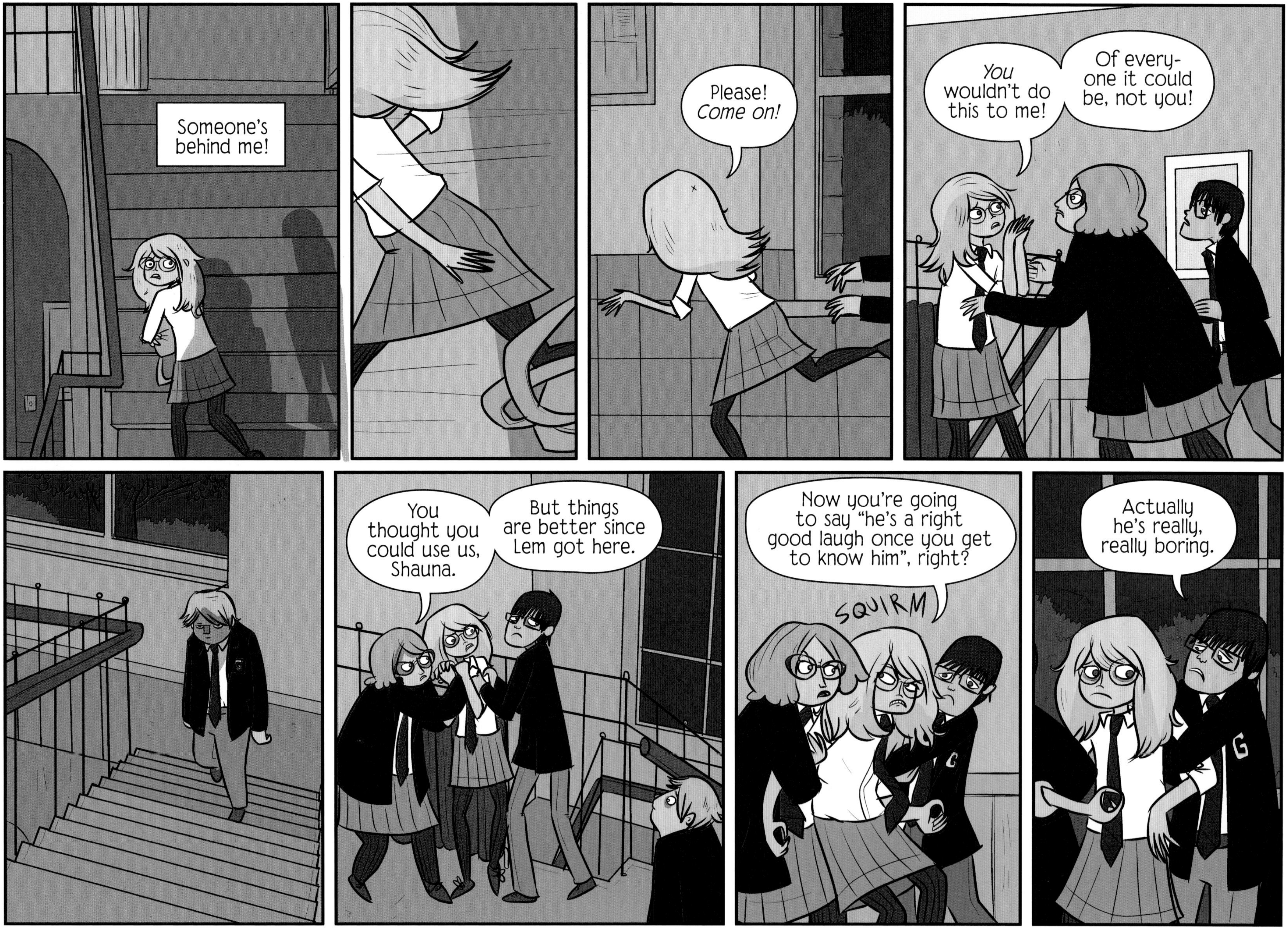
Someone's behind me!
Please! *Come on!*
You wouldn't do this to me!
Of every-one it could be, not you!
You thought you could use us, Shauna.
But things are better since Lem got here.
Now you're going to say "he's a right good laugh once you get to know him", right?
SQUIRM
Actually he's really, really boring.

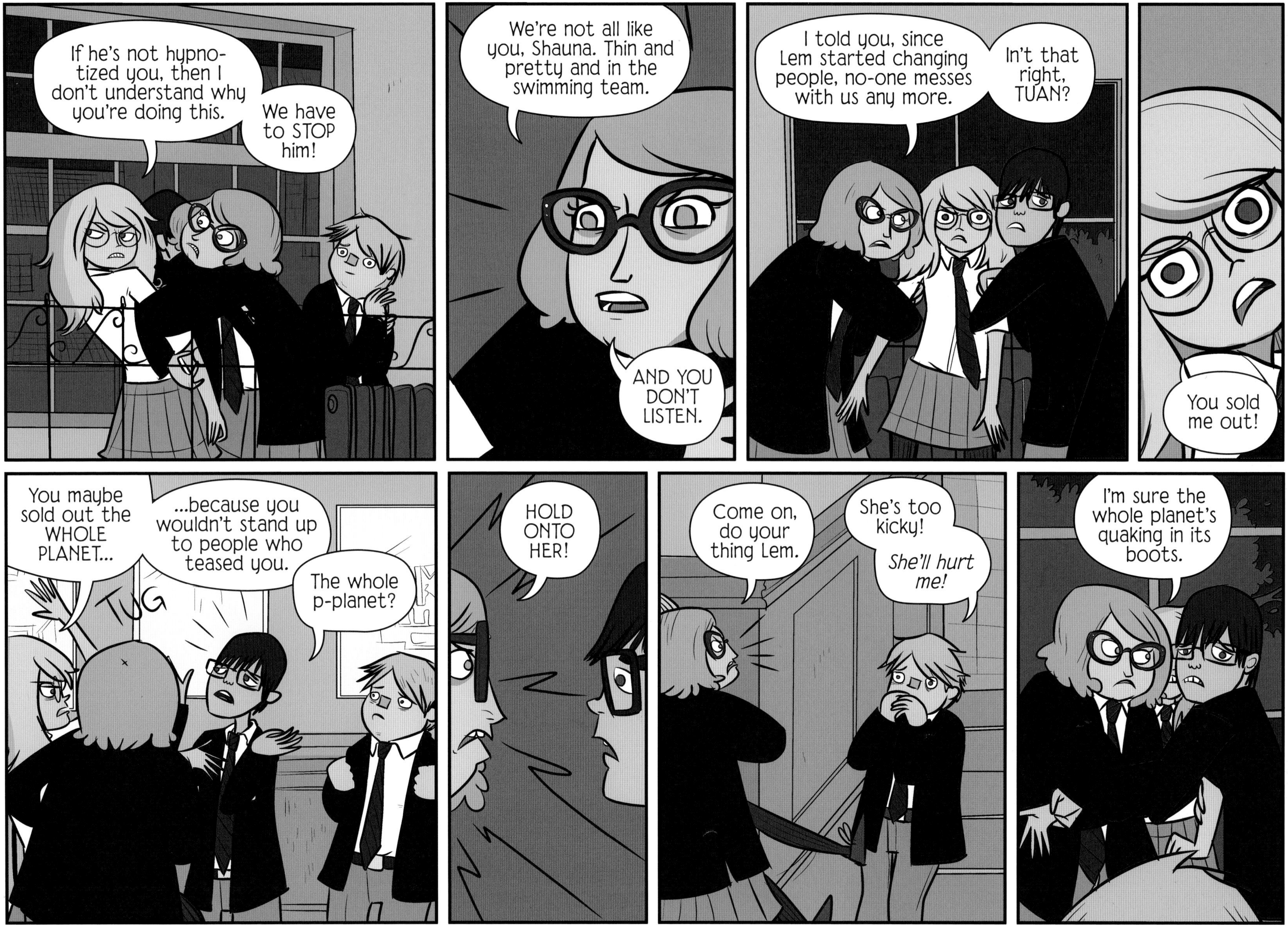
If he's not hypno-tized you, then I don't understand why you're doing this.
We have to STOP him!
We're not all like you, Shauna. Thin and pretty and in the swimming team.
AND YOU DON'T LISTEN.
I told you, since Lem started changing people, no-one messes with us any more.
In't that right, TUAN?
You sold me out!
You maybe sold out the WHOLE PLANET...
...because you wouldn't stand up to people who teased you.
TUG
The whole p-planet?
HOLD ONTO HER!
Come on, do your thing Lem.
She's too kicky!
She'll hurt me!
I'm sure the whole planet's quaking in its boots.

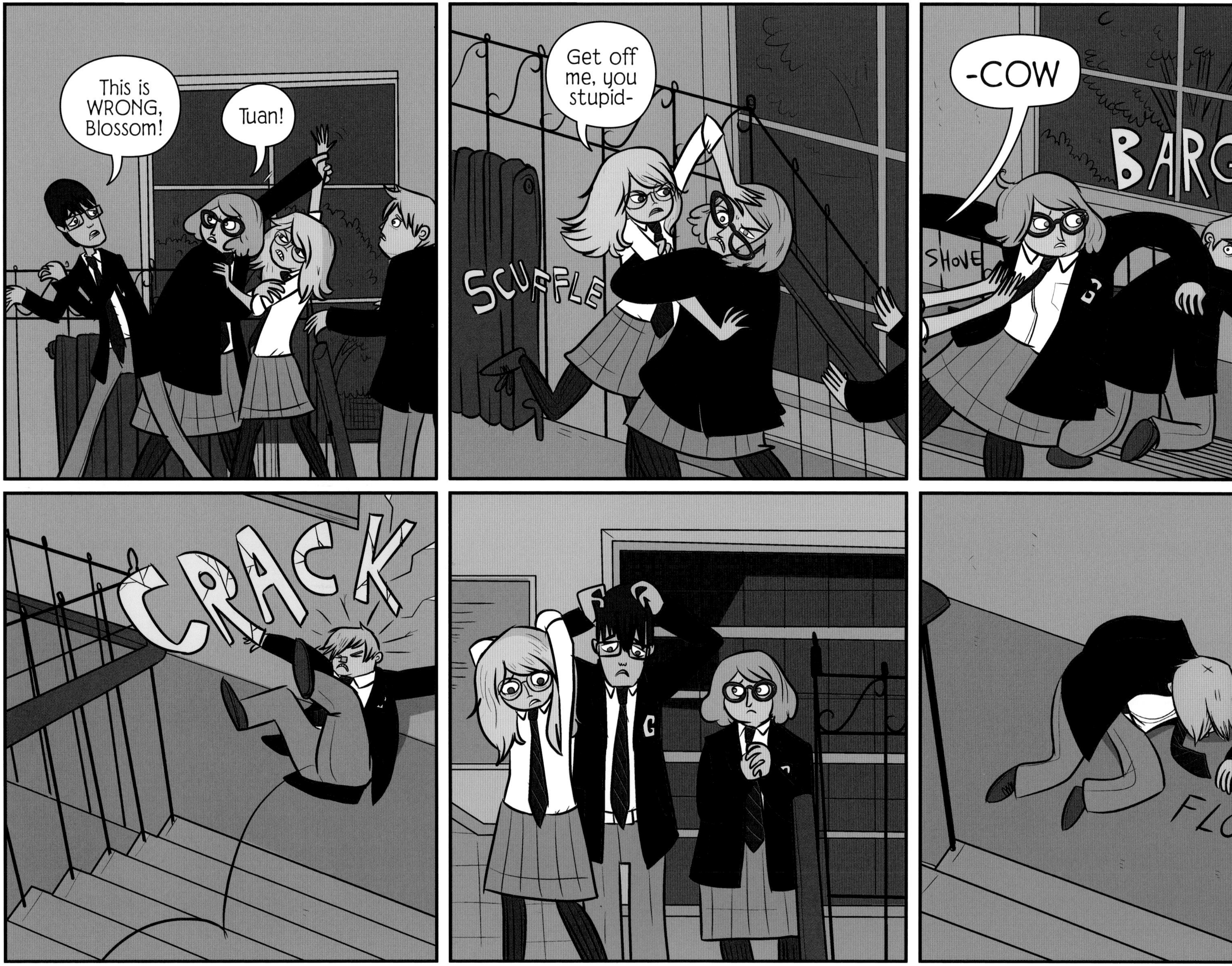
This is WRONG, Blossom!
Tuan!
Get off me, you stupid-
SCUFFLE
-COW
BARGE
SHOVE
CRACK
FLOP

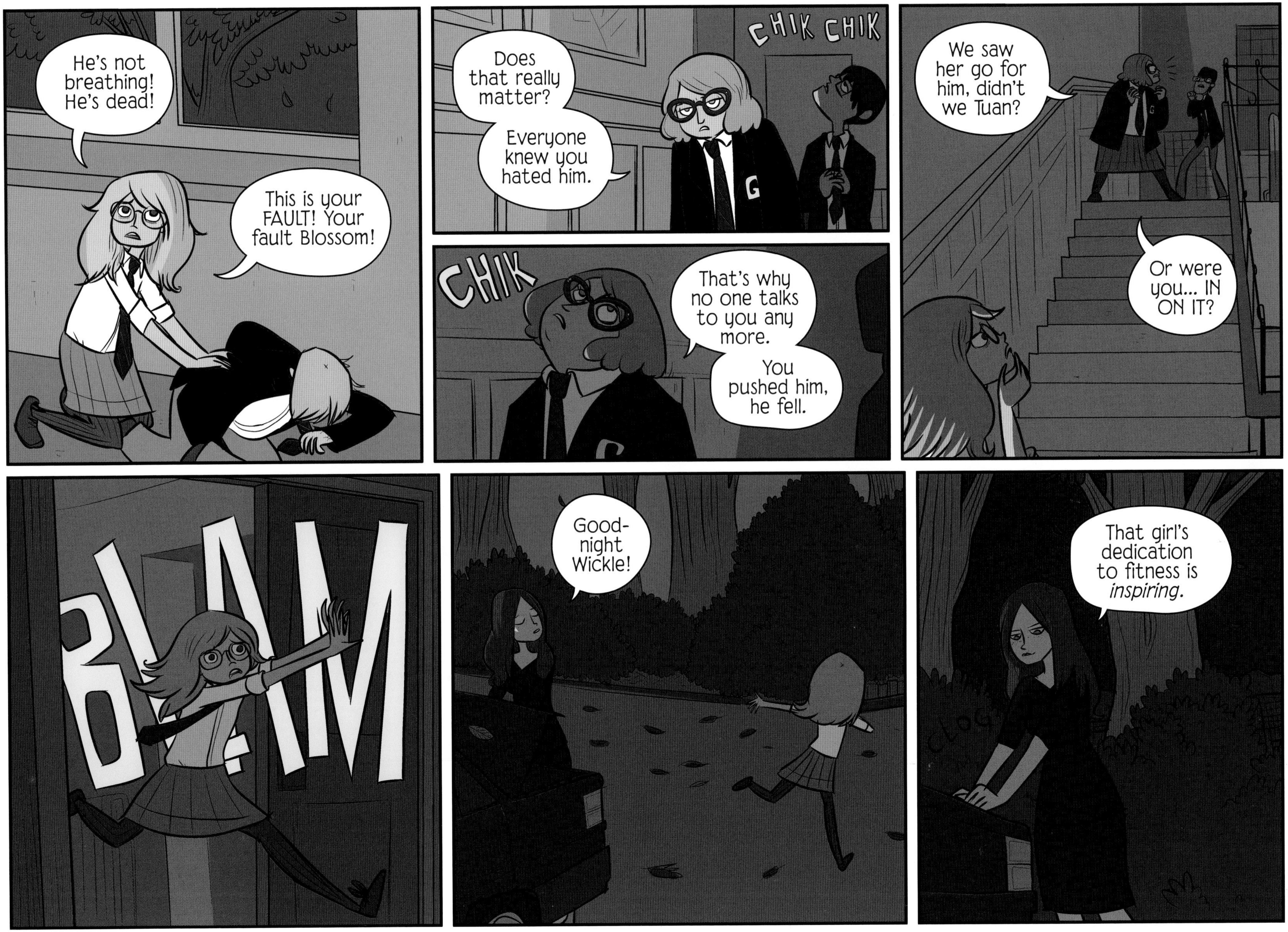
He's not breathing! He's dead!
This is your FAULT! Your fault Blossom!
CHIK CHIK
Does that really matter?
Everyone knew you hated him.
CHIK
That's why no one talks to you any more.
You pushed him, he fell.
We saw her go for him, didn't we Tuan?
Or were you... IN ON IT?
BLAM
Good-night Wickle!
CLOG
That girl's dedication to fitness is *inspiring*.

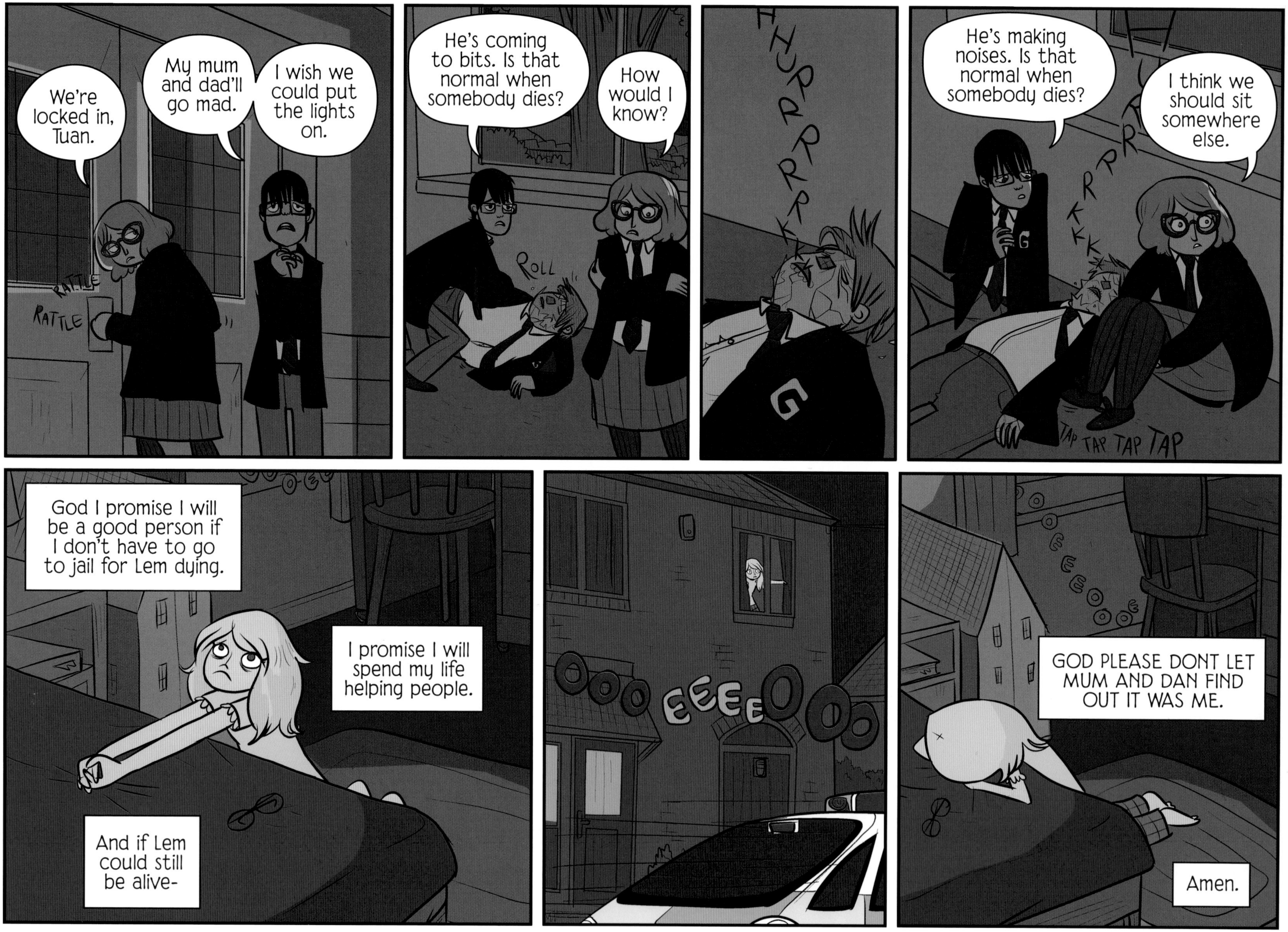
We're locked in, Tuan.
RATTLE
RATTLE
My mum and dad'll go mad.
I wish we could put the lights on.
He's coming to bits. Is that normal when somebody dies?
How would I know?
ROLL
He's making noises. Is that normal when somebody dies?
I think we should sit somewhere else.
TAP TAP TAP TAP
God I promise I will be a good person if I don't have to go to jail for Lem dying.
I promise I will spend my life helping people.
And if Lem could still be alive-
OOO EEEEOOO
GOD PLEASE DONT LET MUM AND DAN FIND OUT IT WAS ME.
Amen.

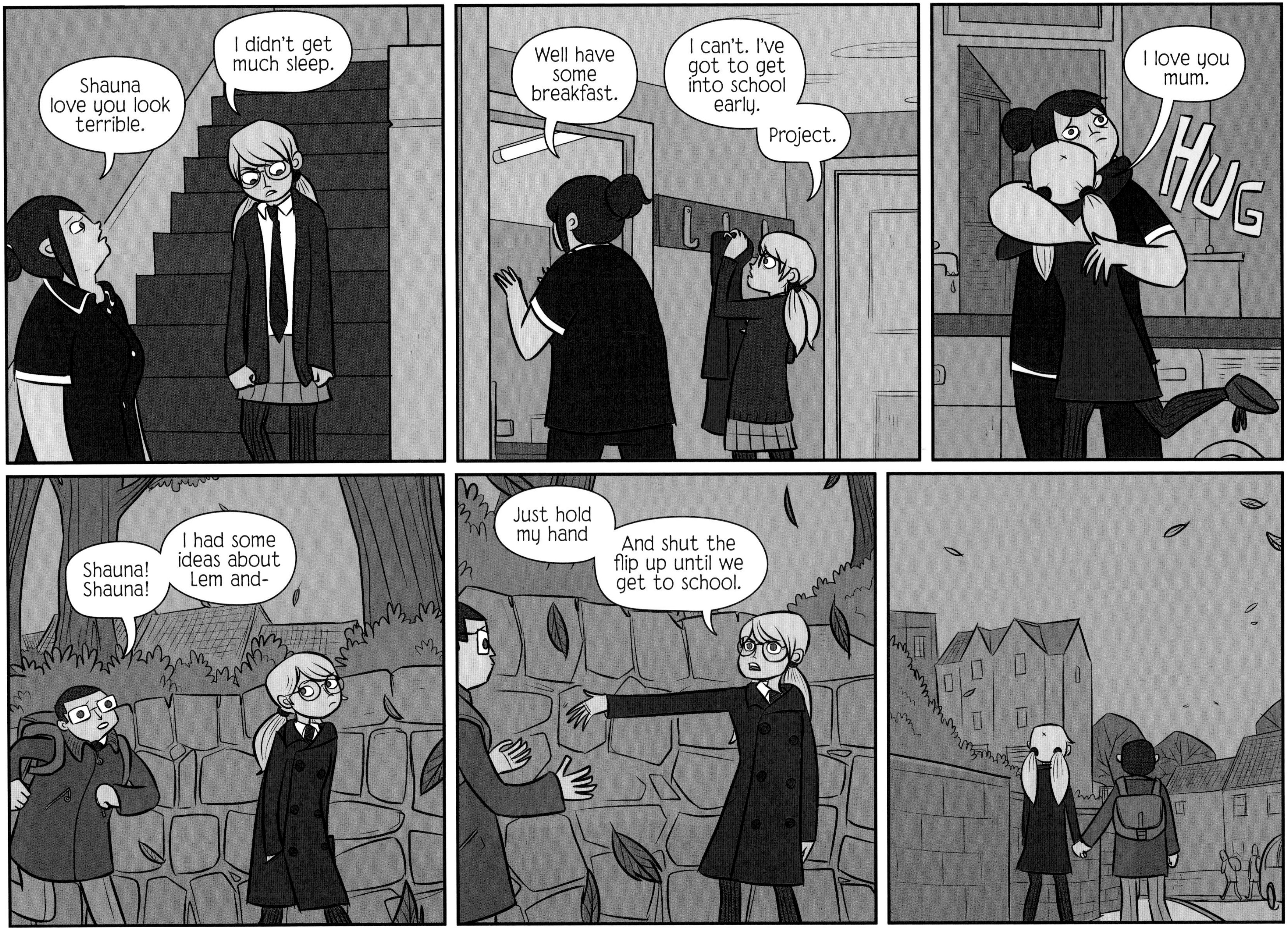
Shauna love you look terrible.
I didn't get much sleep.
Well have some breakfast.
I can't. I've got to get into school early.
Project.
I love you mum.
HUG
Shauna! Shauna!
I had some ideas about Lem and-
Just hold my hand
And shut the flip up until we get to school.

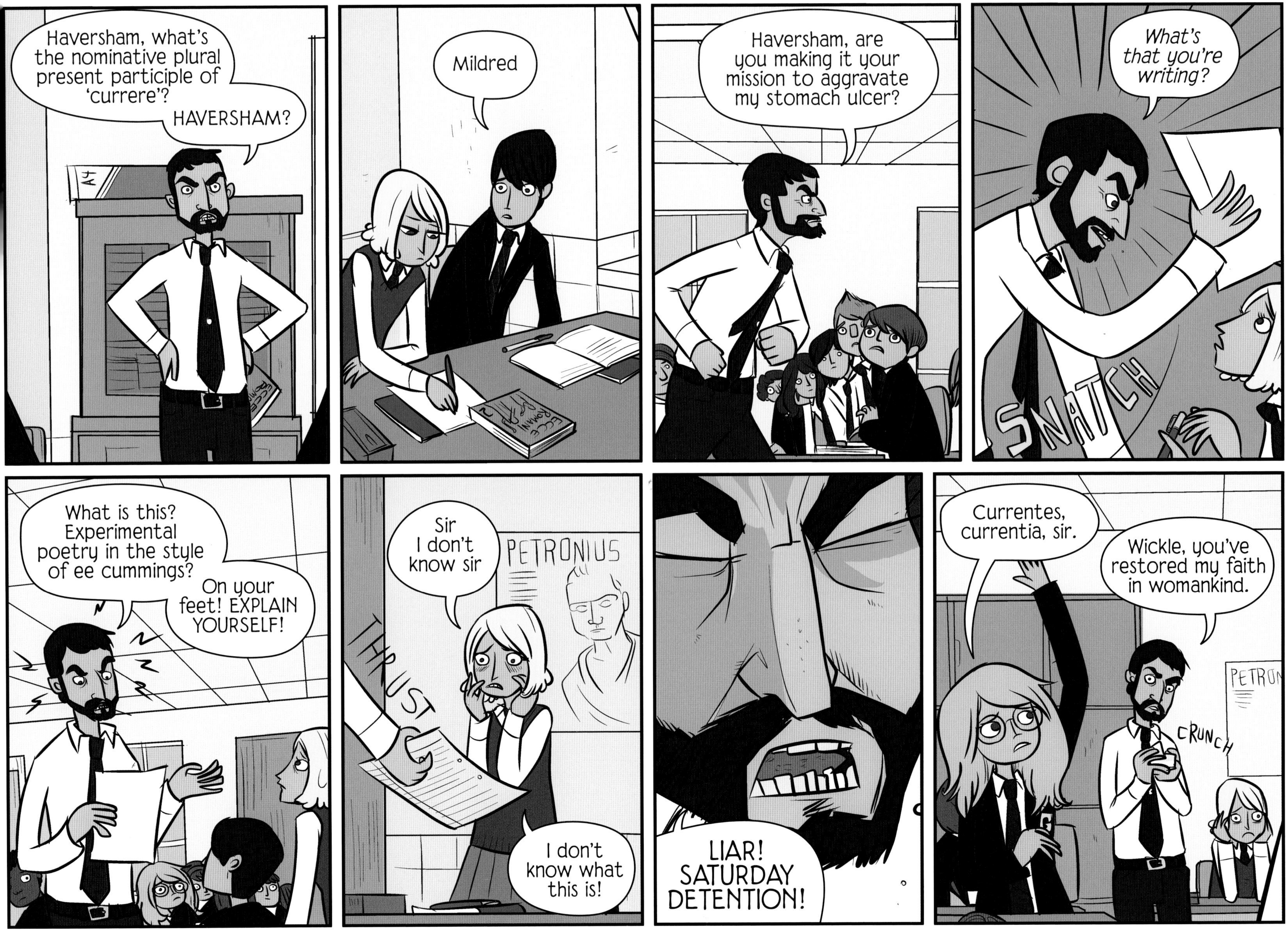
Haversham, what's the nominative plural present participle of 'currere'?
HAVERSHAM?
Mildred
Haversham, are you making it your mission to aggravate my stomach ulcer?
What's that you're writing?
SNATCH
What is this? Experimental poetry in the style of ee cummings?
On your feet! EXPLAIN YOURSELF!
Sir I don't know sir
PETRONIUS
THRUST
I don't know what this is!
LIAR! SATURDAY DETENTION!
Currentes, currentia, sir.
Wickle, you've restored my faith in womankind.
CRUNCH

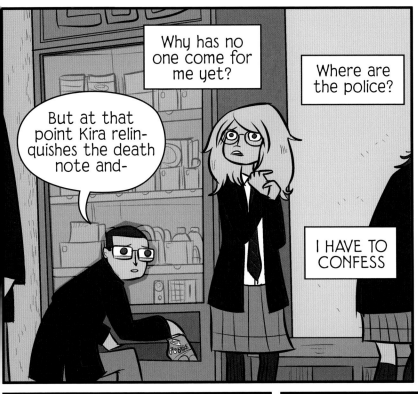

But at that point Kira relinquishes the death note and-

Why has no one come for me yet?

Where are the police?

I HAVE TO CONFESS

Corky last night I-

HE'S ALIVE? AM I GOING MAD?

Is this my pash?

Be gentle with me, Shauna.

Detention? I've NEVER had detention.

What did I write on that paper?

FISH FISH FISH

I must have developed a split personality.

AND SHE'S COMPLETELY MENTILE

Exclude non onion eaters
Never reveal the secrets of the onion farm
Lem is a right good laugh once you get to knowin
Onions are delicious
Exclude non onion eate
Never reveal the sec
the onion farm
m is a right
you o

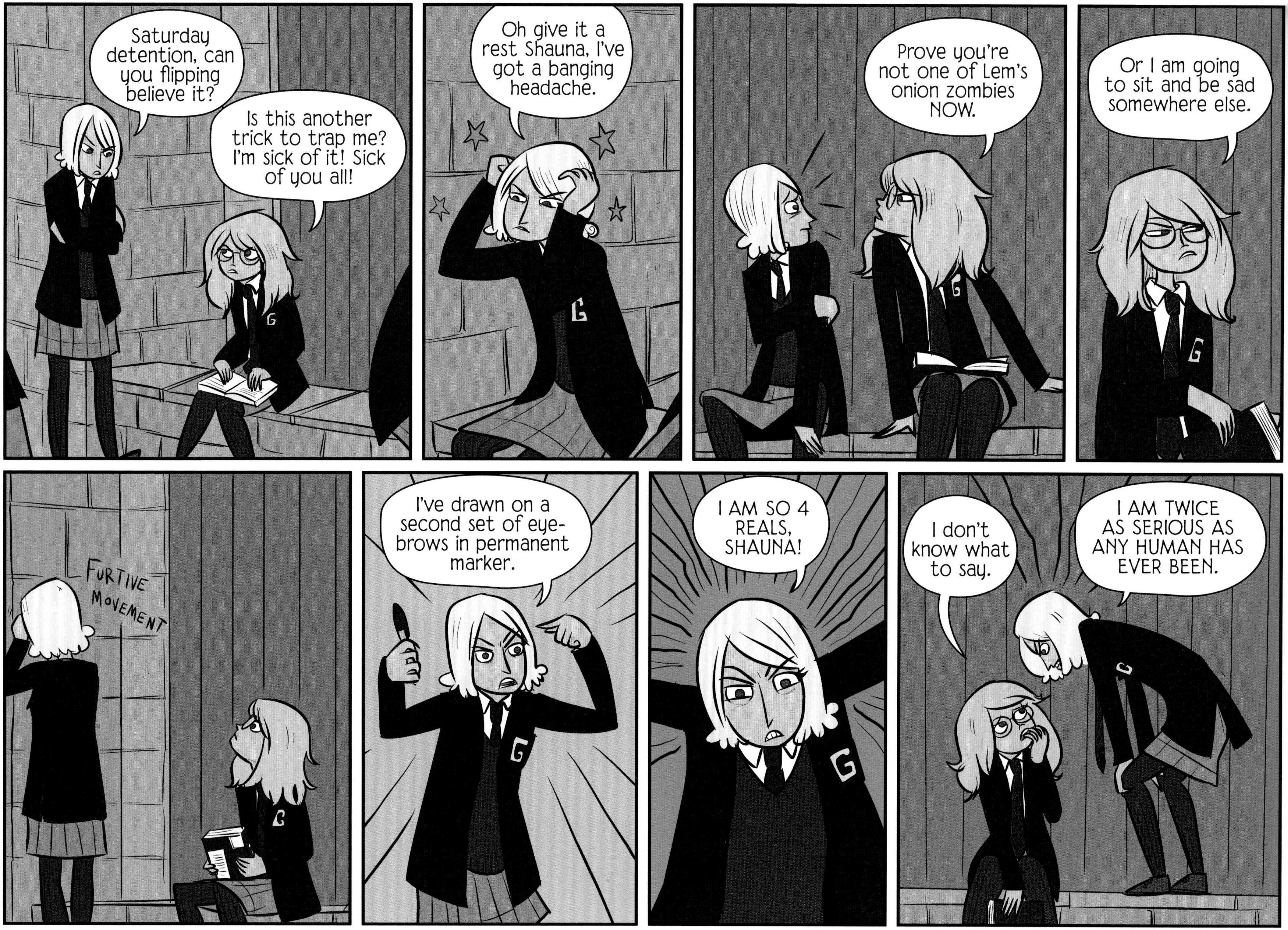
Saturday detention, can you flipping believe it?
Is this another trick to trap me? I'm sick of it! Sick of you all!
Oh give it a rest Shauna, I've got a banging headache.
Prove you're not one of Lem's onion zombies NOW.
Or I am going to sit and be sad somewhere else.
FURTIVE MOVEMENT
I've drawn on a second set of eye-brows in permanent marker.
I AM SO 4 REALS, SHAUNA!
I don't know what to say.
I AM TWICE AS SERIOUS AS ANY HUMAN HAS EVER BEEN.

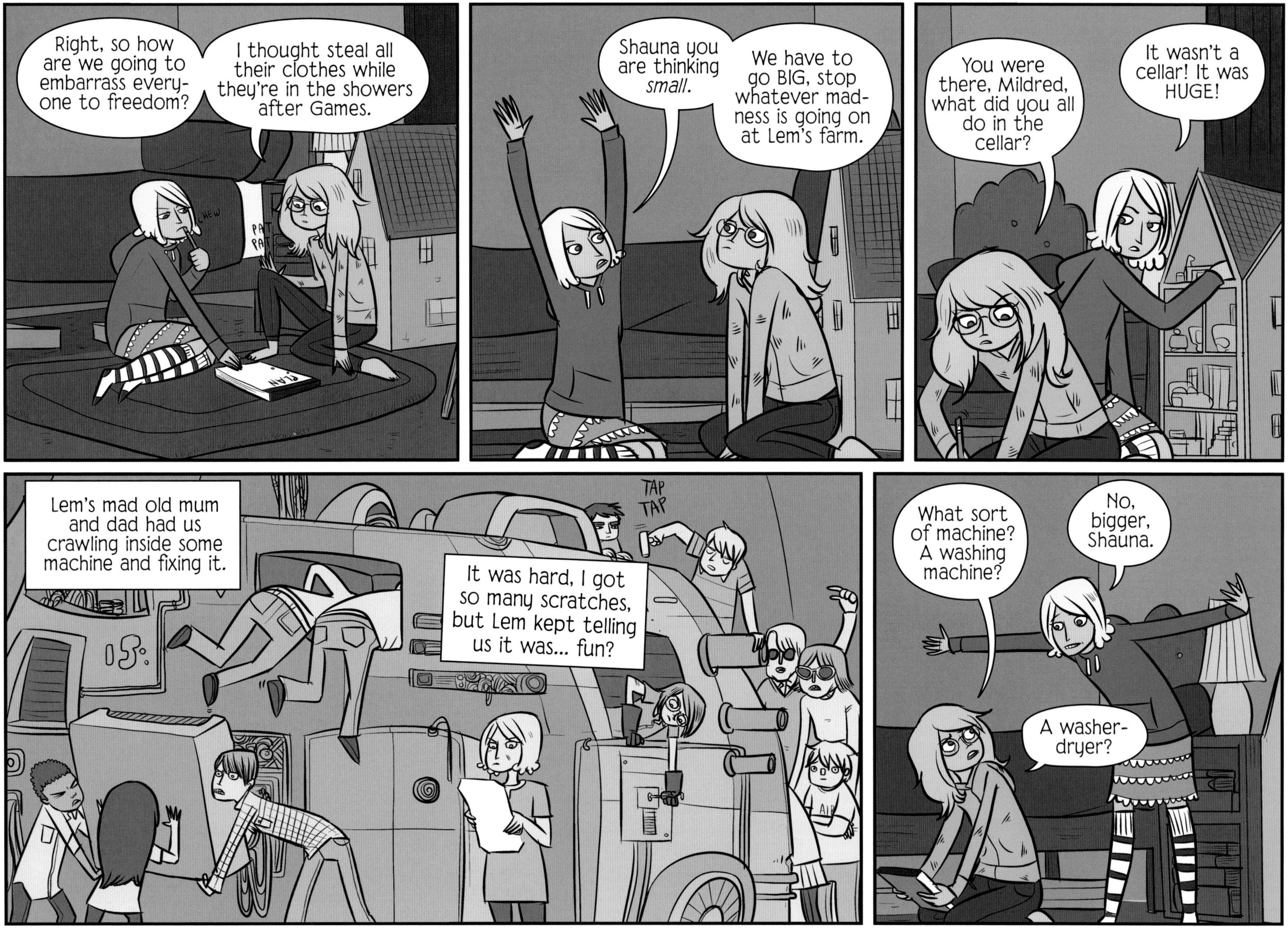
Right, so how are we going to embarrass every-one to freedom?
CHEW
I thought steal all their clothes while they're in the showers after Games.
PAT PAT
Shauna you are thinking *small.*
We have to go BIG, stop whatever mad-ness is going on at Lem's farm.
You were there, Mildred, what did you all do in the cellar?
It wasn't a cellar! It was HUGE!
Lem's mad old mum and dad had us crawling inside some machine and fixing it.
TAP TAP
It was hard, I got so many scratches, but Lem kept telling us it was... fun?
What sort of machine? A washing machine?
No, bigger, Shauna.
A washer-dryer?

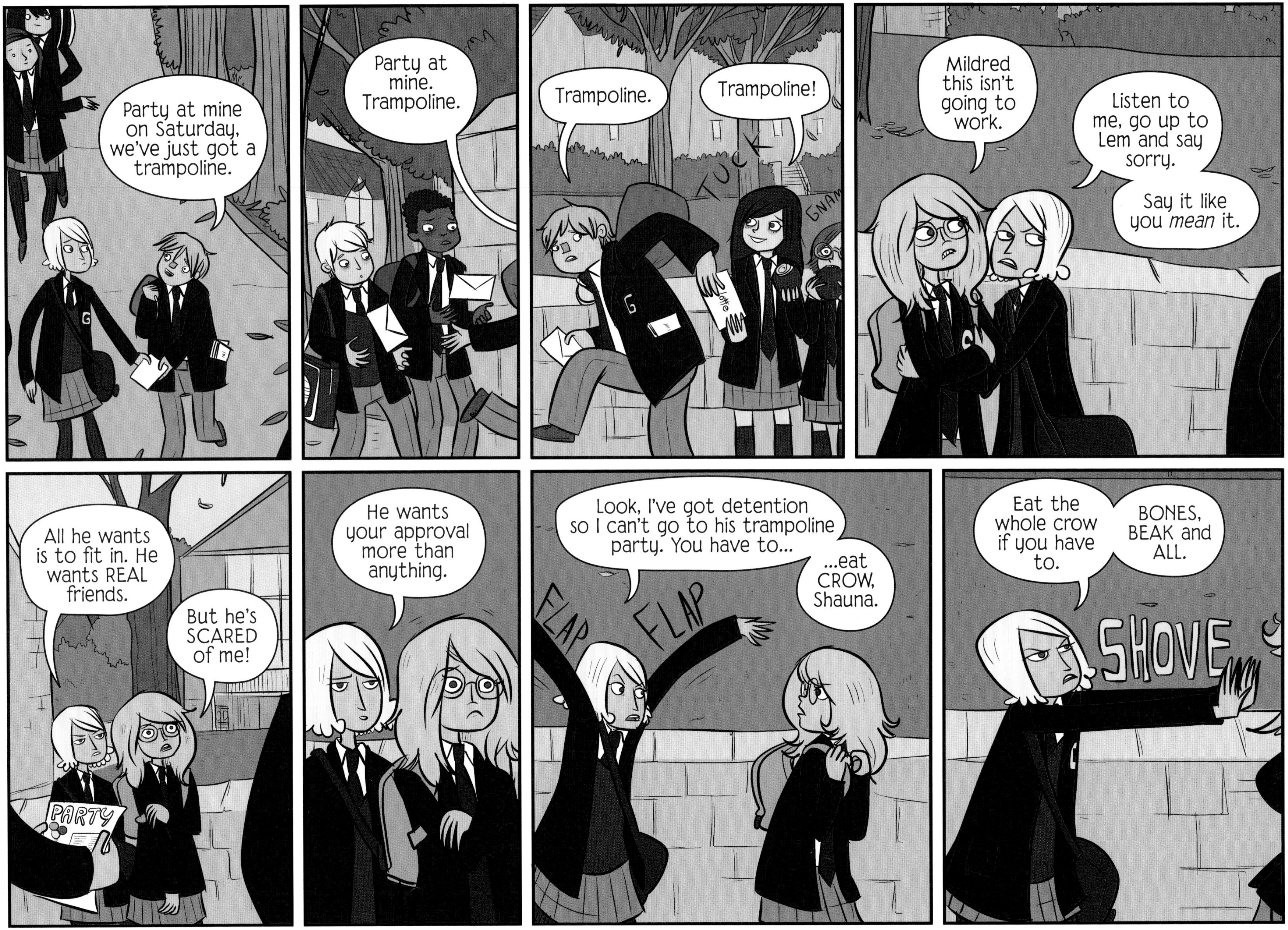
Party at mine on Saturday, we've just got a trampoline.
Party at mine. Trampoline.
Trampoline.
Trampoline!
TUCK
GNAM
Mildred this isn't going to work.
Listen to me, go up to Lem and say sorry.
Say it like you *mean* it.
All he wants is to fit in. He wants REAL friends.
But he's SCARED of me!
PARTY
He wants your approval more than anything.
Look, I've got detention so I can't go to his trampoline party. You have to...
...eat CROW, Shauna.
FLAP
FLAP
Eat the whole crow if you have to.
BONES, BEAK and ALL.
SHOVE

Lem, I just wanted to say sorry for everything.

I hope we can be friends. No more stupid fighting.

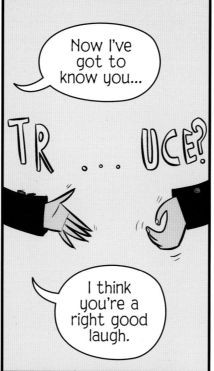

Now I've got to know you...

TR ... UCE?

I think you're a right good laugh.

Make her eat a raw onion.

Including the skin.

Bones, beak and all, Shauna.

Bones, beak and all.

Pretend it's an apple, *pretend it's an apple.*

GNAM

BLAH
BLEH
BLEH
BLEH
BLOGH
BORG
BLAH
BLEH

Ha ha hahahah

HA HA HA!!

SPIT
PTUI
PTUI
PTUI

Party at mine on Saturday.

THRUST

We've just got a trampoline.

Is your coffee working?

I'm feeling quite jangly.

8.50! I have to get a move on!

A-PPARENTLY they kick you out of Saturday detention at 12.

So I'll be at Lem's by *one*.

Write down your observations until then.

I'm scared Mildred!

Me too! Satto detto is full of school's most hardened criminals.

I've got to live through that to get down to how scared *you* are.

Flipping Norah. Worst of the worst.

Filled someone's bag with lab gas.

Drew a willy on the bonnet of Mr Peebles' new car.

Sold her mum's ciggies in the loos at break.

POLDERS

Hid in an organ pipe, no one knows why.

I think your work is really groundbreaking!

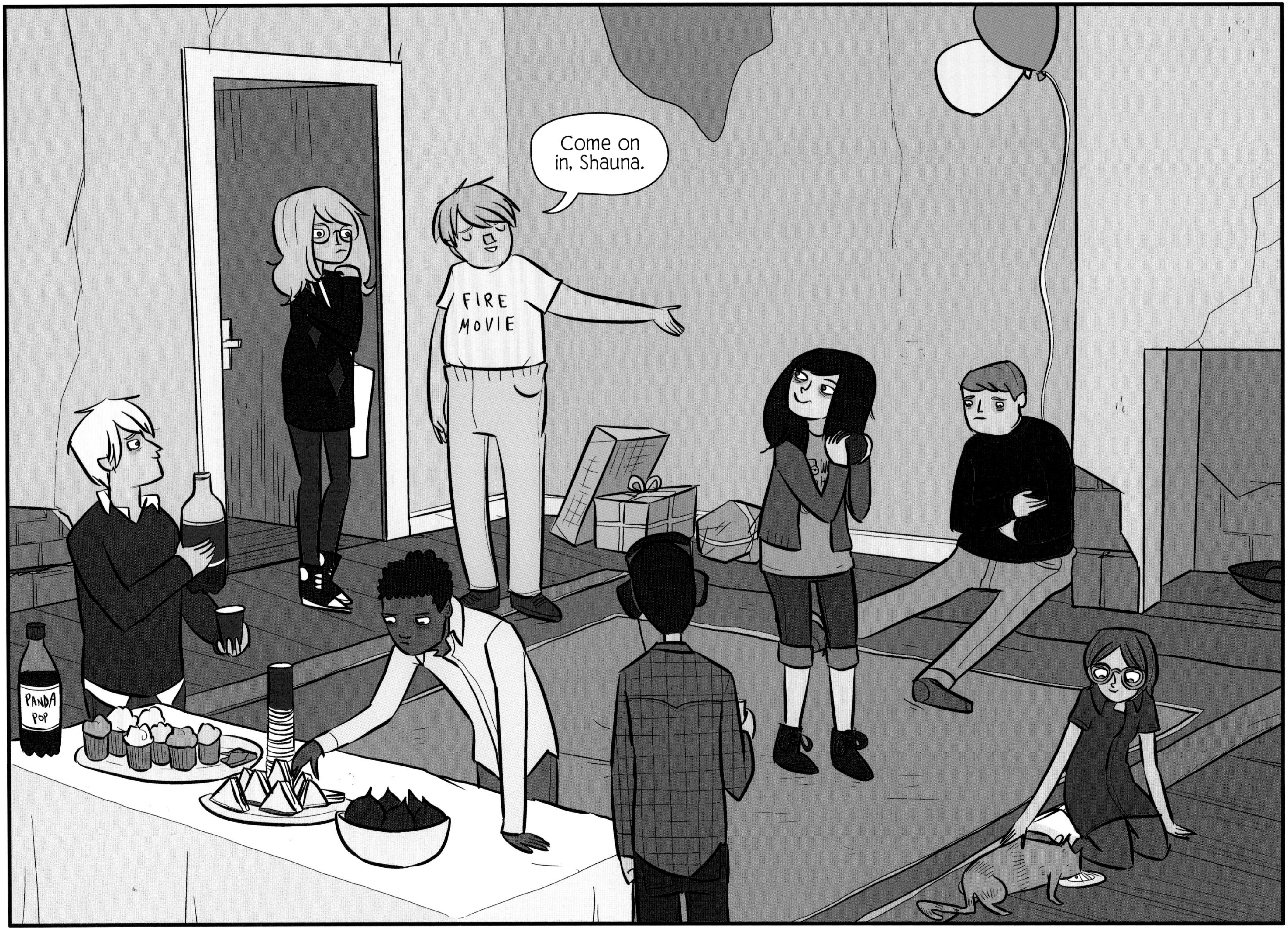
Come on in, Shauna.
FIRE MOVIE
PANDA POP

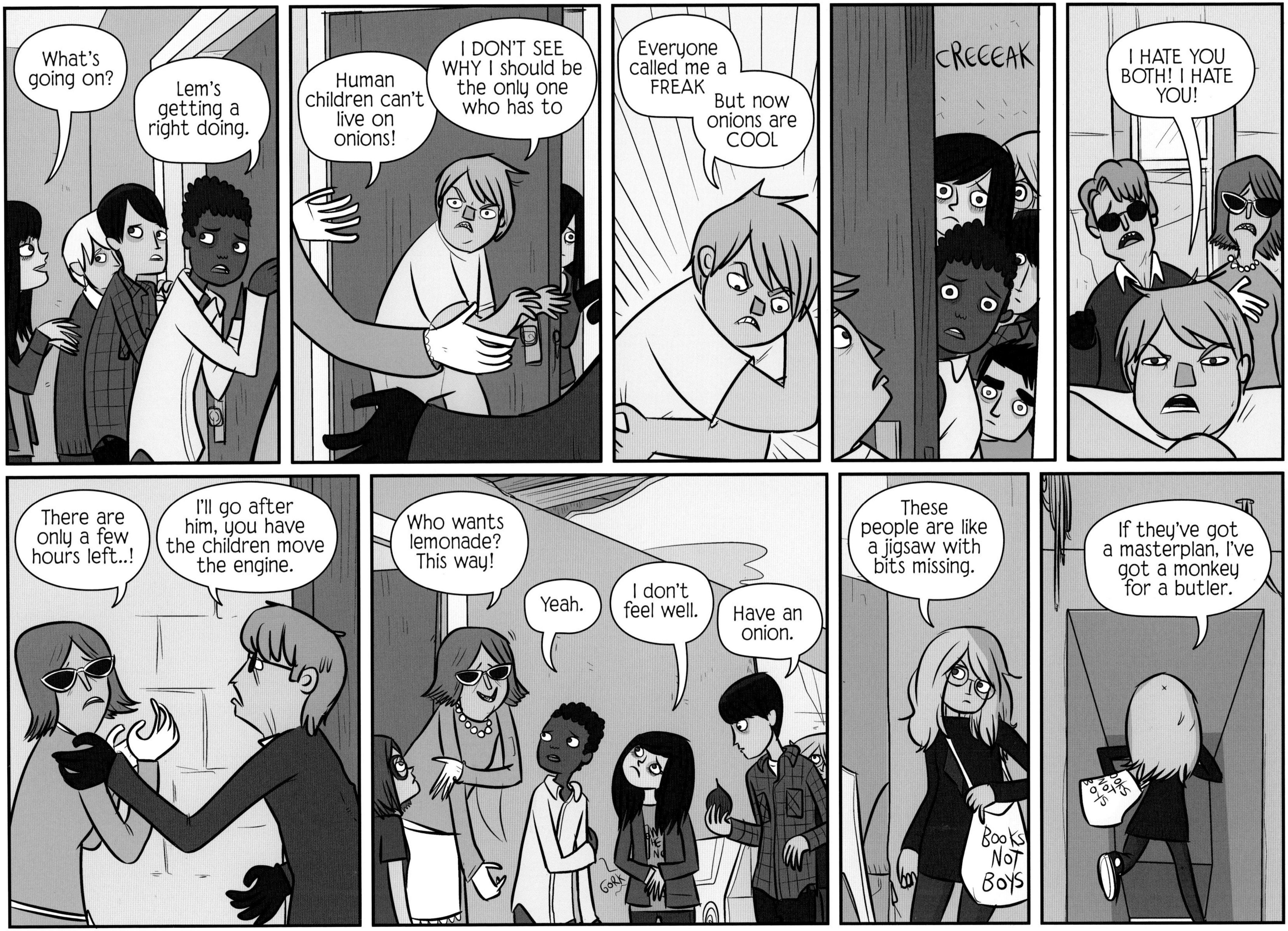
What's going on?
Lem's getting a right doing.
Human children can't live on onions!
I DON'T SEE WHY I should be the only one who has to
Everyone called me a FREAK
But now onions are COOL
CREEEAK
I HATE YOU BOTH! I HATE YOU!
There are only a few hours left..!
I'll go after him, you have the children move the engine.
Who wants lemonade? This way!
Yeah.
I don't feel well.
Have an onion.
GORK
These people are like a jigsaw with bits missing.
Books Not Boys
If they've got a masterplan, I've got a monkey for a butler.

Bad Machinery, Volume Four

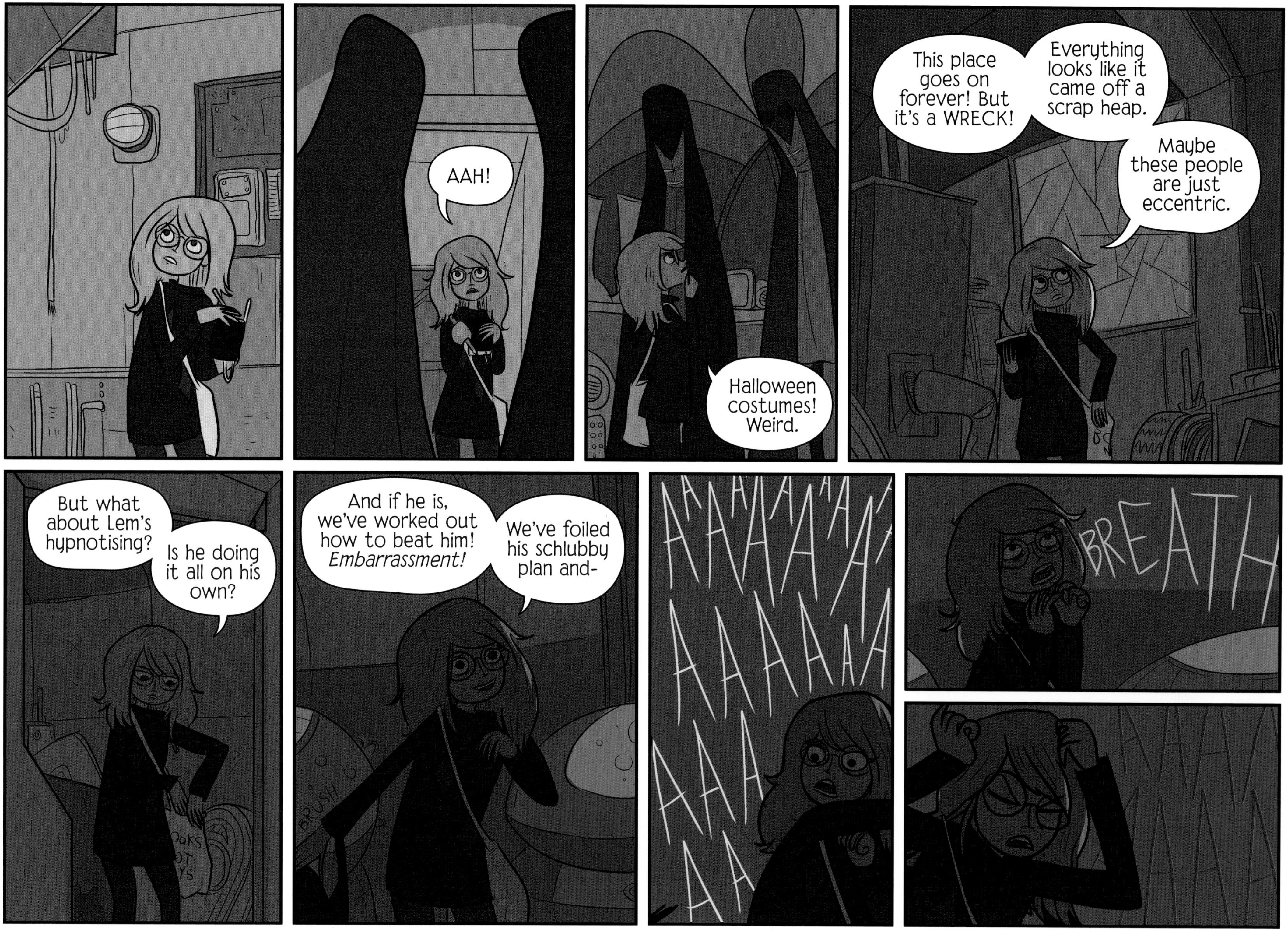
AAH!
Halloween costumes! Weird.
This place goes on forever! But it's a WRECK!
Everything looks like it came off a scrap heap.
Maybe these people are just eccentric.
But what about Lem's hypnotising?
Is he doing it all on his own?
And if he is, we've worked out how to beat him! *Embarrassment!*
We've foiled his schlubby plan and-
BRUSH
AAAAAAAAAAAAAAAAAAAAAA
BREATH

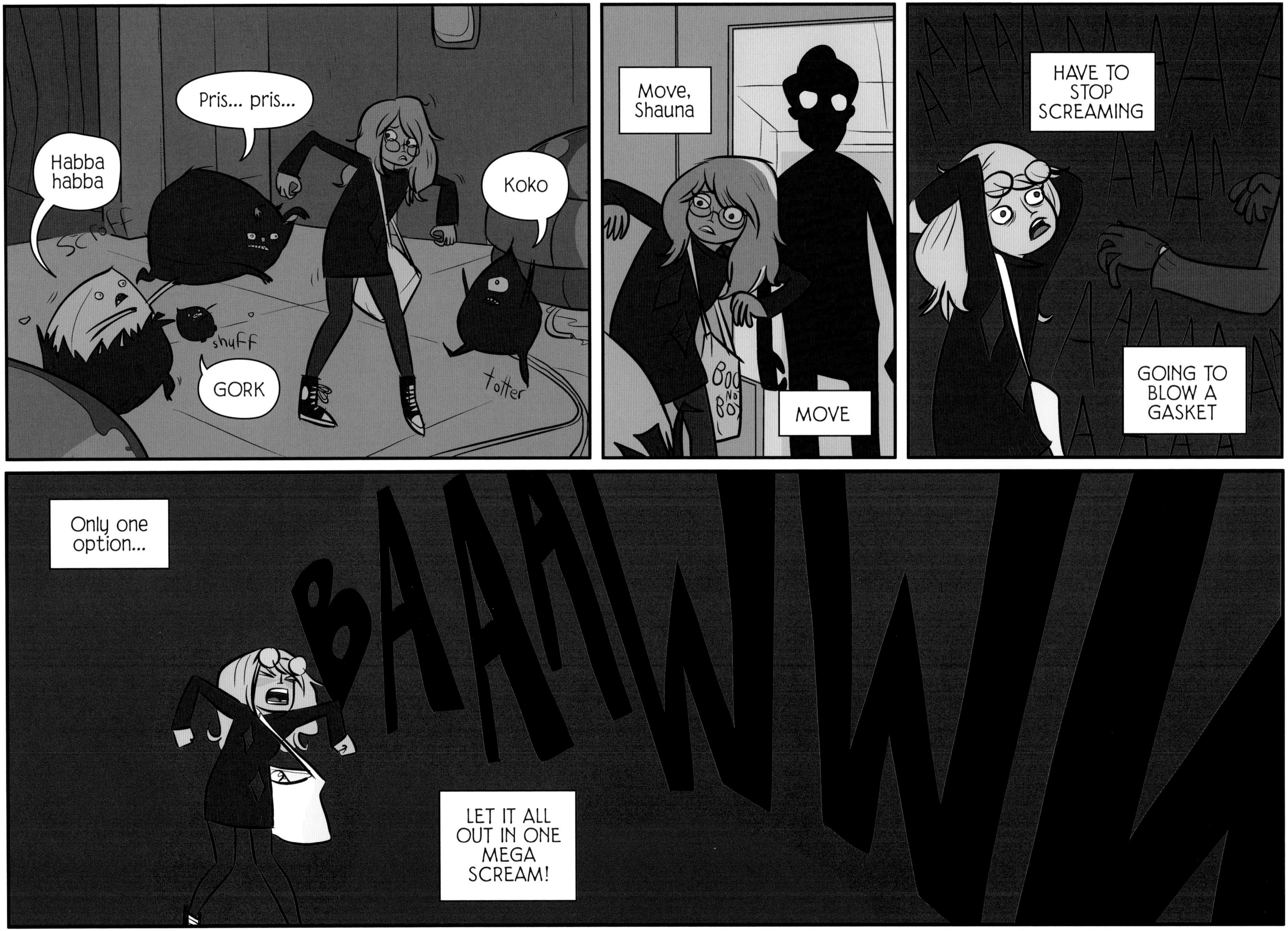
Pris... pris...
Habba habba
scroff
Koko
shuff
GORK
totter
Move, Shauna
MOVE
HAVE TO STOP SCREAMING
GOING TO BLOW A GASKET
Only one option...
BAAAWWWW
LET IT ALL OUT IN ONE MEGA SCREAM!

Bad Machinery, Volume Four

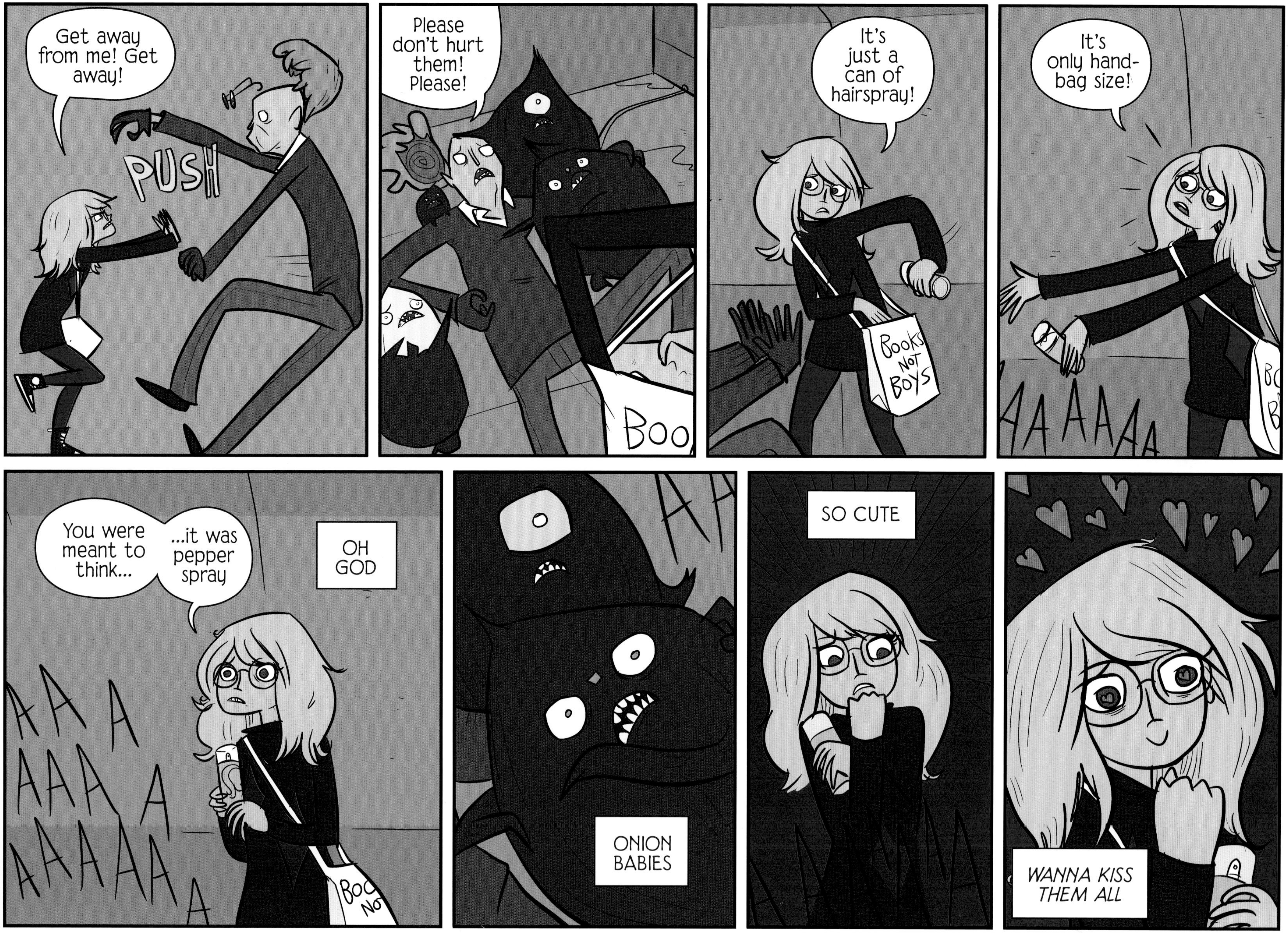
Get away from me! Get away!
PUSH
Please don't hurt them! Please!
BOO
It's just a can of hairspray!
BOOKS NOT BOYS
It's only hand-bag size!
AAAAAA
You were meant to think...
...it was pepper spray
OH GOD
ONION BABIES
SO CUTE
WANNA KISS THEM ALL

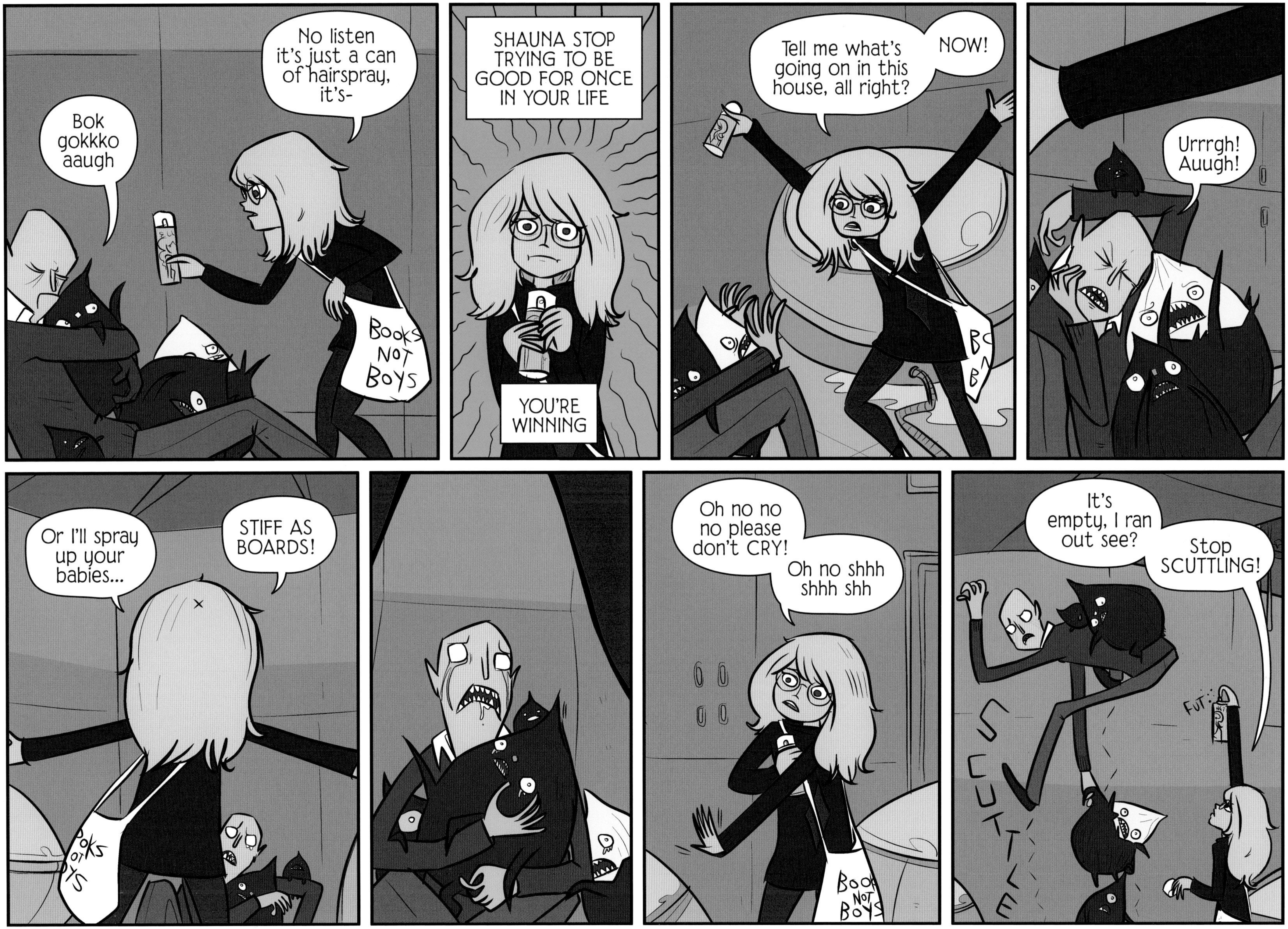

No listen it's just a can of hairspray, it's-
Bok gokkko aaugh
Books Not Boys
SHAUNA STOP TRYING TO BE GOOD FOR ONCE IN YOUR LIFE
YOU'RE WINNING
Tell me what's going on in this house, all right?
NOW!
Urrrgh! Auugh!
Or I'll spray up your babies...
STIFF AS BOARDS!
Oh no no no please don't CRY!
Oh no shhh shhh shh
It's empty, I ran out see?
Stop SCUTTLING!
FUT
SCUTTLE

My wife and I are from the planet Korfus.

It is more distant than you could possibly imagine.

I AM WELL INTO THIS.

Having detected intelligent life on your planet, we were part of a diplomatic mission.

We set off hundreds of years before our intended arrival, and traveled in suspended animation.

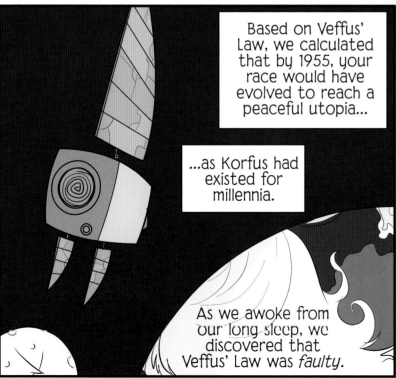

Based on Veffus' Law, we calculated that by 1955, your race would have evolved to reach a peaceful utopia...

...as Korfus had existed for millennia.

As we awoke from our long sleep, we discovered that Veffus' Law was *faulty*.

Yeah because humans still LOVED fightin'?

No. We discovered that our own planet had been destroyed...

...in "The Battle Of Whose Turn Is It".

You'd better not be joking me. *I'm 13.*

I'm not *stupid*. I wrecked these eyes *READIN'*.

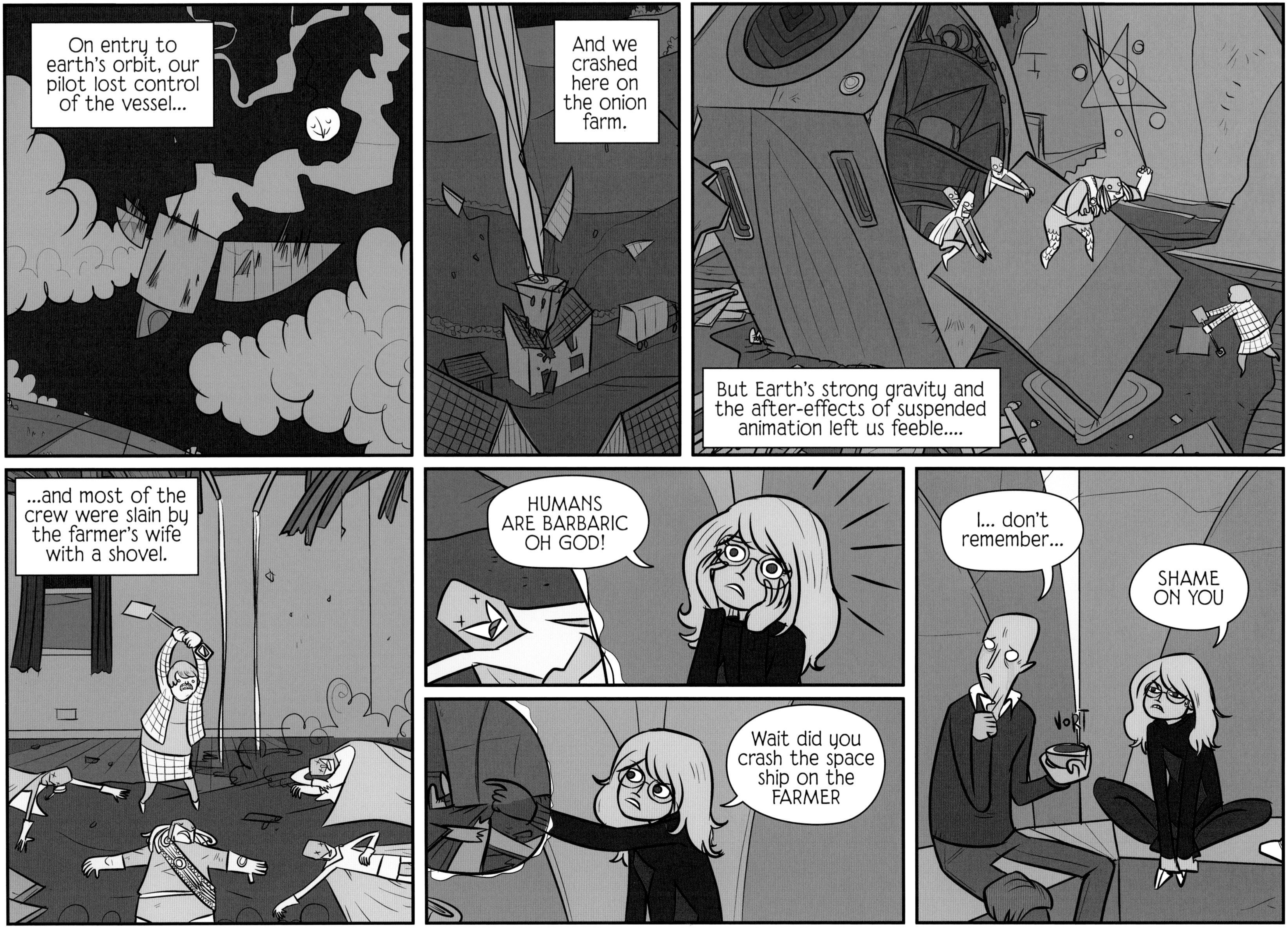
On entry to earth's orbit, our pilot lost control of the vessel...
And we crashed here on the onion farm.
But Earth's strong gravity and the after-effects of suspended animation left us feeble....
...and most of the crew were slain by the farmer's wife with a shovel.
HUMANS ARE BARBARIC OH GOD!
Wait did you crash the space ship on the FARMER
I... don't remember...
SHAME ON YOU
VORT

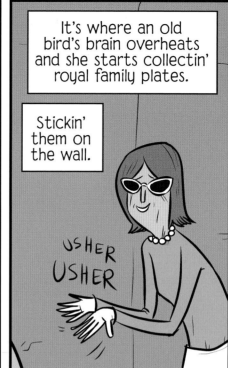

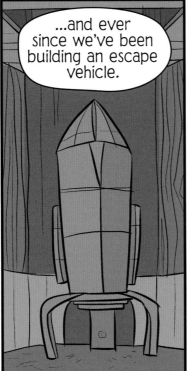

What are you doing?

I'm gonna smash it it! Gonna smash it so we don't have to leave!

Lem! No son! We're going home!

This is my home

POLL!

FIRE MOVIE

He's pretty weak. He's just scratched this panel a bit.

OOKS NOT OYS

But why do you want to go home, isn't it partially destroyed?

We just want to feel light again before we... we...

To feel light again.

Are you... are you... um, pretty old?

LEM WILL YOU KNOCK IT OFF!?

FIRE MOVIE

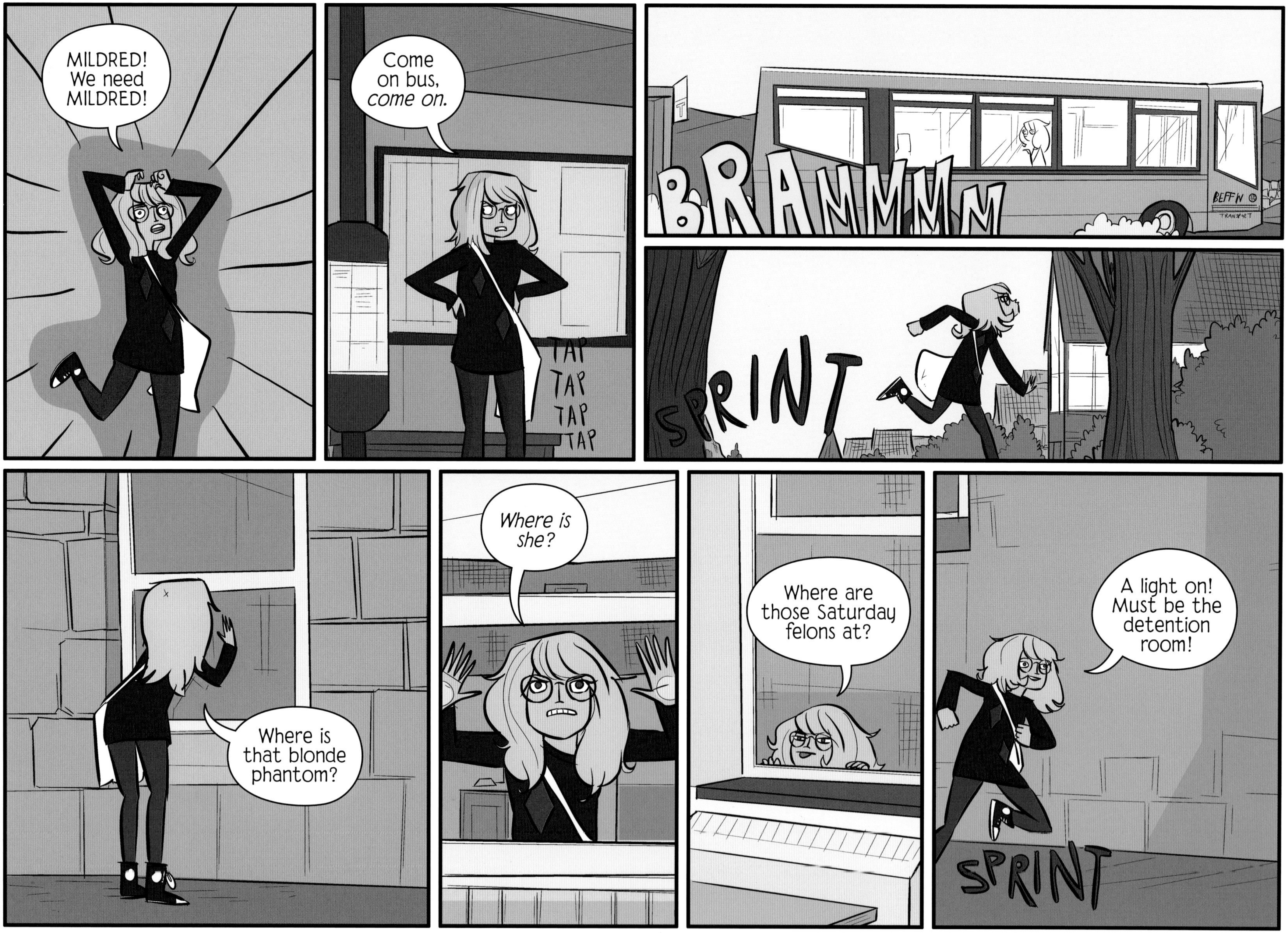
MILDRED! We need MILDRED!
Come on bus, *come on.*
TAP TAP TAP TAP
BRAMMMM
SPRINT
Where is that blonde phantom?
Where is she?
Where are those Saturday felons at?
A light on! Must be the detention room!
SPRINT

Mildred, you're different from the other 2nd year girls.

Taller? I'm tall for my age.

Mildred laaaa!

Anytime you're ready.

Anytime.

So that's Saturday detention eh? PASHING ON 4th year boys!

Mr Carter nicked off for an emergency after 20 minutes.

DRAG

BOOKS NOT BOYS

I'll probably never get to kiss anyone EVER AGAIN Shauna.

I'll be known as Mildred Haversham, KISS-LEAVER.

Those bad kids would've led you into a life of crime.

BOOKS NOT BOYS

They lived life fast. They stayed up late.

WEEK E15·

They'd made moody faces into an art form.

Okay so this is what you want?

C. Huzzah

B. Rocket takes off

ROCKET

A. Engine pushed into hole in rocket

engine

The Case of the Lonely One

We will achieve this using BASIC PHYSICS.

My friends are bravely stomping hundreds of onions into a thin, watery paste.

SQUIT SQUIT SQUIT

HATE ONIONS NOW!

MY GUTS, MAN!

Like a train compressing autumn leaves on rails, this will create...

...a TEFLON-LIKE NON-STICK COATING ON THE GROUND.

Using the last of their strength, they will push the engine into the "skid zone"

It will GLIDE into position.

Do you think this will work?

Well, Mildred seems very sure of herself.

But she was very sure that "the queen can just shoot anyone she likes" too.

STOMP STOMP

STOMP STOMP STOMP

STOMP STOMP STOMP

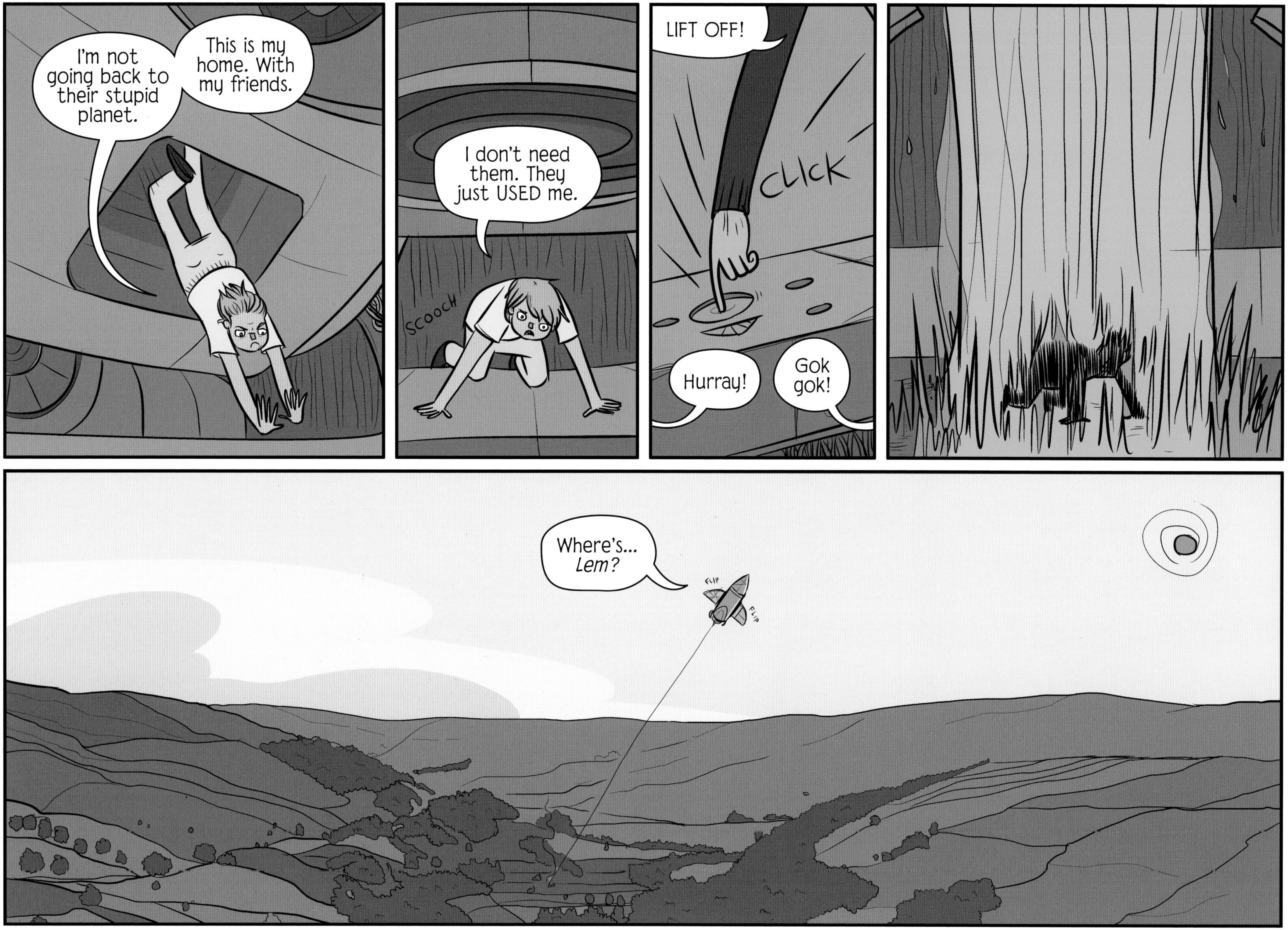
I'm not going back to their stupid planet.
This is my home. With my friends.
I don't need them. They just USED me.
SCOOCH
LIFT OFF!
CLICK
Hurray!
Gok gok!
Where's... *Lem?*
FLIP
FLIP

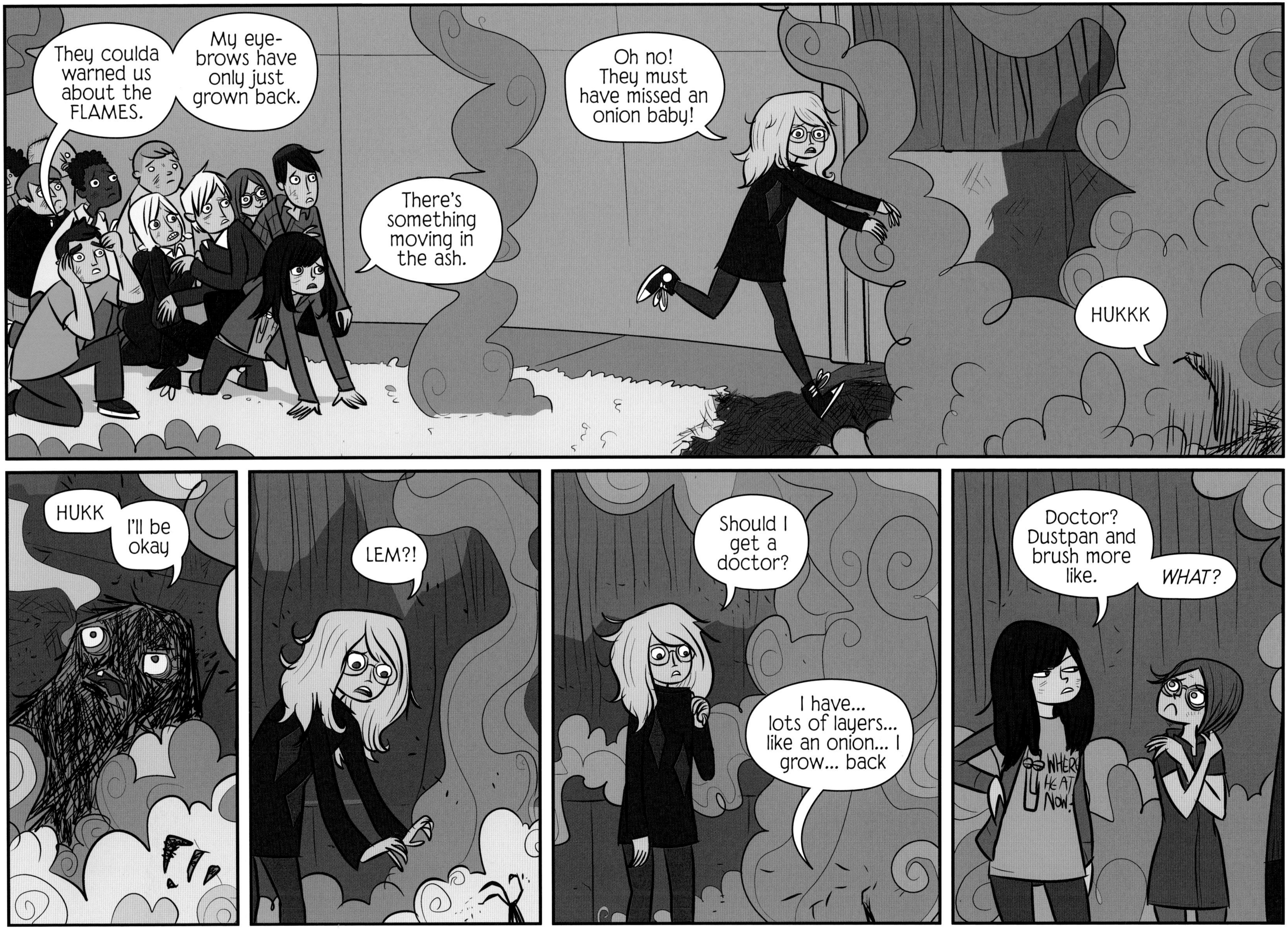
They coulda warned us about the FLAMES.
My eye-brows have only just grown back.
There's something moving in the ash.
Oh no! They must have missed an onion baby!
HUKKK
HUKK
I'll be okay
LEM?!
Should I get a doctor?
I have... lots of layers... like an onion... I grow... back
Doctor? Dustpan and brush more like.
WHAT?

What he's saying... that he grows back? Makes sense.

Little Claire kicked him right in the middle fighting him off.

HURK HUKK HUKK

First he couldn't breathe, then he flaked off a layer and he was fine.

Or, you know, fine for *Lem.*

I think he's hurt worse than he can flake off this time.

Are you still there? I'm cold.

Yes! I just wanted to say, um...

...you were a right good laugh... *once I got to know you.*

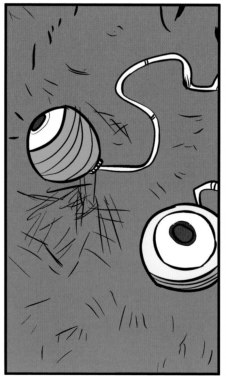

I'm sick of this stupid place.

Let's go home.

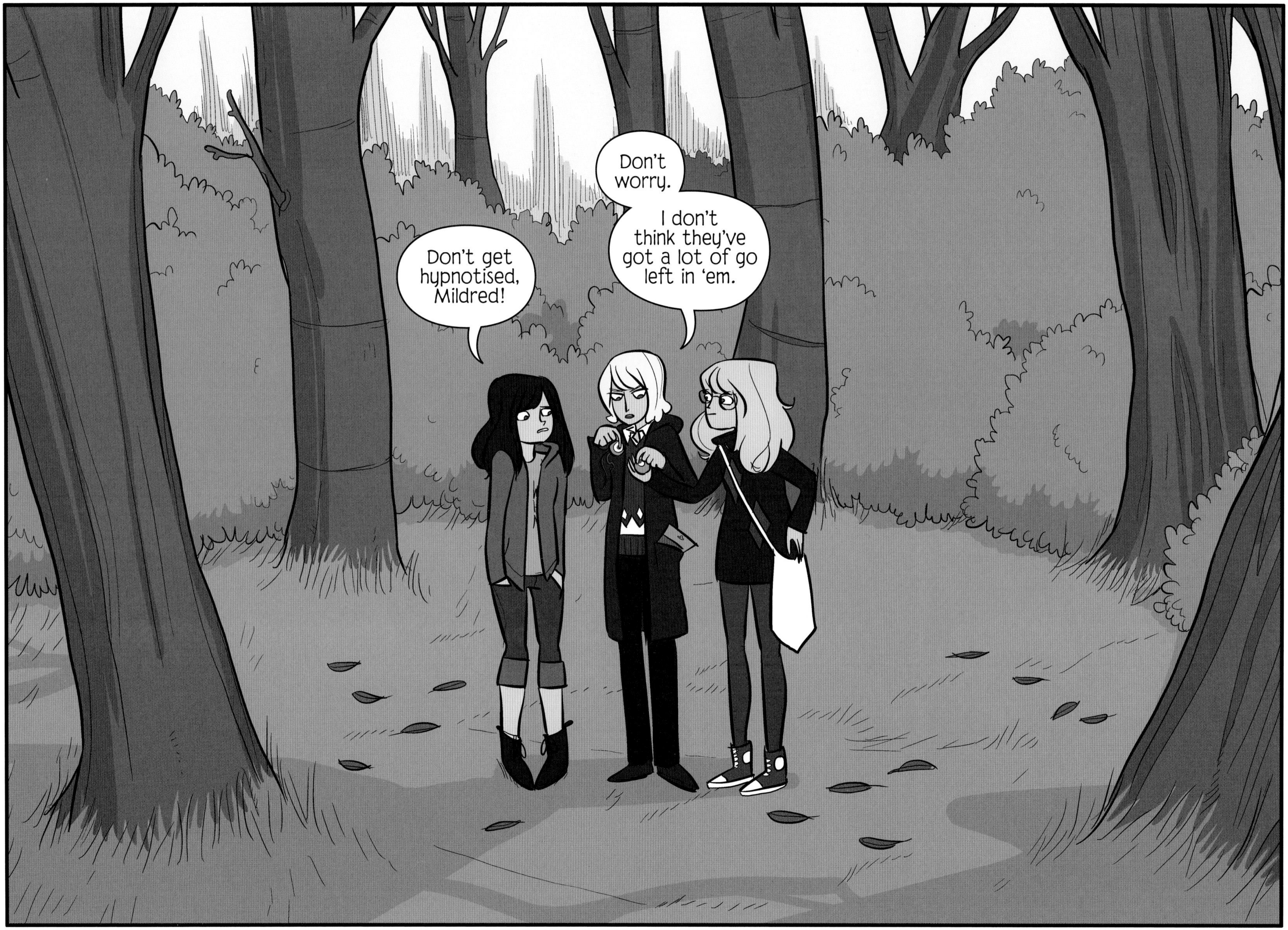
Don't get hypnotised, Mildred!
Don't worry.
I don't think they've got a lot of go left in 'em.

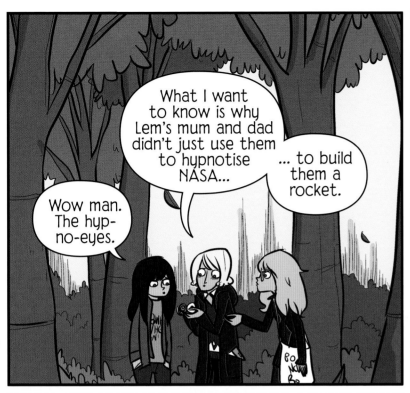

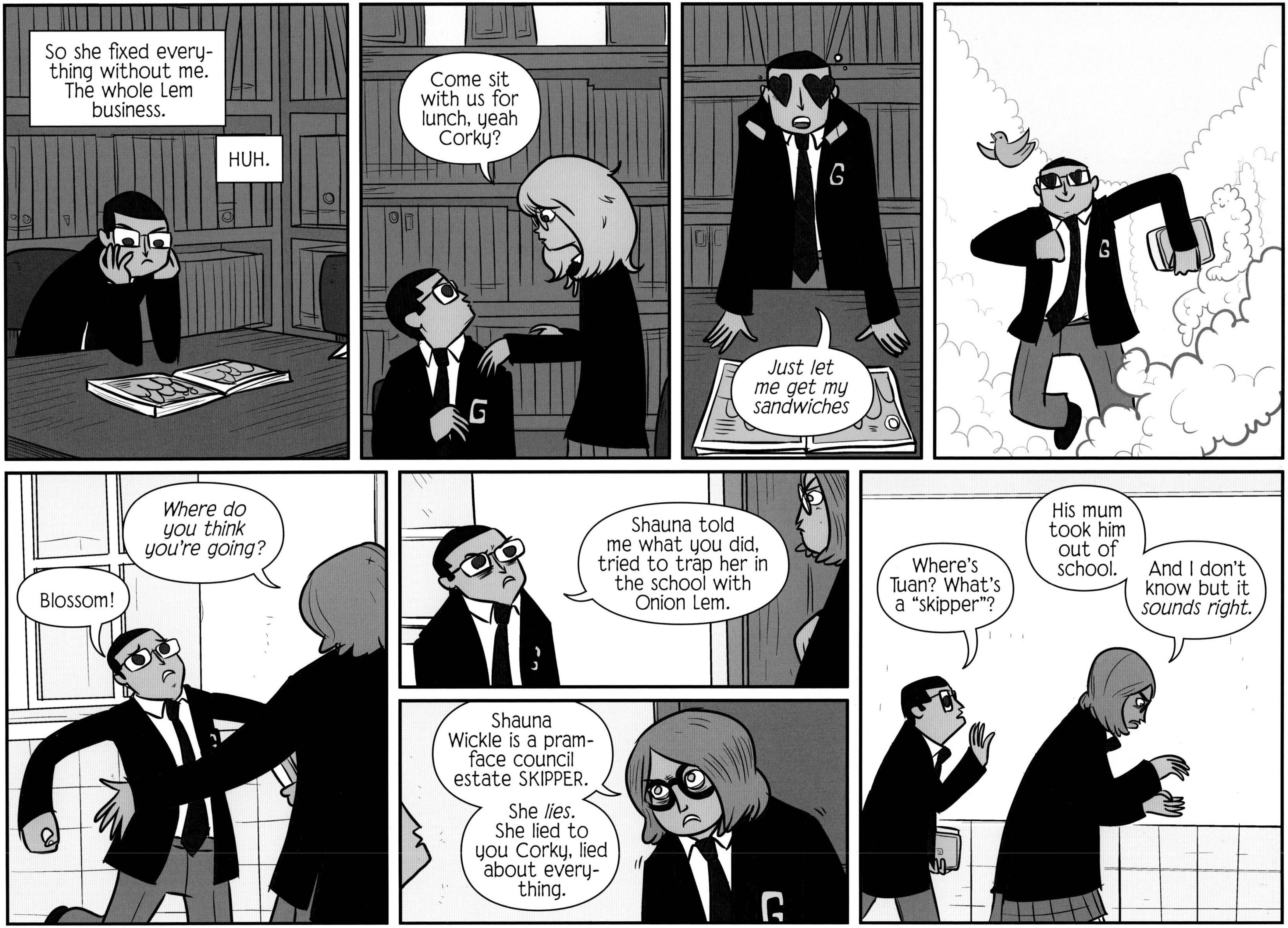
So she fixed everything without me. The whole Lem business.
HUH.
Come sit with us for lunch, yeah Corky?
Just let me get my sandwiches
Blossom!
Where do you think you're going?
Shauna told me what you did, tried to trap her in the school with Onion Lem.
Shauna Wickle is a pram-face council estate SKIPPER.
She *lies.* She lied to you Corky, lied about everything.
Where's Tuan? What's a "skipper"?
His mum took him out of school.
And I don't know but it *sounds right.*

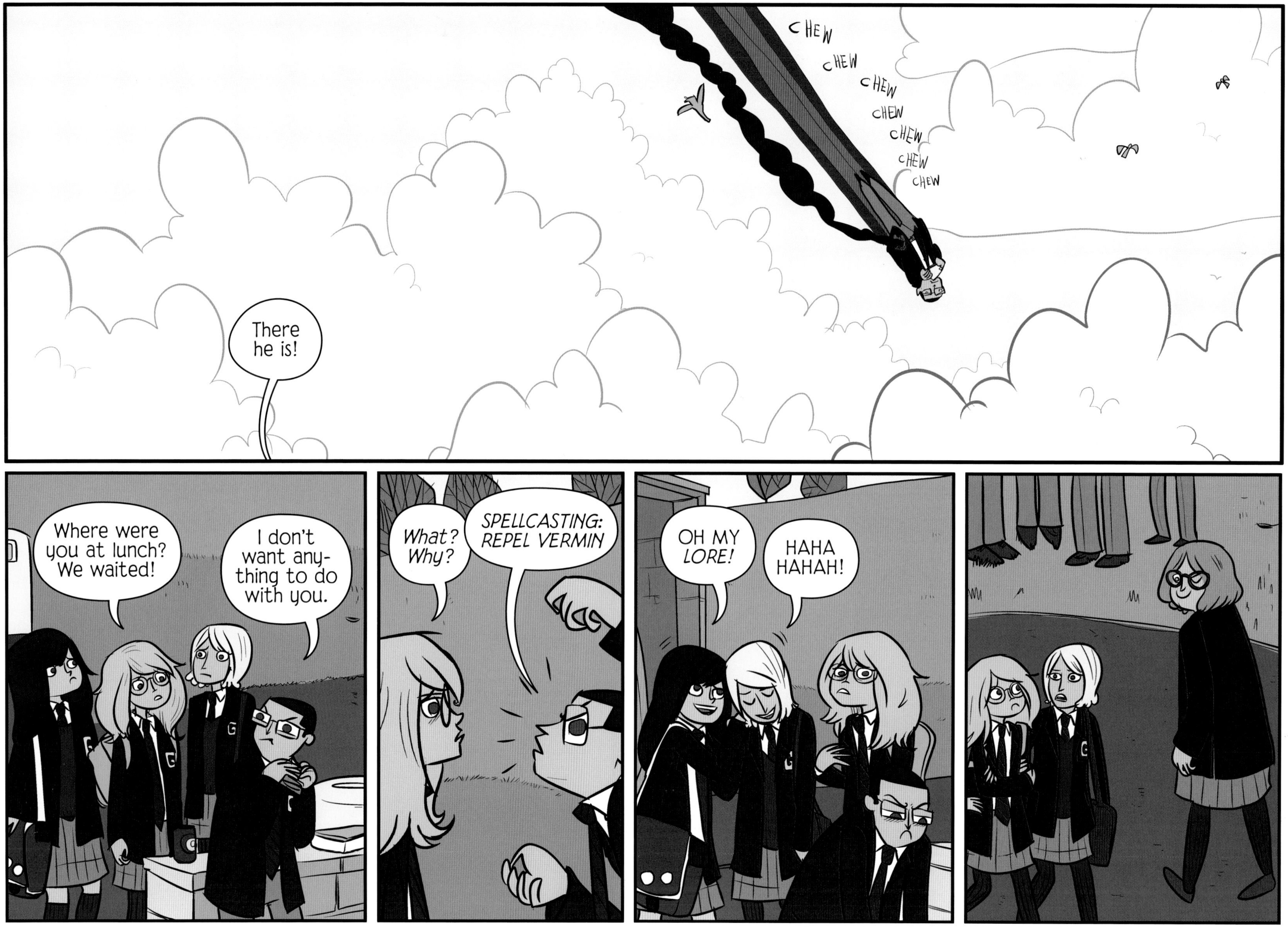
CHEW
CHEW
CHEW
CHEW
CHEW
CHEW
CHEW
There he is!
Where were you at lunch? We waited!
I don't want anything to do with you.
What? Why?
SPELLCASTING: REPEL VERMIN
OH MY LORE!
HAHA HAHAH!

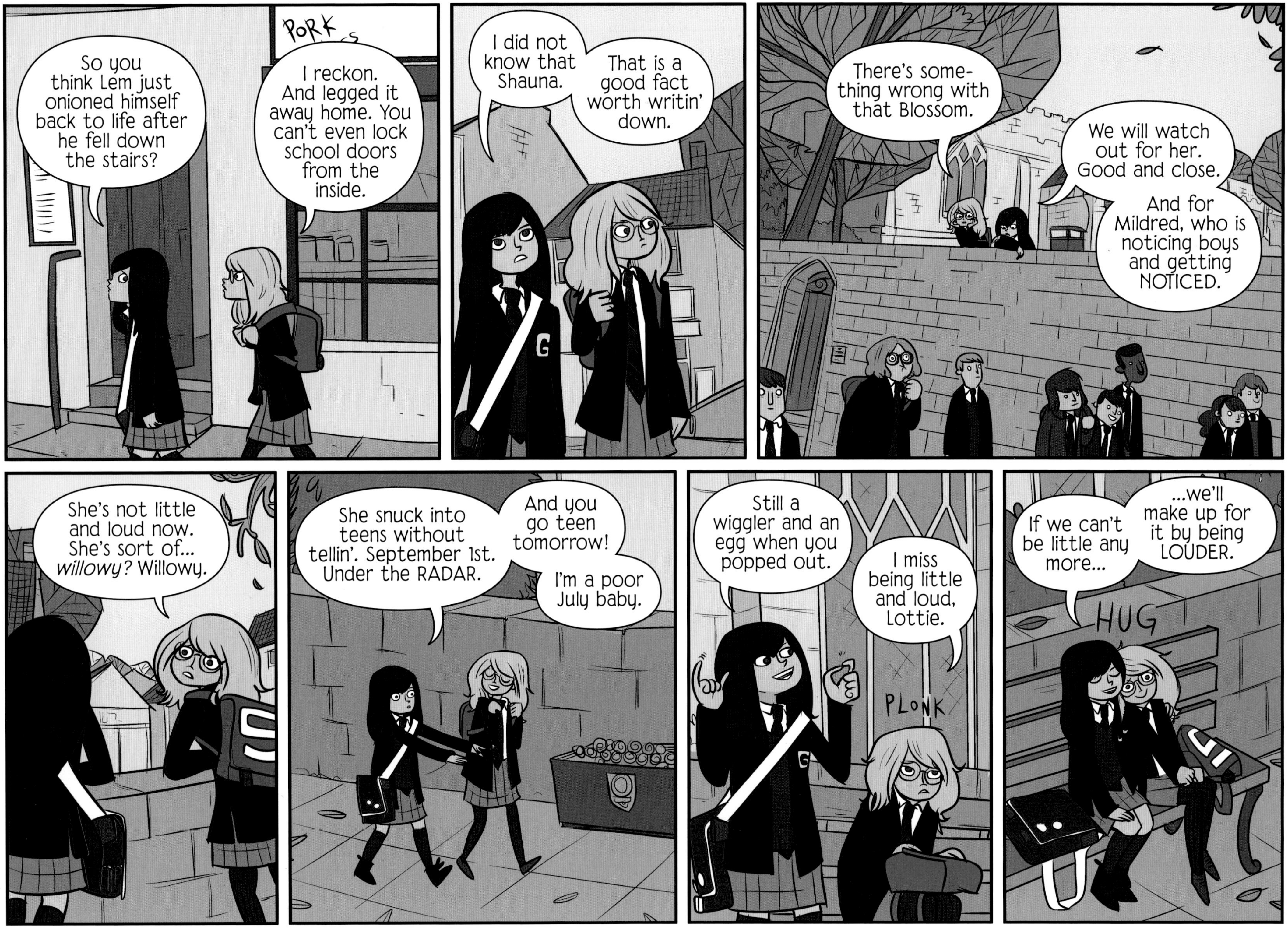
PORK
So you think Lem just onioned himself back to life after he fell down the stairs?
I reckon. And legged it away home. You can't even lock school doors from the inside.
I did not know that Shauna.
That is a good fact worth writin' down.
There's some-thing wrong with that Blossom.
We will watch out for her. Good and close.
And for Mildred, who is noticing boys and getting NOTICED.
She's not little and loud now. She's sort of... *willowy?* Willowy.
She snuck into teens without tellin'. September 1st. Under the RADAR.
And you go teen tomorrow!
I'm a poor July baby.
Still a wiggler and an egg when you popped out.
I miss being little and loud, Lottie.
PLONK
If we can't be little any more...
...we'll make up for it by being LOUDER.
HUG

The Case of the Lonely One

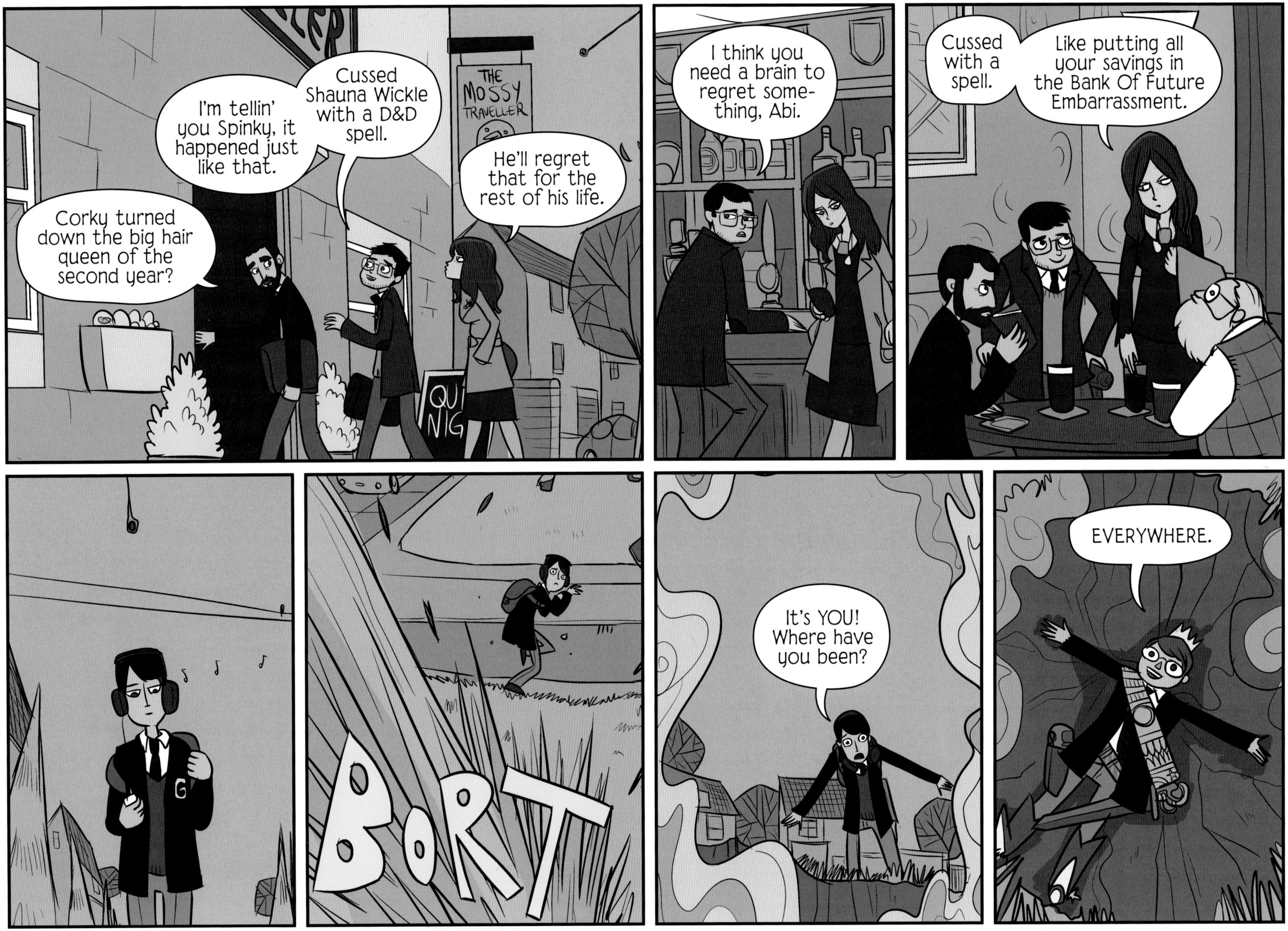
Corky turned down the big hair queen of the second year?
I'm tellin' you Spinky, it happened just like that.
Cussed Shauna Wickle with a D&D spell.
THE MOSSY TRAVELLER
He'll regret that for the rest of his life.
I think you need a brain to regret some-thing, Abi.
Cussed with a spell.
Like putting all your savings in the Bank Of Future Embarrassment.
BORT
It's YOU! Where have you been?
EVERYWHERE.

Bad Machinery, Volume Four

THE 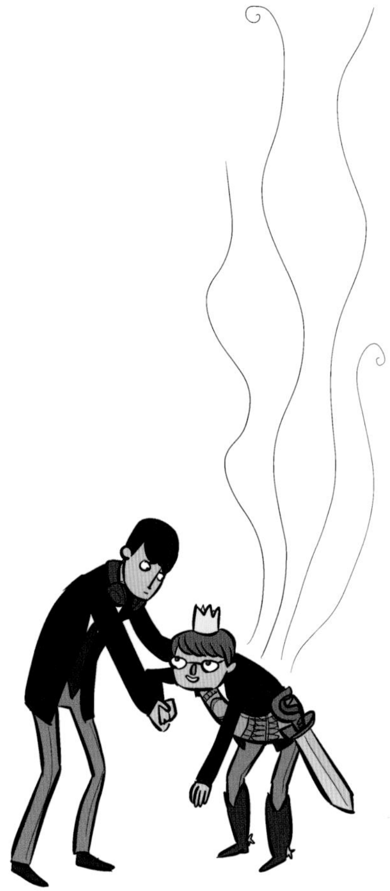 END

SKETCHBOOK

The way I write my stories is always changing, but I prefer to do most of the work with pencil and paper if I can. Writing things out longhand means I can draw alongside my notes, try out visual jokes, rough out characters, and work anywhere without needing my computer or a power outlet, away from distractions. I wrote most of this story on trains in cheap square sketchbooks. Here are some of my favourite rough drawings and what I remember about writing *The Case Of The Lonely One* four years ago.

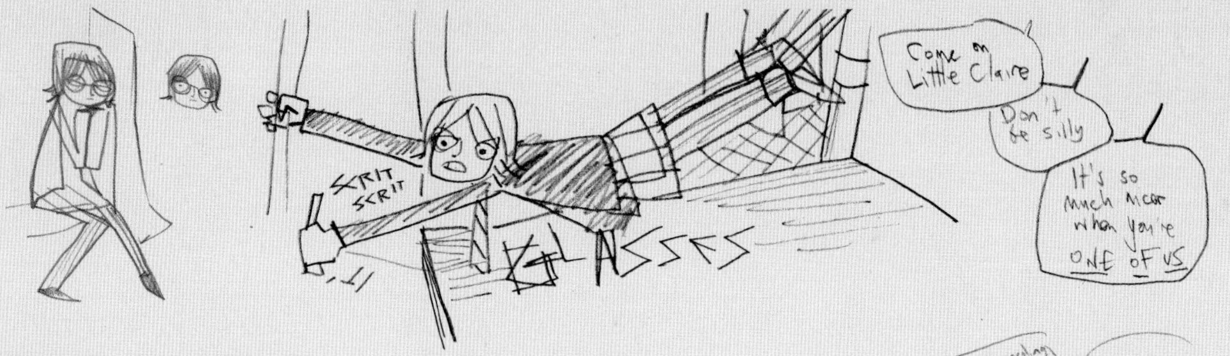

SCRIT SCRIT
GLASSES
Come on Little Claire
Don't be silly
It's so much nicer when you're ONE OF US

LITTLE CLAIRE

I introduced Little Claire in the last case as a fun character (admittedly, a fun character who has a slight problem with pyromania). I still thought of her that way until she started helping Shauna. Although she's little, she's not fragile. People underestimate her in almost every *Bad Machinery* case.

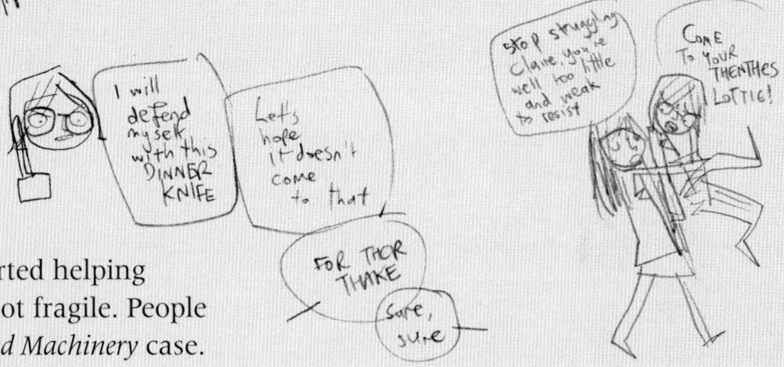

I will defend myself with this DINNER KNIFE
Let's hope it doesn't come to that
FOR THOR THAKE
Sure, sure
Stop struggling Claire, you're well too little and weak to resist
COME TO YOUR THENTHES LOTTIE!

SHAUNA

This is the first *Bad Machinery* story where one mystery solver has to do it (almost) all on her own. Shauna is one of the quieter characters, but I think that made this case more interesting. Juggling six characters often means that the sensible ones keep the plot moving while the nutty ones deliver some hot jokes. Leaning on someone who couldn't just fool around while being abandoned by all her friends meant that I had to change how I told a story. Anything that forces me to not to be lazy is good.

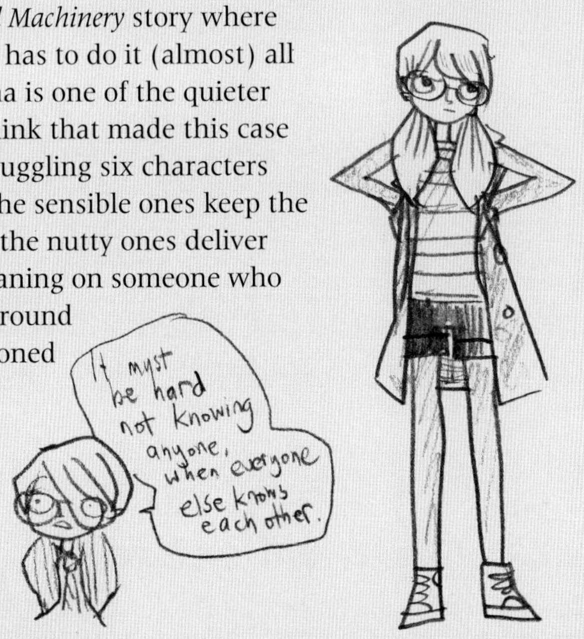

It must be hard not knowing anyone, when everyone else knows each other.

CORKY'S HOUSE

Drawing fancy houses is a treat. I go on real estate websites, type in a price that I could never afford, and have a snoop around all the photos. It's free fun! Don't judge me!

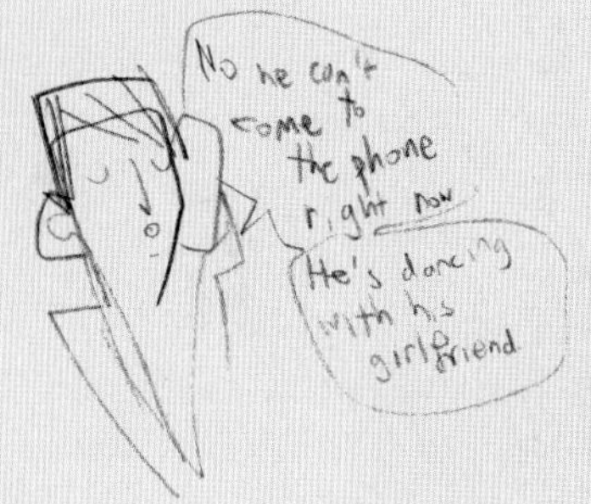

No he can't come to the phone right now
He's dancing with his girlfriend

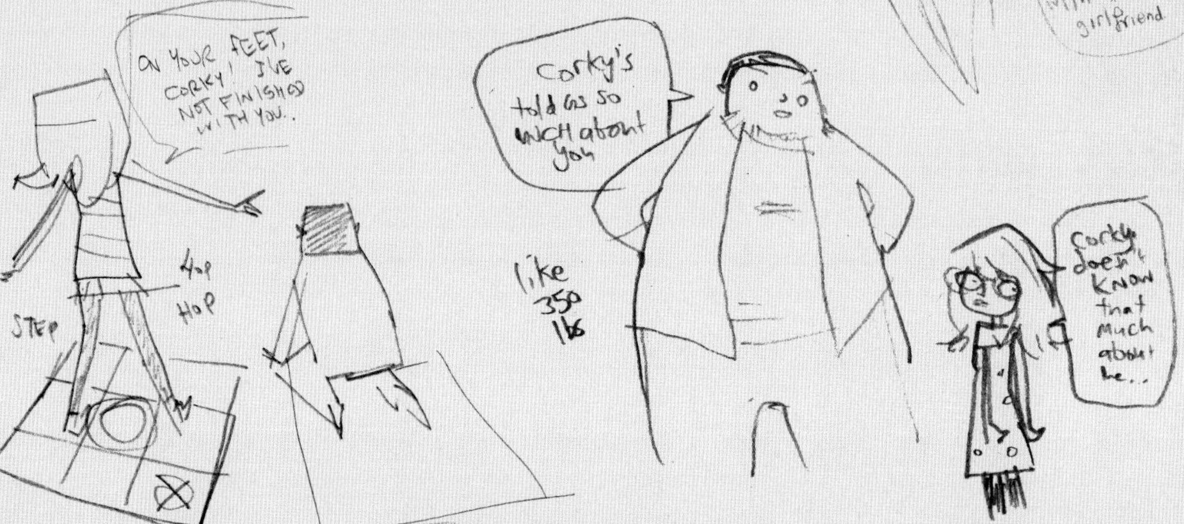

ON YOUR FEET, CORKY! I'VE NOT FINISHED WITH YOU.
STEP
Hop
Hop
Corky's told us so much about you
like 350 lbs
Corky doesn't know that much about me...

BLOSSOM, CORKY & TUAN

When I start drawing a story, the details for the later parts are very loose, so that anything that occurs to me as I'm working can be slotted in. This often means that characters who start with small parts get built up if they work well.

Tuan, Corky and Blossom didn't even have names when I started, but they all got their own little backstories. Cork and Tuan play as standard nerds, but Blossom is my favourite of the three. Nobody is going to mess with her and get away with it. She's a much more formidable enemy for Shauna than poor pitiful Lem the onion boy.

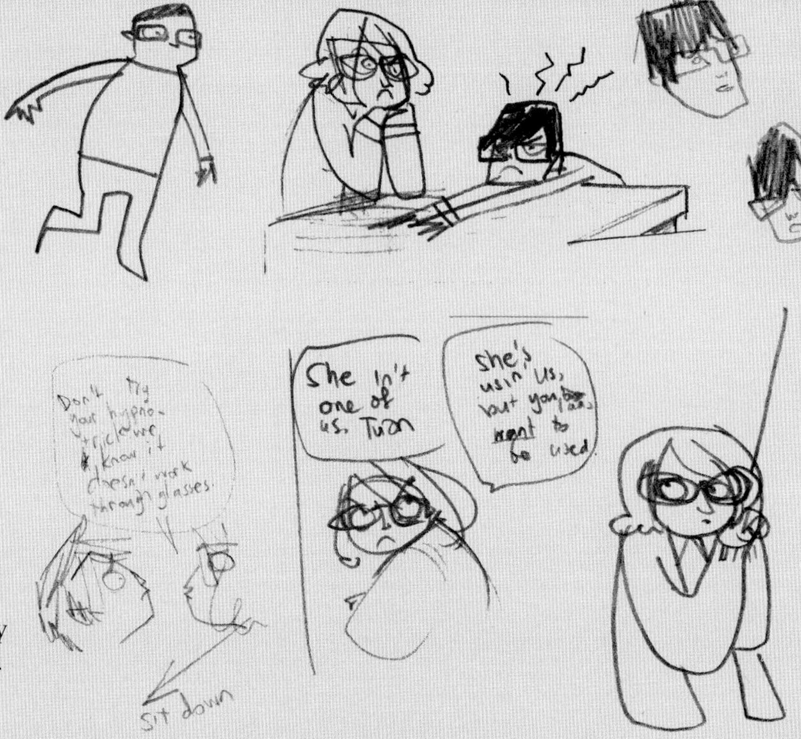

She isn't one of us, Tuan
Sit down

THE ONION FARM

I grew up next to a farm. On the plus side, the neighbouring field often contained the same animal you were eating for your dinner, which bred a healthy respect for "livestock". On the downside, one was regaled by some of the most ferocious biological odours imaginable if the wind was blowing in the right (wrong) direction.

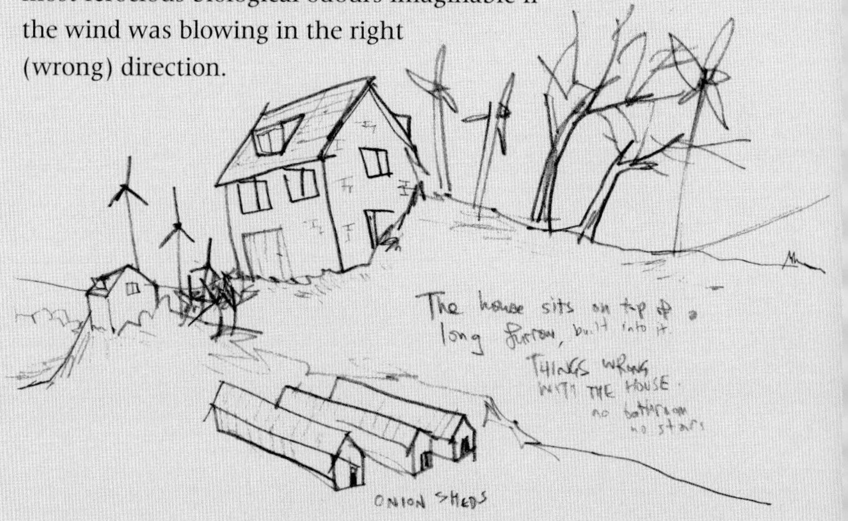

The house sits on top of a long furrow, built into it
THINGS WRONG WITH THE HOUSE
no bathroom
no stairs
ONION SHEDS

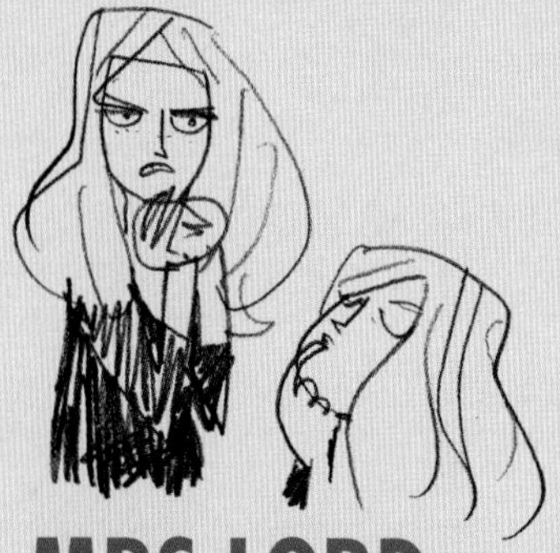

MRS LORD

Mrs Lord was just a name in my notes for this story until the day before I had to write her first scene. I think she's the sort of person who no one has ever said "no" to. I had a little drawing of a French actress in my sketchbook. "That'll do", I thought.

THE MYSTERY KIDS

The mystery kids change a little bit in every story, but this is the story where the girls start to become little women. They're trying on slightly more sophisticated ideas for size, while the boys are probably still swapping stickers and throwing loose debris at each other. On the first day of the second year of grammar school, I remember seeing the new intake, and they looked almost impossibly little.
A year ago, that had been us. Social norms and rules and expectations seemed to change so fast during that time that you were never sure what was right and wrong. I think I spent about 50% of the second year of big school absolutely livid, burning furiously with embarrassment.

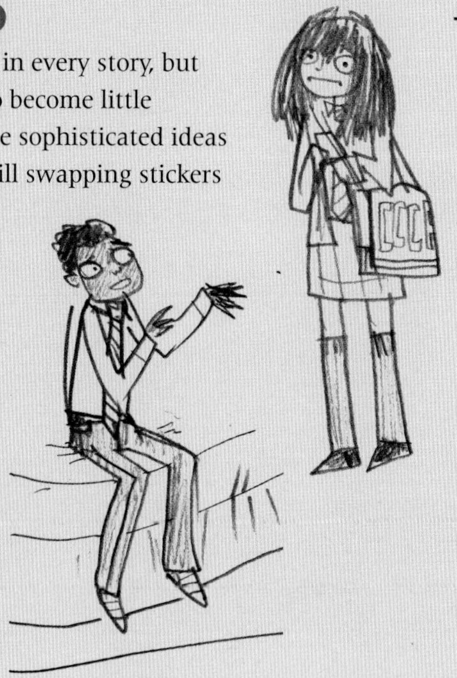

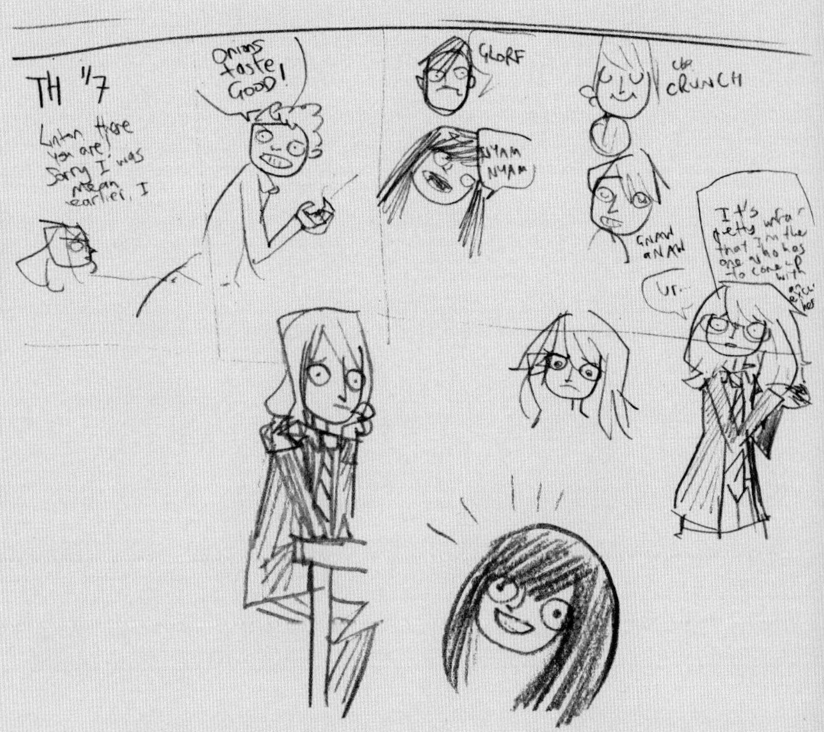

Onions taste GOOD!
GLORF
CRUNCH
NYAM NYAM
GNAW GNAW

LEM: EVOLUTION OF ONION BOY

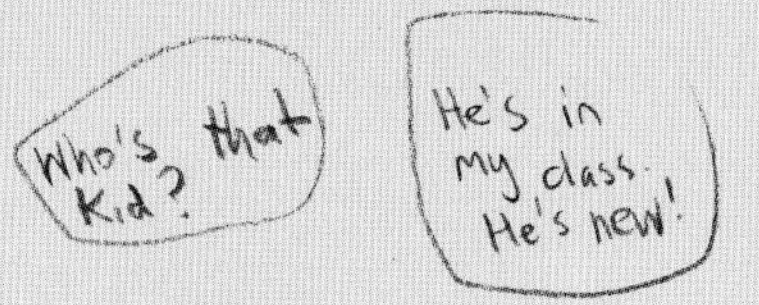
Who's that kid?
He's in my class. He's new!

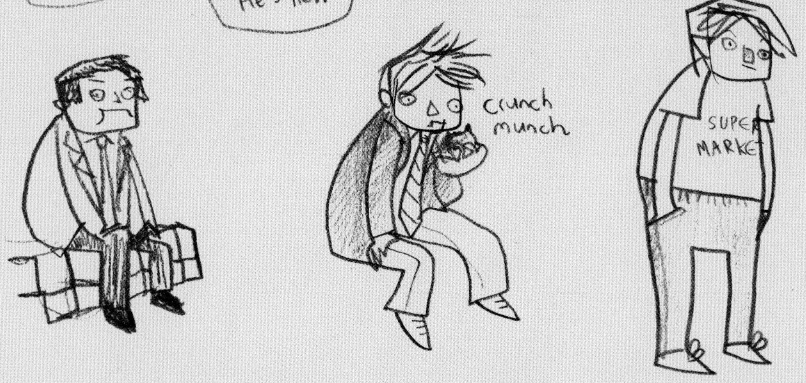
crunch munch
SUPER MARKE

Lem's design came quite easily. Initially, he was meant to be very bland and forgettable, but then I remembered a boy at school who got home haircuts for a bit longer than was probably appropriate. His mother would neatly cut it into a pudding bowl shape, but the natural directions of his hair would turn it into what looked like three haircuts fighting on top of his head. Lem's rounded gait was inspired by the classic shape of a shallot.

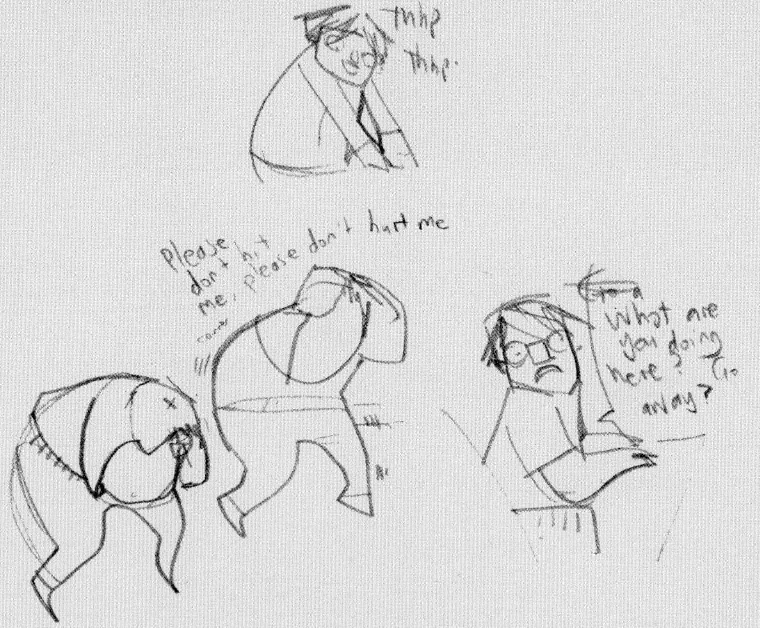
thhp thhp
Please don't hit me please don't hurt me
What are you doing here? Go away?

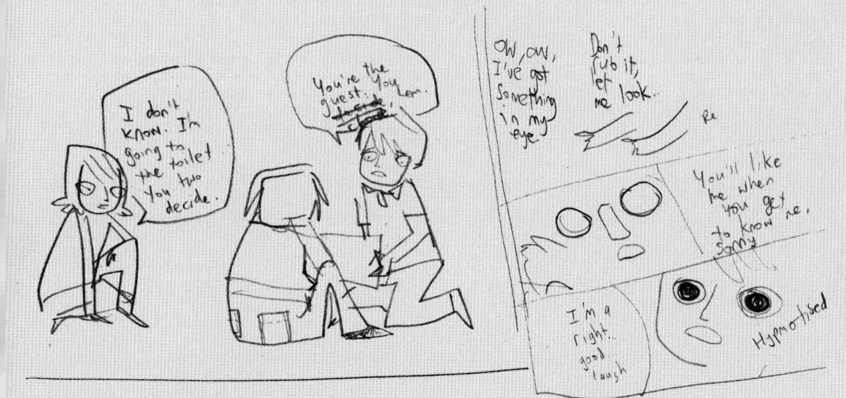
I don't know. I'm going to the toilet. You two decide.
You're the guest. You Lem.
Ow, ow, I've got something in my eye.
Don't rub it, let me look.
You'll like her when you get to know her, Sonny
I'm a right good laugh
Hypnotised

HYPNO EYES

Is there a more magical mesmeric trope than the time-honoured hypno-eyes? From Kaa the snake onwards, nothing says "you are under my power" like a spiral. In fact, it's possible to be hypnotised by almost anything spiral shaped. Queen Victoria was famously put into a three-week hypnotic trance just by riding a helter-skelter at a funfair.

MEET THE PARENTS

I'm particularly fond of Lem's parents, Vizier and Empyrean. I don't think I ever used their names in the comic, so there they are. They're pretty old to be parents, and constantly exhausted by their teenage son. When you want to fit in, as Lem does, no one seems more out of touch with how you feel than your poor parents. When a child becomes a teenager, a parent goes from steering the ship to gripping onto the wheel for dear life and trying to stop the vessel from crashing into a series of ever more dangerous obstacles. And that's when the parent isn't an ancient alien hiding in a wrecked spaceship under a decrepit onion farm.

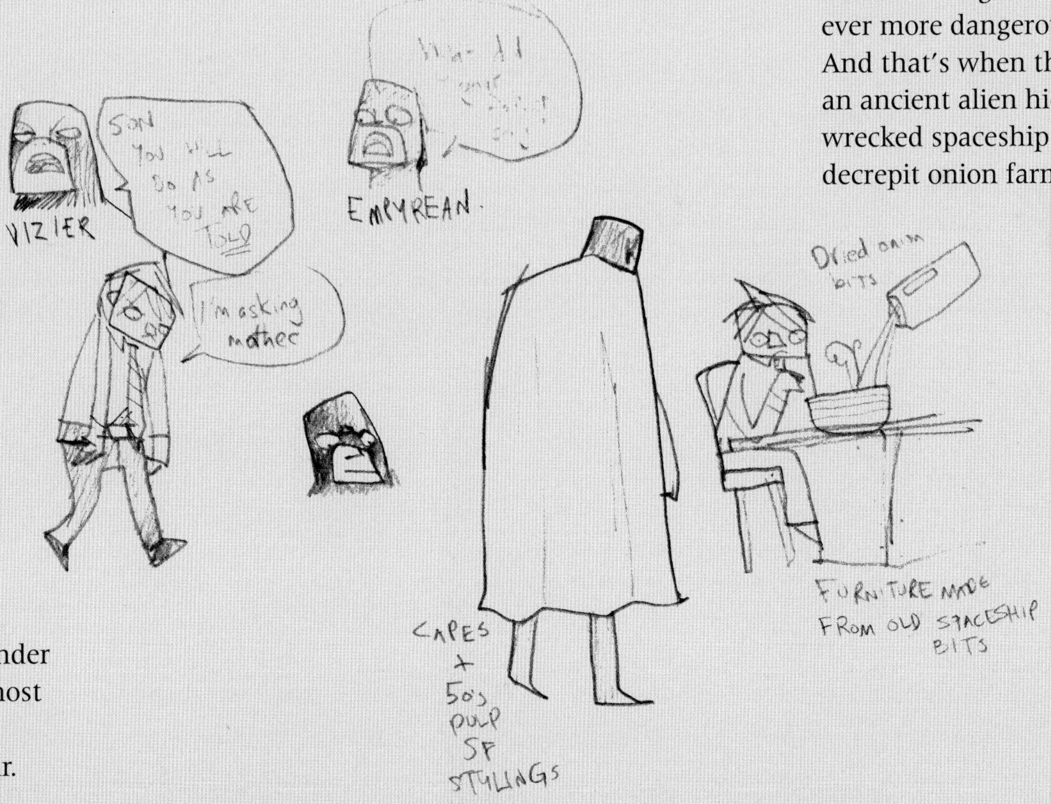
Son You will do as you are told
VIZIER
EMPYREAN
I'm asking mother
Dried onion bits
CAPES + 50's PULP SF STYLINGS
FURNITURE MADE FROM OLD SPACESHIP BITS

I'm so impressed with the girls at your school
Teasing-out like that takes time. It's an art
That's Shauna Wickle. She's a nice one.
But man she don't look right of late.
DRAG
I'm lookin' for distinguishin' marks, wife, making sure it's still you under there.
Let me know if you find any nits.
25/6/11

AMY

In the other *Bad Machinery* books, Amy Beckwith-Chilton doesn't really interact with the mystery kids. She only sees them from a distance, the way you or I might safely view a wasp's nest. Like a lot of adults, she's gone from being a child, to not being a child, to forgetting how to talk to children, to being actively afraid of children. It's a very normal, natural process—like puberty. Children are our future, they will replace us one day, turning our bones into gasoline for their futuristic cars. The fear is entirely justified.

But Amy sets aside the terror of being used to power a flying car by Shauna and takes her under her wing. It's an important day for both of them: the first day that Shauna enters the world of adults on equal terms, and the first time in years that Amy meets a teenager without crossing the street (or crossing herself).

Amy's look in this book is out-there and all over the place. I saw her kicked-out hair, her crazy jacket and her fluffy skirt walking down the street one day and scrawled them down as fast as I could. It was a look that said "confidence", but confidence is just armour for a fragile soul. It's hard to make new friends as an adult, you have to seize the chances when you can. I like Amy and Shauna as friends.

The ablative singular of "servus". Come on fella

MR SPINK

My Latin teacher was a lot like Mr Spink. He was a short man, but every cell of his body was packed with a raw fury that he would unleash upon anyone who got anything wrong in class. He got results: you felt almost religiously compelled to cram the most obscure details of classical grammar and vocabulary into your unreceptive mind. So long as you never got anything wrong, he was quite pleasant. But there was no margin for error, he was wound tighter than a clock spring. He also worked as a barman in a local pub. A pub where, I assume, no one spoke without raising their hand.

A ghastly parade of onion specimens
WORRG

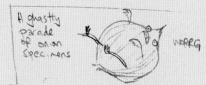

ONION BABIES

I'm not a geneticist, but I'm ABSOLUTELY CERTAIN that if you tried to create an onion that could walk, talk and gibber, your early efforts would look like the onion babies. They're probably not even babies, are they? They're just small. The same size as an onion. "John, why onions?" you may ask, and the answer is simple. Setting it at a horse farm would have made the story much harder to draw.

ALSO FROM JOHN ALLISON & ONI PRESS

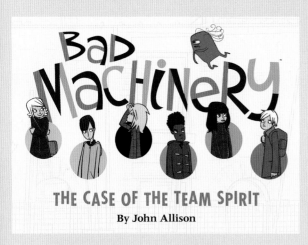

Bad Machinery
THE CASE OF THE TEAM SPIRIT
By John Allison

BAD MACHINERY, VOLUME 1:
THE CASE OF THE TEAM SPIRIT
By John Allison
136 pages, softcover, full color
ISBN 978-1-62010-084-4

Bad Machinery
THE CASE OF THE GOOD BOY
By John Allison

BAD MACHINERY, VOLUME 2:
THE CASE OF THE GOOD BOY
By John Allison
144 pages, softcover, full color
ISBN 978-1-62010-114-8

Bad machinery
THE CASE OF THE SIMPLE SOUL
John Allison

BAD MACHINERY, VOLUME 3:
THE CASE OF THE SIMPLE SOUL
By John Allison
136 pages, softcover, full color
ISBN 978-1-62010-193-3

Bad Machinery
THE CASE OF THE FIRE INSIDE
Coming Soon!

ONI PRESS
www.onipress.com

ALSO FROM ONI PRESS

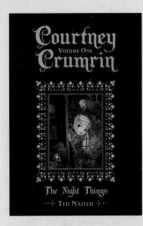

www.onipress.com